BEYOND *TISH*

BEYOND *TISH*

edited by
Douglas Barbour

Edmonton

Vancouver

© Copyright 1991
All rights revert to the authors on publication
All rights reserved. The use of any part of this publication reproduced, transmitted, in any form or by any means, electronic, mechanical, photocopying, recording, or otherwise, or stored in a retrieval system, without prior consent of the publisher is an infringement of the copyright law.

Main entry under title:

Beyond *TISH*

ISBN 0-920897-98-3

1. Canadian literature (English) –20th century*.
I. Barbour, Douglas, 1940 -
PS8233.B49 1991   C810.9'0054   C91-091213-0

EDITOR: Roy Miki

ASSISTANT EDITOR: Irene Niechoda
EDITORIAL BOARD: George Bowering, Peter Quartermain,
        Miriam Nichols, Charles Watts, Jenny Penberthy
EDITORIAL ADVISORS: Robin Blaser, Peter Buitenhuis,
        Shirley Neuman, Smaro Kamboureli
SECRETARY: Christine Goodman
WORD PROCESSING: Anita Mahoney,
COVER AND DESIGN ASSISTANCE: Pierre Coupey and Janice Whitehead
PAGE LAYOUT AND DESIGN: Bob Young/BOOKENDS DESIGNWORKS
PROOFING AND PRODUCTION ASSISTANCE: Tim Hunter

FINANCIAL ASSISTANCE: NeWest Press gratefully acknowledges the financial assistance of
        Alberta Culture and Multiculturalism, The Alberta Foundation for the Literary Arts,
        and The Canada Council.

West Coast Line gratefully acknowledges the financial assistance of Simon Fraser University, The Canada Council, and the Government of British Columbia, through the Ministry of Tourism, Recreation, and Culture.

Printed and Bound in Canada by Hignell Printing Limited, Winnipeg

NeWest Publishers Limited
#310, 10359-82 Avenue
Edmonton, Alberta
T6E 1Z9

West Coast Line is published three times a year: spring, fall, and winter. Unsolicited manuscripts must be accompanied by a self-addressed envelope and Canadian postage to ensure return.

SUBSCRIPTION RATES: [New rates as of January 1, 1991] $18/year for individuals; $24/year for institutions; single copies $8. U.S. subscribers: please pay in U.S. funds. Donors of $30/year or more will receive a complimentary annual subscription and an official receipt for income tax purposes. Prices include GST.

NOTE FOR LIBRARIANS: *West Coast Line* is a continuation of *West Coast Review*. *Beyond Tish*, this special issue co-published with *NeWest Press*, is Volume 25, Number 1, Spring 1991.

CORRESPONDENCE ADDRESS:

West Coast Line
c/o English Department
Simon Fraser University
Burnaby, B.C.
V5A 1S6 Canada

Distributed by the Canadian Magazine Publishers' Association.

COVER: "Variations Done For bpNichol (6)," by Pierre Coupey. Acrylic on canvas, 48" x 48", 1990

ISSN 1182-4271

CONTENTS

ONE: *New Writing*

FRANK DAVEY
Dead in France/ 11

JAMIE REID
Homage to Lester Young/ 22

GEORGE BOWERING
The Stump/ 33

DAVID DAWSON
Four Poems/ 39

FRED WAH
Seven Poems/ 49

DAPHNE MARLATT
The Difference Three Makes: A Narrative/ 53

GLADYS HINDMARCH
Improsements/ 55

LIONEL KEARNS
The Arrow of Time/ 60

DAVID CULL
Six Poems/ 61

ROBERT HOGG
Four Poems/ 67

DAVID BROMIGE
Three Poems/ 74

TWO: *Interviews*/ 81

IRENE NIECHODA AND TIM HUNTER, EDITORS
  A Tishstory/ 83

BRENDA CARR
  *Between Continuity and Difference:
  An Interview with Daphne Marlatt*/ 99

GEOFFREY ZAMORA
  Interview of Lionel Kearns/ 108

THREE: *Critical Essays*/ 113

WARREN TALLMAN
  A Brief Retro-Introduction to Tish/ 115

KEN NORRIS
  How the Tish *Poets Came to Influence the Montreal Scene*/ 120

PAMELA BANTING
  Translation A to Z: Notes on Daphne Marlatt's Ana Historic/ 123

E. D. BLODGETT
  Frank Davey: Critic as Autobiographer/130

LYNETTE HUNTER
  War Poetry: Fears of Referentiality/ 144

JEFF DERKSEN
  Torquing Time [on Fred Wah]/ 161

SHARON THESEN
  *Writing the Continuing Story:
  Gladys Hindmarch's* The Watery Part of the World/ 166

JANICE WILLIAMSON
  *It gives me a great deal of pleasure to say yes:
  Writing/Reading Lesbian in Daphne Marlatt's* Touch to My Tongue/ 171

ED DYCK
  Rhetoric and Poetry and Fred Wah/ 194

LIANNE MOYES
  *Writing the Uncanniest of Guests:
  Daphne Marlatt's* How Hug a Stone/ 203

MANINA JONES
  Log Entries [on Lionel Kearns]/ 222

Tish/Afterword and Notes on Contributors/ 235

ONE
New Writing

FRANK DAVEY

Dead in France

The dead, I jested as I passed through the gates, are smaller than the living. Their houses are smaller, their streets are smaller, there is nowhere near as much traffic. There are no garages or driveways. Just like in French cities.

†

Why not a series of texts on the French cemetery, I wondered, on this odd practice of mimicking the houses of the living in those of the dead, the same architectural styles, grander architectural styles, you can have a style in death that you can't afford to have when living. Most of the dead also have a stained-glass chapel window, a kneeling-bench, are inviting someone to pray for their souls?

†

I have written to my friend Barrie telling him about the cemetery & its little playschool houses. Is he or one of the Horsemen going to stop in Paris & visit on their way to their performance in Tarascon? Gertrude Stein is here in a grave with no house. Oscar Wilde has a large house which the IRA uses for a billboard. I haven't been able to find Apollinaire. I will send one of the new texts as soon as I have a first draft. There are also two fresh daffodils on Wilde's house. Stein's visitors appear to be borrowing plastic flowers from nearby wreaths & planting them among the weeds above her chest.

†

The cemetery is the only large green space in our arrondissement. Tourist buses come from Germany, Britain & Holland. Students sit on benches with their books. Small maps that locate the graves of celebrities are sold from a booth by the main gate. I practice my French by answering, from different streetcorners, 'Où est le cimetière du Père-Lachaise?' Nevertheless there are walls around the cemetery to regulate the living who may not want to play by its rules, who may want to use it too much as a place for living. Some living is okay, picnicking, feeding birds & cats, reading, strolling. Sleeping is permitted, but only in daylight. All residential uses, including cookery, housekeeping, improvised hostels, drinking after dark, are forbidden.

†

I am not sure about the implications of writing about a cemetery. This is one of the questions I want to put to Barrie in my next letter. All this started when I was looking for a quiet place to read & write, away from the flat à-deux-pièces I'm sharing this summer with my son & daughter. Why is it that death provides here one of the few places of repose to the living? Depressives spend nights here to make metaphoric self-declarations. Must I mention Gray's Elegy, Spoon River, Quaker graveyards, Audrey Thomas, John Toronto? In Montmartre there are several graveyards including one with no headstones where the painters pretend to tourists the painters of 100 yrs ago. What news is received when reading the grave of the famous poet?

†

I of course thought I was misreading something when I read that Héloise & Abélard were buried in Père-Lachaise. I knew that they died in the 12th century & that the cemetery was an elaborate gesture by the bourgeoisie who flourished after the Revolution. Translate & maybe it can go with you. Heavenly city, earthly city, avec plan touristique. Grid patterns to facilitate traffic flow. I saw H. & A. marked on the plan touristique but thought this must indicate some sentimental memorial. Each day tour buses from all the prosperous countries of Europe deliver their packages to the H. & A. corner. On Monday August 21st I wander down the trail trampled by the tourists & find genuine 12th century effigies praying upward to the beech & plane trees. An equally genuine government notice.

† † † †

Héloise & Abélard

Abélard was a professor who seduced one of his students. She was a private student & a convent student & in that privacy he began kissing her alabaster neck & rubious red nipples, some 50 years before the founding of universities in northern Europe & 850 before the announcement of policies on sexual harrassment. Before the founding of universities the educational opportunities for men & women, in convents & monasteries, were roughly similar. Some convents & monasteries were coeducational. Héloise's letters suggest that Abélard was an adept & experienced lover. Afterward, convents were gradually dissolved & universities began planning for the admission of their first women late in the nineteenth century. Probably in Abélard's time professors seduced as many students as they do today but:

Héloise was a 'brilliant' student & Abélard regarded 'as the most learned man of his day.' Abélard, it is written, fell in love with Héloise's mind. There was also the matter of her passionate body, a matter which delighted her greatly, & which also became pregnant. The delightful & pregnant body of Héloise was 15 or 16 years old while the unpregnant & yet intact one of Abélard was 37 or 38.

(Find out what Abélard wrote of the mind-body problem.)

Héloise's guardian uncle was Canon Fulbert of the Argenteuil convent. When he learned she was pregnant, he demanded she & Abélard marry. Marriage at the time was a useful social convention which secured the unborn child the financial support of two parents & an unambiguous place in the social order. Marriage was the generally accepted Pauline means of minimizing the archangels' disapproval of sexual intercourse. Marriage could also be a form of punishment since most scholarly positions to which people like Héloise & Abélard might aspire were filled, thanks to the Gregorian reforms of 1075, by officially celibate clergy.

One problem for the uncle was that Héloise went crazy with joy whenever Abélard was inside her but also wrote complex theological discourses & would later become a renowned ecclesiastical administrator. Learning & lovemaking involve different words & different ways of placing words together & have rarely been combined except in paradox & risqué metaphor like the bride of Christ & never chaste lest thou ravish me. While paradox & metaphor may imply oppression, they are always understood to exclude, as the words of medicine would later say, the exchange of bodily fluids. Héloise is a contemporary of Eleanor of Aquitaine. Words also do not make a belly swell unless whispered in the ear of, among others, a sweet, passionate adorable girl theologian.

The uncle's second problem was that scholarship & theology & the words of scholarship & the words of theology are all mixed up. The church has been for a few hundred years the only place most people can get an education & getting an education means becoming a sort of unclassified ecclesiast most often a priest or a monk or nun. Later the state will involve itself in learning & the conventional price of higher education will become a career as a civil servant. But at the time of Héloise & Abélard the bottom line was that scholars are by expectation ecclesiasts but ecclesiasts cannot be married. As one authority writes, "the fact that Héloise could bear a child & later rise to a position of authority in the church indicates the wide range of flexibility in medieval church practice." Or as Héloise writes, "there was no divine call but will alone to throw my youth into the rigors of the monastery."

A third problem was that marriage involves yet more words that have not that much to do with lovemaking, scholarship or theology. Héloise's answer to her uncle, as much we can now decode it from the further words of historians, poets & other romanticizers, was that she enjoyed screwing Abélard & certainly planned to screw him again but didn't want to be married. Like her uncle, contemporary readers have difficulty understanding where she found words for such a discourse or how she managed to conceive herself as a voice which announced she would rather be Abélard's "mistress" than "the wife of Augustus & empress of the world." "I am the sole master of my heart as well as of my body," she writes. The trees & stone canopy allow little direct sunlight to fall on the matching effigies. No commentaries have appeared on the subtext of "sole master."

Being a canon, her uncle did not recognize many of the theological resonances of her words. Her disdain for the secular splendours of Augustus. Her ultimate position among the words of love – "I have kept nothing of myself, if it is not the right to become for all else your property."

Being a canon, her uncle shot off his mouth about shooting off Abélard's balls. One of the things I plan to ask Barrie is whether this is a worthy metaphor for church power, or if it confuses church & the state of Billy the Kid. Gunpowder had only recently been introduced to Europe. Marco Polo & spaghetti were not yet household words. There is a scene in *The Saracen Blade* in which a hole mysteriously appears in the sail of a ship. This hole is the introduction of gunpowder to Europe. The gun, as Barrie & everyone else have been writing since Freud's *New Introductory Lectures*, becomes the sign of the phallus, or an additional sign of the phallus, spears, swords, knives & other cutting & perforating instruments being already very much in service.

Cutting off Abélard's balls was a significant event in the sex life of Héloise's uncle. Marriage was then, as now, an approved way in which people could communicate sexually. When Abélard seduced Héloise, or Héloise seduced Abélard, her uncle had marvellous & terrifying dreams about being in bed with his beautiful niece & one way in which to stop these was to be sure Abélard had married Héloise & the other way was to sever Abélard's balls. To be fair, we must grant that her uncle tried both remedies, although we must also ask whether two remedies is the necessary number, whether remedies indeed were what was called for. We do know that Héloise called for remedies in her dreams. However, these remedies were anything but remedies for the uncle & in fact constituted the ailment he wished to be cured of.

There is no record of the full text of Héloise's view of marriage. "The title of mistress is sweeter than that of wife," she writes, "even those of concubine or fille de joie." The ideological subtleties of the female service industries are evidently of no interest to her. Or possibly they are, since she is marking 'wife' here as at least as much a term of slavery as 'concubine' or 'prostitute.' "I prefer love to marriage, liberty to a chain," she writes. Possibly she had worked up arguments on marriage as legitimated prostitution. Possibly she had asked awkward questions such as why should one matter, such as who you liked screwing, become the determinant of your education, career opportunities & living situations for the rest of your life. These are of course not her actual words but as close as anything else that has been written as her words.

She also didn't want Abélard to have to stop being a scholar & a teacher & become a husband & father, activities which used different & unmixable words.

At the same time Héloise's imagination does not extend beyond being a man's "property." I'm hoping Barrie will tell me something about the financial problems of Coach House Press. While linking 'wife' & 'slavery' she also curiously links 'mistress' 'concubine' & 'fille de joie' & being Abélard's property to 'love' & 'liberty.' Women & theologians have often had to resort to rhetorical figures to imagine themselves free. The only other role Héloise can see open to women is that of "empress of the world."

Abélard was not an emperor but a man of his times & agreed to marry Héloise. Abélard figured that as a well-known scholar he could get enough work as a private tutor to support a wife & so agreed to marry Héloise. Abélard was afraid Héloise might be hidden away by her uncle, or be sent to a nunnery, & that he might never get to enjoy her brilliant passionate young adorable girl body again & so agreed to marry Héloise. Abélard was confused, like we all can be when we enter into the life of another & want to do what both we & the other want to be done, & so agreed to marry Héloise. All this 'agreeing' of course he did with Canon Fulbert. Abélard couldn't see Héloise & couldn't talk to her & despite being the most respected scholar of his time imagined her grief & desire & confusion & desire & imagined all these would fit into the institutional structure of society if only he were with her & so agreed to marry her. After many muddy & confusing walks across medieval Paris, Héloise & Abélard secretly marry. Gregory VII was the first pope to successfully centralize church authority. No one knows why Héloise would consent to marry. Afterward, unknown to Abélard, she continues to tell her uncle she refuses to marry.

Such issues & events have the makings of a gripping romantic plot, & have been seized upon by a variety of narrators. Even those who know the outcome can become gripped, seized or grabbed by the anguish & pathos of lovers who act at cross-purposes, who follow contrary systems of belief with which each thinks the other would agree. Grippe is French for influenza. In these narratives the words of love triumph over those of theology, propriety & scholarship despite the fact that they could not so triumph in Héloise & Abélard's actual lives. Probably also in the narrators' actual lives, or in your actual life. Adding to the pathos & confusion is one more matter. Héloise's uncle cannot believe that a woman can be an independent thinker. His words for woman cannot mix with her words about her own independence. He thinks she is secretly corresponding with Abélard who doesn't want to marry her, who is coaching her, who is giving an impressionable girl bizarre words about the sanctity of her self & the absence of necessary links between eros & the institution of marriage.

♥ ♥ ♥ ♥

The day I stumbled upon the tomb of Héloise & Abélard I wrote to my friend Barrie describing the tomb & remarking on how many different motives & desires had brought the pair to Paris & a bourgeois graveyard, & the next month he is also dead. I had written to Barrie because they were in the same graveyard as Gertrude Stein & Apollinaire & the semiotics of these names all work differently from out of the ground of a single graveyard. I was thinking of Barrie, & of his thinking about the falling of saints into the words of people & of what words Gertrude would have given to Abélard & Héloise.

✂

Believing Abélard had not married Héloise & was refusing to marry Héloise, her uncle hired assassins to kidnap him & cut off his balls. Castration is a primitive method of birth control. The language of violence here meets the languages of eros & logic. In some societies castration has been used to enforce the paternity demands of others. In *The Arabian Nights* eunuchs are expected to have recreational intercourse, with the ladies of the harem. There is no record of how "this barbarous act" (*The Encyclopedia of Philosophy*) affected the sexual performance of Abélard. I like to imagine everyone in medieval France believing that the sex life of him & Héloise was over & meanwhile over & over they are enjoying what later would become fashionable as "sex without fear."

♥

The humanism of Abélard has been misread because of his relationship with Héloise. Abélard held that sin does not reside in single acts but in the overall shape of a human life. I didn't ask Barrie about the sex life of Héloise, I merely indicated I would send him a copy of the text I was writing.

♥

Various plot lines run through events. You & I are two of these plot lines, & sometimes these plot lines become mysterious & sometimes they appear to stop altogether. I went for a walk through a Paris cemetery & along the way counted eleven well-fed cemetery cats. The plot line of Canon Fulbert runs through the text life of Abélard & Héloise. One fine morning by the Gregorian calendar. The day I left for Paris Barrie said he would miss me, & I said I was going only for a year & he replied sensibly that you never know what will happen in a year.

♥

Jim Morrison I now hear is also buried in Père-Lachaise although his grave is not recorded in the official words of the tourist map. Crowds are supposed to gather around it drinking & playing guitars & leaving empty bottles & lunch bags on the adjacent graves, although the only crowds I saw were five people at the grave of a Serbian nationalist, the busloads walking to & fro the tomb of Héloise & Abélard & 3 cats at their food dishes at the tomb of Marguerite Berthillon. A cemetery is a complex proposition on ways & means for honouring the dead.

When Père-Lachaise was first opened early in the 19th-century Héloise & Abélard were moved here by the developers to give panache to the new graveyard. What was a shock to the bourgeois sensibilities of Héloise's uncle was high-class stuff to the inheritors of the Revolution. A cemetery is a complex proposition on how the dead can enter the discourses of the living. Héloise had moved Abélard's body to the convent of which she was abbess shortly after his death in 1142, & was buried beside him when she died in 1164.

After Abélard's castration, both Héloise & Abélard joined religious orders. In the fall that Barrie dies, the big cultural event in France is the release of Nuytten's film *Camille Claudel*. Héloise named her son Astrolabe, although there is no record that this helped her find her way or even of where the son got to. Camille Claudel was the sister of Paul Claudel, *q.v.* "Canon Fulbert made the unwilling Héloise become a nun at Argenteuil." In the sixties, many unmarried California girls named their kids Sky or Heavenly Love. "In shame," reports the *Encyclopedia Britannica*, "Abélard embraced the religious life at St. Denis." The cause of Abélard's shame is not specified, being presumably self-evident. Abélard argued universals could reside in things, which were necessarily unique. Héloise & Abélard had varied ecclesiastical careers, which converged in 1129 when he founded the convent of Paraclete with himself as abbot & her as abbess. He also argued that sin is not a substance or an act, but a consentment to evil. In the early 1130s he & Héloise composed a collection of their love letters & religious correspondence. At this point in the text the reader & writer can themselves compose erotic fantasies. Abélard came very close to arguing that all things & events, including sin, are composed of words, that universals are constructions of words, but as abbott of St. Gildas had poor relations with his monks & was nearly murdered.

I've checked my map & there seems to have been been no grave in Père-Lachaise marked 'Auguste Rodin.' Rodin, Nuytten's film suggests, is the sentimental & melodramatic French sculptor who stole the heart & best ideas of his girl pupil & became, like Abélard, acclaimed as a genius. If you stroll the graveyards of France, you can detect many of the master narratives of French culture. Have we been missing something, Barrie, about our students? Freud owes a prodigious debt to his hysterics. 'Dead' seems a reasonable adjective to modify Héloise or Abélard or Auguste Rodin but is painful to place in front of the name of a close friend. For this reason the movie-goers weep incredulously as Camille is locked away into thirty years of dying by her mother & brother.

♥

My daughter observes that all the film reviewers write of Rodin & Camille & not Auguste & Camille or Claudel & Rodin & certainly not Auguste & Claudel. I reply that maybe they read 'Claudel' as a previously assigned signifier. She does not look satisfied. Rodin gets a 2-column entry in most encyclopedias but Claudel gets none except in the *Britannica* where the full entry reads "Rodin's mistress and model." This story of my trip to a graveyard doesn't look like any poem or novel I've read. Maybe it shows too much concern with death or too much fascination with the seduction of talented young women. Although Barrie didn't get to the Tarascon festival, feeling too ill to travel, the rest of the Horsemen did, & one of them, Paul Dutton, came to my little apartment 2 blocks from the cemetery. Camille & Abélard as victims of phallocratic justice. My son opened a bottle of Bordeaux. Héloise & Camille as victims of phallic inscription. No, said Paul, I think I prefer to remember Gertrude as someone living.

Auguste & Claudel

When Camille Claudel was a little girl she embarrassed her mother all to hell by wanting to play in the mud. Her brother Paul would soon write his own ticket as symbolist poet. The Gregorian reforms were an unquestioned part of church doctrine in the nineteenth century. Camille's father is said to have thought the mud on her face looked cute. The main element one sees in the psychosis of Mlle. Claudel is that no matter how useful her suggestions were to Rodin, or how personally satisfying her own sculpture, she experienced herself as without meaning or identity unless also his lover. By World War II Rodin was dead, but her brother lived on to help others collaborate with Germany. Perhaps Camille foresaw the criteria of the *Encyclopaedia Britannica*. Claudel & her worried younger sister are contemporaries of Jane Avril. W.H. Auden, who did not write for the *Britannica*, wrote "Time will pardon Paul Claudel." Should Héloise have a surname? The lead actress of *Camille Claudel* first came to attention in Truffaut's *Adèle H*.

Camille Claudel was a modernist artist whose work was marginalized by the melodramas of late French romanticism. Camille Claudel was the daughter whose efforts to validate herself to her parents competed inevitably with similar efforts by her brother. Camille Claudel was a paranoid schizophrenic whose early symptoms included her failure to notice sculpture was a field socially forbidden to women. Camille Claudel gave all for love. Camille Claudel was a woman whose acute perceptions of female persecution were termed 'paranoid' by those more accepting of nineteenth-century values.

In the movie Claudel strides pluckily through the Paris streets oblivious to the impossibility of her dream & couldn't you just hug her & Auguste did. Her work will be forgotten without signature. Her brother can go to university, become a diplomat, write his verses within the frames of 'career' & a bowler hat. Time will pardon Camille Claudel. She is "un soufflé de la passion" for a tired sculptor already becoming businessman who will soon feel this 'soufflé' as his own. Auguste's hands roam over her body as if it were a wet soufflé. Paul grows a diplomat's mustache. Auguste's hands roam over her body as if it were wet clay. Intertextual references to Pygmalion. You are mine, he screams at her, or Gerard Depardieu has him scream at her, or Bruno Nuytten has him scream at her, at the very moment that the hard difference of her stone assaults him.

Movie semiotics: mud on Claudel's face; Auguste's hat & cane; Paul's ocean liners, postcards, his & Auguste's warm carriages. Claudel walking. Mother's black dresses. Father's study. Claudel kneeling in a ditch. Bourgeois ladies in pastel dresses. Rodin's house & garden. Claudel drinking with *clochards*. Pedestalled Art. The cinematic beauty of Claudel's scarred hands.

When Camille Claudel ran away to Paris she knew she would become a sculptor. The concept of the *artiste maudit* was an invention of nineteenth-century French romanticism & particularly prevalent among the bourgeoisie. The adequacy of her clay modelling led some of her teachers to compare her to Rodin. "In those days, an artist in the family was a social disgrace. People like Camille's mother felt threatened by it and did not know how to cope." Claudel first heard of Rodin from her art teachers. Everyone was reading *Fleurs du mal*. One of Barrie's first career steps was to establish his trademark 'bp.' Rodin must have found it unusual to encounter a female model who could also carve stone as well as himself. "Before him, Camille, eighteen years, is dizzied by adoration, adulation and passion." Rodin was a professor who seduced one of his students. "Il est d'emblée séduit par sa beauté." Rodin was confused by Claudel's versatility & unsure whether to see her as model, student, or colleague. Rodin was the son of a policeman & hoped by screwing Claudel to raise his social standing. Claudel & Rodin were physically attractive people who shared a passion for sculpture & fell in love. When Camille Claudel ran away to Paris she was sure she would become a sculptor.

Over the years Camille Claudel developed a paranoia that Rodin was stealing her work. "Une révolte de la nature: la femme de génie." In western society women's labor has usually been co-opted by men through their translation of it into domestic or leisure activity. Claudel would not only arrange Rodin's models but carve substantial portions of his commissions. Rodin often talked to her about the 'inachéves' of Michaelangelo, which had recently been installed at the Louvre, & had undoubtedly himself heard stories about the Sistine Chapel. Claudel demanded several times that Auguste give up his housekeeper & mistress Rose Beuret & marry her. Marriage was the price most girls of her class expected to receive for their identities. Claudel lived out her brother's bohemian fantasies. Although we know that all art is social, inasmuch as it is produced through & in relation to conventions collectively developed by a culture, one of these conventions is that the individual who produces art through combining these conventions get personal 'credit' for the work. Claudel's aborting of Rodin's child constitutes a rejection of his aesthetics. "Housekeeper & mistress" was an emotionally charged concept to nineteenth-century men. Claudel's aborting of her own child reflects her understanding of her future. Very likely Rodin signed work 'done' by Claudel. After leaving Auguste in 1894, Claudel rented studio space on beautiful Ile Saint-Louis, now one of the few remaining intact areas of seventeenth-century Paris.

One of the problems faced by Rodin was that Camille Claudel damaged his social reputation. Prominent among the subjects of 19th-century French art were harem scenes, women being taken as war-prizes, & mythological scenes like Hercules & Hippolyta & the rape of Proserpine. He was a responsible citizen who fulfilled government contracts. Among the advantages & disadvantages facing French sculpture in the 19th-century was the practice of monumental state architecture that required uplifting statuary. "Ma pauvre soeur Camille, sa mort sera une délivrance." The Seine frequently flooded parts of Ile Saint-Louis. One of Claudel's most accomplished later works is "Persée et la Gorgone."

Another problem for Auguste were the feelings he had when he thought of Claudel. Women in Rodin's work are usually naiads or nymphs, or goddesses to whom the man comes in worship. His letters to her were probably destroyed by her mother. When drunk, Claudel would stand in the street shouting curses at his windows. Auguste sent friends to offer her financial help. The packages of catshit she mailed to the Ministre des beaux-arts would have helped mythologize many a male artist. "Camille Claudel est une invention récente." He worried about her, he remembered her beautiful. Claudel thought his friends had been sent to steal her work. He worried about her, her carelessness about her appearance & her annual destruction of her work denied the erotic & the monumental on which the value of his own productions rested. Clay figures of working-class subjects.

♥

"Une difficulté somme toute banale." Barrie & I would have talked about the juxtaposition of Héloise & Stein, the juxtaposition of those names, of unmarked Héloise & her who interrupts the march of the phallic sentence. Claudel's mother signed her into an asylum in 1913, a week after Père Claudel died. For 3 years she kept her studio tightly sealed. Some readers will wonder what Héloise & Claudel have to do with Canadian culture. Barrie & I would have perhaps talked about our daughters. Claudel's mother had detested her since the first mud pie but cannot act until herself freed by her husband's death. People thought she was crazy, but an unrecognized part of Claudel's art had been her annual smashing of what she had produced & carting it off to the Paris dump. "La boulimie de création qui l'incite à multiplier les tirages et à réutiliser les fragments et les chutes." The movie version of Camille Claudel offers a Rodinesque ending in which she pathetically claws at the windows of the ambulance. For the next thirty years she refused to work the clay she was offered, convinced that anything she produced would enrich the reputation & person of Auguste Rodin.

The dead are dead because they have at best problematical access to discourse. Half-born, my daughter tracked the obstetrician's instruments, gazing, it is said, as only the law can. Claudel was buried in a common grave which by 1964 when her nephew wrote to claim her body had disappeared. Her funeral had been unattended. Although it will be known as a Nuytten film, *Camille Claudel* is actually the 'creation' of Isabelle Adjani, the lead actress, who after reading Claudel's biography created the production company, Lilith Films, purchased a script & hired Nuytten to direct its filming. The only surviving texts by Héloise are those she wrote to Pierre in 1117-18. To possess Abélard's cock & balls, the girl must obey the law of the uncle. I can find little else to say about Claudel's sister. The centralization of church power under Pope Gregory & the formation of the Third Reich. No one had yet told my daughter she could not see. And God knelt by a riverbank & fashioned Adam out of clay. My friend Barrie had never accepted the inevitability of fellowcentrism. The death tolls of the Inquisition & the Holocaust. "C'est une véritable conspiration des femmes qui tire Camille de l'oubli." Translation is a weapon & a duty. Numerous women knitting & reading in the sunshine of Père-Lachaise. The roles saved for women by Marie de Champagne & Camille's mom. Nuytten is the father of Adjani's son Barnabe. Locking one's sister in prison for the last 30 years of her life then watching Jews shipped to internment camps in the Hautes-Pyrénées. The roles offered Camille's mom. The metrics of Auden's poem are also problematical. All sculpture is political. As Nuytten knows, a major element of bourgeois art is the forcing of the watcher to identify with the afflicted. Centralization of power invites the disempowering of the different. Abélard's balls & priestly celibacy. In the nineteenth century, most of these weeping viewers of *Camille Claudel* would have been parents troubled by a daughter who played in the mud.

Paris – Villefranche/mer, August-December 1988

JAMIE REID

Homage to Lester Young

I
Rhapsody: Lester's Sound

Here are notes like the motes of the last dappled sunlight,
    melting like gold on the clusters of leaves.

Here too is the singing light of the dawn on the same leaves,
    reawakened in the eyes of the man who has not slept
    throughout the night.

Here are the first stars of the evening like emeralds embroidered
    on velvet, and here are the last stars of the morning,
    like ice melting on silk.

Here is the light in the smoke of the nightclub, where the
    feelings of lovers and lonely ones float to the ceiling
    in spirals.

Here is their love of the music, which they cling to because
    they despair of anything else to rescue the heart of man.

Here is the sound of the heart purely in love, loving nothing
    in particular, but all of the particulars of the world
    in which that heart is alive and beating.

Here is the sound of the heart and breathing, alive to the nuance
    of just this precise unalterable moment and no other.

Here is the joy of pure desire which desires nothing
    but to be lost amongst all of the things which are.

Here is the permanent moment of rain remembered.

Here is the flurry of notes like snow, strangely warm, into which
    the voice of a woman suddenly enters to comfort you,
    but which is just as suddenly smothered again.

Here is the ache of the air from which her voice has been
    so cruelly withdrawn.

Here is the milky luminescence of fog spread and reflected,
>   droplet by droplet of wet, until nothing is seen but
>   that silvery shining, the same as it was at the beginning
>   of things.

Beyond this, there is a darkness barely seen, beyond which again
>   is another and more perfect darkness unseen.

Here is the pit-a-pat-pat of counting, in which the spaces
>   between the numbers are never the same length
>   and are never the same shape either.

Here is the moment when time stops and goes back on itself,
>   when all the gestures and reachings of past life
>   are repeated as though in film reversed.

Here is the single damaging phrase flashing like a tongue
>   of terrible flame into the darkened room
>   where a door has been opened by surprise.

Here is the flickering static of atoms and electrons jostling,
>   sounds which began their journey to earth
>   ten million years ago and more.

Here is the annihilating honk of the great black holes in space,
>   ravening for loose matter and light, so dense with being
>   they annihilate all being, all becoming and all knowing.

Here is the drone and cry of the creatures beneath the sea,
>   the clatter of billions of claws drowned in sea water.

Here is the love between particular men and women,
>   transcending sex and generation, but locked in that same
>   shuddering medium out of which the new is constantly coming,
>   smelling like roses.

Here are the eyes of the trees glancing at you without smiling
>   and without pain.

Here are dresses and suits lined up in racks on a city street,
>   the shoes piled in bins, which will never be worn,
>   while barefoot men and woman are walking
>   the sides of the river, half-naked and hungry.

Here is the sound of coins in the pocket. Taken into your hand,
>they speak with an echo of Hammurabi and Caesar, and of
>the old man recently found dead in the street.

Here, strangely, there are no flowers, except for the odor
>of those roses, and a single very white gardenia,
>perched in a woman's hair.

Here is the sound of water wherever it appears. In its lapping,
>you hear the sound of languages unwritten and forgotten.

But here too is the voice of a language not yet spoken
>by a race of men and women not yet born.

II

Lester died on purpose. The president
>could not command the real world
>>to behave
according to his imagination
>of what it ought to be
>>and what he knew it could be, because
of what he knew
of what he was himself,
and what he knew
of what he wished
he might at last become.

"Hear this," he'd say –
and then he'd play it
note for note so they all could hear.
But they didn't hear it
as he played it –
in the same way
that what he thought he heard
was different
from the way he played it.

THIS IS ONLY THE ECHO THIS IS ONLY THE ECHO THIS IS ONLY THE ECHO THE ECHO THE ECHO OF WHAT I HEAR I HEAR I HEAR AND WHAT YOU HEAR IS ONLY THE ECHO THE ECHO THE ECHO OF WHAT I PLAY I PLAY I PLAY.

III

Poor Lester put on his best grey suit and called for the barber to come to his house and cut his hair because he had decided to die and expected his friends to come and pay their respects at the last.

Lester acted this way not out of respect for death, but out of fear for what the living would think of him should he go to his grave with his hair uncut and his suit unpressed. Even in death, he was a professional.

Lester always had money. Well, not always, but later in life he always had money. He made more money than any man alive in his profession while he was alive and he continues to make money for others even today while he rots in the grave.

Lester was never a rich man because he gave all his money away. He kept his sidemen alive so that when the time was ripe, they could play with him again. He'd sidle up to them like a thief from the shadows where they stood at the bar hungering for a drink or a gesture and say to them, "Have yourself a good time man," slipping them half a yard and slipping away before they could protest or refuse or even say thanks.

Lester invented his own language because he was bored with the words and meanings of the words of the language he had already heard and the world he had already seen.

He used words like candles to illuminate the hidden corners where nobody else was ever looking. Lester then slowly taught this language to everybody else who could hear him, and millions who couldn't. But it was not the words he wanted to teach. It was the habit of looking into corners.

Lester was the original inventor of the word cool, and he invented the word while jazz was still hot.

Lester was the most relaxed man on earth. When somebody spoke in the ordinary language of curses and slurs, Lester said, "I feel a draft," and then he would leave the room because the draft was uncool.

Lester invented the word threads to describe a suit of clothes. In the same way, Democritus invented the word atoms to describe the matter which surrounds us and of which we are made.

Lester called his horn a motherfucker,

because Lester would not be
what somebody else already was
Lester would not be
Lester would not
Lester would be
Lester would be
Lester.

IV

Lester's language is the language
of people who do not sleep at night.
Being guilty of nothing, they still
cannot sleep, because,
like children,
they are always desiring
what they cannot have.

Ray Charles was not born blind.
Staring at the sun at the age of three,
he burned his eyeballs, connected
to his brain.
"I loved that motherfucker," he said,
"My mother said I'd go blind,
and I did."

What did he want?
Did he want the blinding summer light of Georgia,
or the permanent night of New York?

The night is supposed to be quieter than the day.
But not in New York, where some people
never sleep.

The waking heads of men in daytime,
Heraclitus said, are turned toward
the self-same light, while in the night
their sleeping heads are turned
towards as many darknesses
as there are heads.

Lester worked the nightshift and kept his eyes half-open
so people would believe that he was half-asleep.
One half was dreaming, one half was wide awake,
so he saw everything,
including all those tunnels into the darkness.

He had to work the nightshift,
because the ones from whom he took his orders –
King Oliver, Count Basie, Billy Holiday –
also worked at night.

Then there were the listeners,
in America, supposed to be the real boss.
Who did not need Lester to listen to.
Who were only in love with the beat
and what it did to their feet.
Dancing until the dust rose in clouds from the floor,
they put sweet rhythms into Lester's horn.

Later, when everybody fell exhausted into bed,
Lester listened to the sound of the lightbulbs buzzing
in the hotels where they allowed him to stay:
WHAW-WHAH-WHAW-WHAW – the buzzing of the blues, the sound
of dead jazzmen, still paying their dues.

These apparent necessities and certainties
do not yet explain
the after-hours sessions in the cities
where unpaid jazzmen tested out each others' powers.
Some sank, some floated,
and some flew right away.

Nor do they explain the sounds
from country woodsheds,
where poor jazzmen, unemployed,
bent their heads and blew their brains out
and emerged alive.

V

Lester and Billy Holiday
loved each other
like no other two human beings.

They loved each other
while each was in love with others.
They were like sister and brother.

People said they were like
Siamese twins
joined at the head.

Lester would outline a figure or a·line
or rather half a figure, half a line
and then Billy would sing the other half
word for word and note for note,
never having heard before what Lester played.

Four lines later, all the others,
Buck, Mal, Jo, Teddy, or whoever else was there
would come in for the chorus,
which by this time
was completely obvious.
On ten different nights,
it would be obvious
ten different ways.

VI

Lester is the opposite
of Dexter.

Dexter
is the right hand man, the man
whose every move is right, the move
that is required
at any time,
in any given situation.

Lester
is the left-hand man,
who speaks with a lisp or a stutter
and understands nothing
of what is ever said to him.

Lester dances to a different drummer
and never pays the piper, because
he is the piper.

Lester, in all his life,
was never late for a date.
This comes as no surprise,
because Lester was known all his life
as one of the slowest men alive.

Even when he was late,
Lester was always
right on time.

VII

Lester drank
        the fermented fruit
                of the juniper tree, letting
the fumes of this potion,
        or poison, seep
                into the cells of his brain,
where it mixed with his
        to create that sweet, foggy ease.

What came up was then not pain,
        but balm, incense, clouds
                of pleasure, air, fragrance, the breath
                      of infants and their easiest laughter.

There was also the laughter
        of knowing adults, knowing
                better than to weep,
because weeping creates only weeping,
        while laughter
                creates life.

In the silence of that night,
Lester was listening, listening
to the slow, easeful gestures of women
deeply in love, listening
to the music of their conversation
when they were alone together
without men. Listening, listening . . .

That helpless,
        knowing laughter.

VIII

Lester is patient and takes the time to frame each note and phrase and link it with the note and phrase which went before and the ones which will come after.

The notes, like molecules of water, always the same, move within a stream, or rest as though in a lake, or shoot up in a fountain, imitating flame.

Lester is patient with the music and takes his time, laying on his notes as a painter lays on colour, layer by layer until the picture is logically complete and glowing – perfect, as it were, or as it will be, then, when the world of people will at last look differently, all its ordinary ugliness within the mirror of the music all transformed.

Being impatient with the real world, Lester takes his time to make the music perfectly and so transform that real world.

IX
Lester Speaks

You think I do this
        because I like it –
stay up all night, drink
        until my head aches and my hand shakes,
speak politely to strangers
        who are blind
            to what is right in front of their eyes,
whose very word
        is ignorance and insult;
            spend every blessed night
        waiting to hear
            and then to reproduce
that sound,
        the sound which approaches the sound
            of a real human being,
instead of this incessant
        barking and clucking.

You mean
        I have to feel like this,
            so somebody else
                can feel wonderful?
Some of them even have the nerve
        to worship me.

I know,
>   I ain't no dog, but
>   >   I ain't no angel either.

I've got all that I can do
>   just to pretend
>   >   that I am
>   >   >   a real living man.

Dogs bark. Chickens
>   cluck. Men
>   speak.

All I do
>   is feed words into the saxophone:
warm words, hard words, cold words, hot words, round words, fat
words, colored words, words of love, funeral words, sharp words,
pointed words, words like burps and farts.

I shape my lips just right, and from my lungs, I push
this thread of air right through this reed, and then,
I move my fingers, bending air inside this tube, my horn,
and it all comes out here,
and goes in there.

I do not expect to be understood, because
I do not understand myself. Understanding
is not the point. Poetry
is the language of the country
beyond the understanding.

Do not understand that I understand
that the world is not real. If
the world is not real, why
do I want it different from what it is? why
do I dream of another and a better place
that is not Hawaii or heaven,
but is this same New York in which I live
and feel like this?

If I had made this world up,
it wouldn't be like this, you
would not be living the way you do,

and me neither. I play
because there is nothing else to do,
and nothing else to be.

I drink to remember what I am and to forget
what I am not. I forget
that I am not Beethoven or Mozart or Bach,
or even Debussy, who are real heroes of civilization.

I am only Lester, a poor left-handed black man
whom even the army wanted to forget.

They gave me a rifle, and took away my saxophone.
They said I was anti-social, and when I raised my voice,
they put me in a cell.

The rifle
has a single trigger. Press this
and a man is dead. How powerful, it can make
wives and children weep.

The saxophone
carries 18 to 21 brass keys,
and as many keys of harmony
as two and a half octaves can contain.
Press these keys, people dance
and dream of children
and the means to keep them alive.

GEORGE BOWERING

The Stump

I can see him now, as if I were in that house and watching him from some invisible advantage. Human eyes in a fly on the wall. He shakes his abundant flaxen locks, and rises from the swivel chair in front of the old beaten typewriter with the Spanish keyboard. He is wearing no shirt, and his narrow hairless trunk rises out of his blue jeans like that white German asparagus prized by people who wait for it in cities with airports all over western Europe.

His name is Robert Kroetsch, a poet with a jittery mind, never married because his metabolism is too quick. When he was a whiplash boy, growing up in the little orchard town of Lawrence, B.C., he imagined himself as a science fiction writer, a science fiction writer so successful and famous that he would be invited to join the first crew of earthmen bound for a second planet.

But he has inexplicably fallen into poetry. Maybe poetry was sitting around waiting for someone with a pulse as fast as his, for this quick lad who could not grow a whisker on his long narrow chin. His first few poems had fallen somewhere into the crack between typewriter and magazine, but eventually his burning veins produced a breath that worked its way under a lot of people's collars, and in the eighth decade of the twentieth century he became the most famous poet in the land.

Now he was trying to dodge some imaginary shrapnel, and write a poem that would save his life.

He was not a kid any more, but he could not put a centimetre of suet on his back. He could not slow his heartbeat. The birds recognized him, and stared into his house through the wide window in back. They watched this creature stuck inside, who should be pulsing and wind-ruffled on a branch of the cherry tree.

But he was stuck inside all right, and that is what this story is all about. That house on the sweetest street in Nanaimo is the subject of all this care.

I wish you could see it, it is that important. What people do, in a tale we tell each other, or the life we see developing uncomprehensibly around us, is shaped by the contours of the place they are doing it in. It is environment if you are a social worker, setting if you are a playwright, landscape if you are a gardener.

If they put a little square box around each infant tomato, the adult tomatoes will grow square bodies, and will thus pack nicely into a bigger box. If you abandon a baby boy to be brought up by wolves, he will be a wolf boy, and howl at the full moon, wont he?

So do you remember the times you have read a novel, and then when you saw the movie you were disappointed because they had not got the house or the street or the farm or something the way it had laid itself out in your reading mind? Sure. The horsemen turned and rode the wrong way once outside the gate. Oh, is that what plane trees look like? In the movie Catherine Barkley has dark hair. Really.

Are you old enough to remember detective novels and cowboy novels as reprinted by Dell drugstore paperbacks? On the back cover the detective books had maps, an aerial view of the house where the murder took place, with the roof removed. The cowboy books had maps of the whole valley, showing the big ranch and the road to town and the mesa and so on, the box canyon, remember? I think it was Dell books. Maybe Popular Library. Dell, I think. Remember the detective novels had a keyhole with an eye looking through it on the front cover. I dont recall what westerns had.

Anyway, remember how you used to read through that book and notice your picture of the place differing from the map on the back cover? You would try to keep it the way it was shown, but soon the earth would be rolling away under your eyes, and the bartender was fat, even when the book said he was lanky.

I have been thinking for a while about what I said, how skinny Robert Kroetsch became the most famous poet in the land near the end of the twentieth century. I said that, didnt I? Something like that. So I'm thinking. There was some poet alive in the seventeenth century, say John Donne, and here we are still reading him now. Can you imagine someone reading a twentieth century poet three centuries from now? I think people have a hard time imaging that the world will last that much longer than they do. I know I do. I think Robert Kroetsch does. One of his poems starts: "I wonder, by my trough, how I lived airing our love,/ and how my teeming brain will gleem/ down past my time."

That, though, is neither here nor there. I am thinking of Nanaimo, of the Nanaimo that appears in lanky Kroetsch's short poems, and the one in which I am imagining him at his desk. It is an outdoor desk, by the way, fashioned from the lowest meter of the trunk of a huge tree that once towered over his bluff-side property.

For you people on the prairie, a bluff is not, at the west coast, a little copse of trees on the bald-headed, but rather a kind of cliff made of soil, something a suicidal horseman might leap his pony from.

You see? Even when I explain it, the southern Saskatchewan reader is still going to have a clump of willows in mind when he sees the word "bluff," or maybe a clump of those scraggly things called prairie oaks.

All right, I said earlier that he rose from a swivel chair, and I implied, perhaps, that he was inside his cedar-shake house on Vancouver Island. Nanaimo used to be a coal town and now it is a motorcycle-magazine town. Kroetsch lives there because he was brought up in the Okanagan Valley, which is more or less the opposite of Vancouver Island. Here he is now in Nanaimo, trying to finish a poem that will prolong his life. Actually, he isnt so much trying to finish it as he is trying to get the middle of it going. He always writes his poems in three sections—beginning, middle and end. He has finished the beginning. He wrote that indoors. But the middle wouldnt come this morning. He moved to his almost natural outdoor desk and tried for a middle. No luck. He was stymied, you would say. Up he stood. He ran his cigarette-stained fingers through his flaxen hair.

"Stuck in the middle," he said.

He murmured.

If you want, he breathed.

If he can finish this poem, and that includes rendering a boffo ending, such is his esthetic, he will have finished a book of poems called *The Stump*. He will be able then to proffer this book to his publisher in Toronto, Marty DiSalvo, who will publish it without question, because he has never before published a poet so successful. Even Doreen Seaweed the west coast shawoman never reached the public with such an impact.

And as soon as *The Stump* is published, Kroetsch's forlorn lost loved one will read it. She will understand the clues he has left about his house in Nanaimo, the whereabouts of the weapon, the note, the schedule. She will get across the country, if she is living across the country, or she will hie down from the Skeena Valley if that is where she has her tent. She will get there in time, and she will save his life.

"DiSalvo has never seen such a relevant manuscript," said Robert, sitting down again, staring at the Underwood.

He decided it was time for lunch. He could find his way to the refrigerator with his eyes closed, which he did. He reached inside, with his eyes closed, and brought out the first thing his hand closed around. It was a carton, or most of one, of pink grapefruit juice. That was lunch, then. He drank it all, and opened the carton and stood it on the sinkboard. Later he would empty his ashtrays into it and chuck it into the garbage can.

She has never been in this house. She has to pick up the clues in his poem *and* imagine the place. Poetry books do not have maps on the back covers. In the sixties a lot of them had maps on the front covers, because an American poet named Charles Olson had a map on the front cover of his first widely-distributed book.

Usually blond Bob didnt have anything resembling writer's block. He had once written twelve sonnets in a day. He loved sonnets. He loved the way they resembled a small house, with a bigger room for cooking in and a smaller room for sleeping in. He liked to put a sonnet to bed. He loved the couplet at the last. He felt like a shoemaker with the polishing rag covering his hand during the voila.

Now regarding *this* house. In poetry it was perhaps not usually so serious a thing as in a novel, this problem of seeing the place. On the next island over there is a woman novelist who wants you to see exactly the kitchen she sees, exactly the wharf she looks at through her kitchen window. But poetry, in poetry you are directing people more to words than to floorplans, isnt that true? More to the inside of the ear than the furniture in the living room.

"The deep recesses of her odorous dwelling/ Were stored with magic treasures – sounds of air,/ Which had the power all spirits of compelling,/ Folded in cells of crystal silence there." There's Shelley and the kitchen he gives to the Witch of Atlas. It is filled with sounds, and isnt that what poetry is made of?

But Robert Kroetsch was not Shelley. He was not any poet in the great tradition. He had come to poetry from the odorous Okanagan Valley, with a deep duty, he thought, to change things. For over a decade he had been trying to make readers see what was in front of his eyes.

He wanted to make the stain on the table before his eyes unconditionally present to his reader. He was bedevilled by absence.

When he was a kid playing guns they didnt shoot real bullets. Billy the Kid didnt shoot real bullets. Billy the Kid is a present they give you when you are young. When he read the many biographies of Billy the Kid, he always tried to imagine the ranch exactly, no matter how the authors described it. Once he went to New Mexico and it was noisy with low-flying black air force jets.

Once in a poem he seemed to break into the lyric, or maybe break out through the lyric, with anger, with impatience. He declared that he wished he could present an actual orange to his reader and watch the reader peel it and get juice on his thumb knuckle, and so on. It is one of his best poems ever. I have just spent an hour looking for it, and couldnt find it. But I know I have it there somewhere, in that pile of Kroetsch's poetry books.

I went to a lecture about Kroetsch's poetry one time. A professor from Kingston said that the orange was a symbol of Irish Protestantism and explained Kroetsch's political stance. He brought in the House of Orange and the Orange Free State, and California and Florida and Walt Disney. He said that Kroetsch's poem was about his desire to return this country to monarchy and strict order.

It was a pretty good lecture. I didnt believe a word of it.

But to return to the poet sitting in front of his patio table. He had raised the stakes. He had decided to put his mimetic powers to the test. The last poem in *The Stump* would be a treasure map, except that the treasure would not be a pot of gold. It would be the body of the poet. If the woman in question figures out the poem and then figures out the map, she will find that body warm. If not, someone else will eventually find it cold.

"My poetry is my life," the poet said in his first ever national interview.

But what if that intended reader should happen to miss Kroetsch's poem? How long a time is he giving himself after the publication of his book, after it finally appears in the nearest town to that place she lives in such a long way, perhaps, north? Do poetry books find their way up there? Of course, with a poet like Kroetsch and a reader like her, that book, *The Stump*, will find its way into her hands, and there will be enough time to find the warm thin blond somewhere on his property.

But if she does happen to miss that poem – what if she is reading the book and somehow doesnt get to that poem, or decides to skip it? Will she read this story? How will I see that she gets it? I dont even know who she is or where she lives, up north there somewhere. Will time run out on me, on her? On the poet?

And if I can get this published in the right place, and she happens to read it in time, so what? I have not read Kroetsch's poem. Yes, but if I did read it, I would not imagine the house and yard the same way she imagines it, much less the way the poet imagined it. But let's worry about place later. What about time?

Well, actually, that problem is pretty well taken care of, when you stop to think about it. Time will not run out. This is not a football game. It is a fiction. Fiction has its own time, and the perpetrator of the fiction is in charge of it, and this life-saving prose is after all a fiction.

So wait, if these are fictions, this story of mine, and the one she will, one hopes, read, and the poem-puzzle he will write when he gets over his block, what have these to do with saving lives? Lives, or at least the lives in question here, exist outside the stories. The stories are there to make life interesting in one's leisure moments.

It seems to me that there are two approaches I can make to helping the poet help the reader save his life, which he need not, remember, put on the line this way. Poetry is my death, he might as well say, if the signifier is really more interesting than the signified, as the hippest critics have been saying about his recent work.

Two approaches. I could fix it so that he gets over his writer's block and produces a poem of almost eyeball-wracking clarity and nerve-exacting detail. A poem that any somewhat intelligent reader with a patient heart could follow to its breathing climax. I could tell about his smacking his forehead, say, with the palm of his left hand, the one he writes with, and sitting himself down at the stump and writing without blot for hours, producing the first long poem of his life, so to speak. I could turn pages into poem:

At one o'clock on equinox a shadow from that fir
Fell on the floor and up the wall and reached
Into the open drawer of spoons. There your eye
Would find one error, one misapplication of doubt,
One silver item that belongs beyond this wall . . .

And so on.

Or I could write a story about the gaunt poet at his outdoor table, feverishly yet quietly laying down unheard runes. In the story I could describe his domicile to its smallest detail, fix every mote so carefully that when you, I mean she, when she reads the poem she will have an exact duplicate of the real building, the real rooms clear in her head.

If I can get the story written by the time he gets the poem written, and if I can see that it gets into print and distribution as quickly as his book does, I might be able to save his life. I do not know who this particular woman reader is, not exactly. But if I can make the story somehow glamorous as well as precise, I will reach a great number of potential life-savers. As Kroetsch would say, that would be sweet. That would make writing worth living for. Too often it has seemed worth dying for.

So I have to make a glamorous and precise story, and I have to write it in such a way that the magazine with the widest circulation in the country will want to print it. Why dont I just go to Kroetsch's place and watch him for day after day, until I see what he has in mind, and just stop him, just make him go on living? Even without her. Even without her there is a reason to live and a reason to write. If she wants to leave everything and go up north, why not let her? Or if it is not up north she went to, if she went to Nova Scotia. And especially – what if she went to Tokyo? What if she is browsing in the glove section of a Seibu store right now? In Japan they dont read stories or poems by Canadian writers from Nanaimo or White Rock. Oops.

Well, I cant think about that. I have a poet's life to save. I had better just get to inventing, I mean describing his house exactly, so that any reader could find her way around in it. And not worry about metaphors, for instance. We still dont know what he has in mind regarding his physical person. He hasnt finished the middle of the poem yet, much less the denouement.

I'd have to say that the chances arent great.

But that skinny baby-faced hay-haired lad is the best poet in the country. You have to do what you can.

Here goes.

The kitchen is painted a kind of Granny Smith green. But before you get to the kitchen, there's the walkway that goes from the front gate around the side of the house overlooking the ferry terminal. The front gate is made of old waterlogged and crumbling four-by-fours, probably cut before World War II. They are nearly black, and smooth from decades of rain. There is no actual gate, just these two posts, about waist high to an average woman. You have to picture two posts that are not any longer parallel as they rise from the earth. Their tops, where their heads would be if they were people, lean away from each other a little, say ten degrees off the parallel. If you are entering the yard between these posts you are facing just about north, perhaps ten degrees off true north. If you are looking straight in front of you, you will be seeing at about seven meters (though it will look different depending on whether there is fog or overbright sunlight and overdark shadow) an old rusted screen partly covered with a grape vine. If we are nearing the equinox, as we are while I write this, there will be many clusters of Concord grapes that have reached nearly their optimum size but are still uniformly green. Let us say that at this angle you can see twenty bunches of grapes, though the number will not register in your consciousness.

I hope you are seeing this right. You've got to be picturing it exactly the way I am imagining it, I mean looking at it. My life, or rather I mean his life depends on it.

Maybe two-thirds of the rusty screen is covered by the grape vine, obviously a very old vine for these parts. One time an old lady came by and said "I remember that grape vine from when I was a little girl." If not two-thirds, certainly sixty percent. In the summer time no one can see into that porch, but then there is never anyone on it. That is why we are looking at the walkway around the side of the house, because the back door, the kitchen door, is the only one used by anyone. Now the grass is usually long and obscuring half the walkway, or making it, let us say, narrower than it need be. But what is the walkway itself composed of? Let's see.

DAVID DAWSON

small forms in a thicket

      (variations, in a progression)

                            even in the dark
                  there are birds summoned by words

    i

in the dark
night will echo
to birds, summoned
by the sounds we make.

wordless presences
inhabit the thicket
from which flow
melody.

              ii

        bird voices sound
        in a thicket.

        a first-quarter moon
        informs this shadowless
        durational.

                        iii

            in-
            cantatory,
                    steps out
            beyond small
            intricate ferns,
                      beyond
            the midnight silent
            green

                                of these woods, this
                    forest
                                : bird sounds.

    iv

even in the night,
bird voice sounds
recur. the moon again
is a poetic slice in the dark

as one by each –
    songs
    earth murmurings
    even night winds smelling of the sea –

echo.

        v

    in the cold night bird voices call.

    leaves rustle in a light
    breeze, all

        is in motion
        beneath
        the silent dispensation of the moon.

        vi

        leaves
        are birds

        & the moon sounds

omage

for Louis & Celia Zukofsky

      whose household stands
      on rhythmic recurrences.

a poem, he said,
for the pleasure of its recurrences,
while Celia
sets syllables to music, she
weaves a mosaic

out of whose loose ends,
forms
    (each tufted shred,
each torn & ravelled fragment
drops into place)
              fall
into form as it forms.

    & then there is the way the language lies
    not unlike a landscape   to the eye
        (given all those tricks of perspective
          & the play of light)

    so that   I can imagine
        "an action whose words are actors."

the ground
we have come to see these famous mimes
perform upon
is not level, but rolling
up from the shore, & thereupon
those celebrated dancers show
that step by tide it goes.

she & he, they
                        move together
    (one crafty bower bird
    with berries, beads
    of turd, with petals, leaves,
    with pebbles, even
    feathers)
                make
                             a sunlit mosaic.

in Celia's odd hours, she sounds bells.
each note tells, accounting for,
her daily changes.
                        clear the air she sings.

the mistress of his song, she moves
in other rooms, he hears her
note by note
                    : a patchwork quilt.

moon poem

      i   (picture postcards)

looking at the moon,
it is
      lovely in its rising fullness
as it drifts behind delicate
oriental brushwork clouds
to reemerge
with a single, clear star beside it
in the twilight sky

but this bright love sign, luminous
moonstone hung over earth
in centuries of poems

constant
in its varying shapes,
fair in her reflecting

fades now, fails
under the cold scrutiny of television cameras
which beam back to earth
(by way of orbiting satellites)
images of the barren surface of our moon.

      it is rock

    which in its dance with earth makes a music still:
    earth feels   vibrations,
    motion
    of her phasing shape against what we take to be night,
    against a darkness swept by solar winds.

        o moon,
        moon of all my dreams   shine for me

        pale stone, opal   shine for me

        remote, cold night form   shine
        shine in your phasing
        shine for me
        now.

ii   (and the cow jumped over, mundanely)

Not only the terrestrial tides and female monthly phases, but perhaps even the ebb and flow of bodily fluids depend upon the reciprocal pull of the earth and this, its co-planet. Each lunar month, as the moon nears perigee, that point in its orbit closest to earth,

> there are moonquakes,
> tremors
> along the rim of the Sea of Tranquillity.

At this nearest point, land tides raised by the mutual pull of the two bodies are at their full, presumably moving residual pools of still molten rock deep within the moon.

We know now too that in the pause between transmission and reception of information sent from the moon, the moon has stepped back from earth. Subject to its own laws, this ancient form is no captive satellite entranced in earth's orbit:

> it recedes,
> propelled
> by tidal interaction with earth
>
> at an estimated
> three centimeters a year.

iii   ("bad moon rising")

          moonscapes
now made visible
are not as my dreams have had them,
silent   and mysterious.

Men have walked upon that bleak surface, brought back pictures and rock samples in sterile canisters, left footprints, plastic bags of feces, now frozen . . .

> dead planet, in retreat   shine for me
>
> earth's only moon   shine for me, now
>   and as you go.

In my dreams of her dying, the moon loses all ancient computations, cannot maintain quarterly phasing, and accelerates her present removal, drifting slowly, perceptibly off into the dark with her cargo of rock, all the garbage from earth's space machines with centuries of accumulated meteoric debris, the heart of her molten still.

        o moon, moon
        you do well

        to flow
        as you do

        away from me.

    iv   ("moon shadow moon shadow")

Memory stirs in the pale morning light of a late moon risen and before the sun. Lines I had composed and then committed to memory twenty-five years ago flow back, come to me now. They seem to have found their place after all this time:

    the moon in all its possible continents
    rounds the black of sky –
    in such full turning, in the world's dream
    lacks only the rustle of bamboo leaves
    to make it oriental.

    v   ("look for me by moonlight")

today
I watch for that pale shape
in the noonday September sky

again. I am
obsessed.
                (moonwords of a dream
                cool as stone in my ear
                reach me
                from across a great distance)

    this song
    stumbles through fragments of moonlight,
    moves slowly to its end.

casting out demons.

I have waited for a comet,
a volcano, for some
phase of the moon to make palpable
this sense I have
of my body caught
in a living dance of whirling constellations

entranced. nor have I come
so far to now turn back,
playing out here this oldest
art of spell casting

as I step toward
the end, resolution

last gesture of my obsession

to enact
at last a closing phase,
a dance of dances done

                    all by the light of

upstream, at one remove: 6:02 am

speechless at Matsqui, he stood on the bank
of the river, watching it flow,
stood watching the river go down to the sea

and waited to dream.

        then he heard it again, that far-off murmur
        as of thunder on a cloudless day
        he knew well,
                      he was
        talking to himself again, inside his head,
        this time about Heraklitus
        (as who would not by a river in his frame of mind)

thinking
how the river
had swung back and forth in gradual meander
these thousands of years, to alter
the surface features of the glaciated landscape,
a broad funnel of a valley, its sea-end delta
cross-cut by channels, mudflats
a body of light in a low tide under the slanting sun
                                            he imagined
                  (though he couldn't see
              round the river's nearest bend
        south and west past a small wooded island)

waiting to dream.

the shape of the whole thing is imaginable:
                          downstream the unseen
islands, and east beyond the valley
a deep canyon,
              confluence
of two rivers, and behind that another

finally to a snowy watershed,
to headwaters a thousand miles inland.

the long flowing form of a river he had seen
between trees, below bridges, and out across the valley
over the years, from its source
to the sea
        held
in the late buzz of sunlight he was
dreaming
        (he suddenly realized)
                        of a river
made all of a piece, his mind
for now at least at ease
in the contours and peripheries
of an imagined afternoon reverie
(in the dark before sunrise)

by the slow bent sweep of a river at his feet.

FRED WAH

Seven Poems

                          I get up in the morning
                and the cloudy skies are in my legs.

                          The news on the doorsill lies
        under the guise of someone else's pulp mill.

                        In the shower I smell creosote,
     my brain drinks up the pressure-treated ions.

You choreospect around the kitchen all egg,
          you say my eyes have dreamed nothing.

Your eyes. Mine squint from the winter sun,
      they read about the world, foothills in the
                                    distance.

            They read languageless heads subtract
              language. No more poems until.

Your tall body twirls, bone-rippled ankles lift.
      We could count, we could dance all day.

      Each day depletes a little more mith (sic),
      mouth logged – logos scaled and decked.

ə

Aghia
      An easthope on that boat going three times as fast as can
                                                    should
                                                    tessera
                                                    puht.

Gallini

The harbour is for the ear and the view. Out there a minor fourth fog horn claims large chunks of life. Sun glints off a windshield. Someone waves, falls, drowns. Boats bob. Staring at the water's risky.

ə

April or maybe March

just this chance touching of you each night
this build-up in our bones under sleep's murky plans
this reservoir of unfamiliar language
near you this disturbed tug of body limb
heart-logged this shore or that
this flailing mind behind your tired sighs all that
core, root

all night the assizes of the years
holds this life at revised angles and intervals
this clamour for America's eyes
all around us "small month's meagerness"
every day precious tonguings accent a fever
words float through the dark freer than ever
know what I mean, this
feeding at the creek mouth
while we wait for the final coordinates

ǝ

You want to know until I found you and your skin which sits in itself language was to me a system out there others thought up but I couldn't.

That story of the moon about her eye knocked out isn't what they told me.

You see I don't remember any other than the sun and moon stuff or mountain mystery almost as "truculent fingerless chamaco" better to be the bird or owl of poetry so I could just do it by itself without being surrounded by these masters of the "arrow" I don't know the surface of unless "it" literally is techne I mean it art is the only environment this paper and all the touch brought to that skin I know the action I'm capable of'll only get done by blood as the life of the mind thought not so silent just thinking of God rather the log sun scooped out his boat from or the cedar Enki drummed with I know exactly every time story happens I remember.

ǝ

for hidden behind glass and silent too walked footsore for years just to have a look led up/on to smouldered tortoise-stoneshell rocks for eyes night seen by day sudden silence stole stolen in the middle of a stealed conversation borderline of a crowded room wealth taken spoken presence is there a kind of after-trauma of the duplex mode not quite sudden recognition more like being struck dumb loss of memory just brushed dust just passing through

ǝ

MAP/FISH/MIND

"quantity" or size in the fish is really only some souvenir of memory that climbs the map-ladder fingers sensate fighting not to be taken keyhook of print thought out over the paper-blue ocean map of the fish which contains the plat of a world spawned river map harboured in its fight against its mind making the size of the fish-flesh cranial and quantity of the brains going at the fish in the fingers feeling out oceans, ocean getting into the arithmetic double the trouble or nothing into fish story fish map pocketing place and genesis genetic so even if "a" map gets carried to the fingers there's prehension ahead just like driving bridge get back to the creek and smell mind.

Ə

the "permanent spirit" turns
pages, the lexicon turns to
numbers, names, and outlines of names

(bare birch of November) nothing
remains after the words
except words, wet leaves

cold substrate of the precessions
motions of the stars
the tongue literally sings through those signs

(buzz)-frost without the body
unable to unscatter the scatter
tremendous volume of light

this is their white bark which coheres
to each phrase, the rest soil
mountain, root-rock

clean tatters shed the mouth
book of the forest uncut hillsides
self-interviewed what fork, sweep

DAPHNE MARLATT

The Difference Three Makes: A Narrative

        for Mary S.

In the dream we argued about a preposition as if in French Emily held the key to the whole story.

you wanted it to read: The Family of Emily Courte is Tired from *The Family of Emily Courte is Tired* – how do we translate?

not that i remember translating so much as turning the page in a kind of hungry absorption and then backing up to reflect, as one does, about the message of the title, i thought – (this was all about framing, for instance the kind of framing a table of contents does) – what's the point of repeating, je me tue à vous le répeter (how many times?) unless it's of . . . tired of . . .

"the family romance."

because the bed had framed you/us watching her slide out into this room so full of women and her father too. three midwives three wise women around your Mary. three the beginning of family, Emily at the end...

there's a chapter within the book from which it takes its name you explained, as the child does the family. or the family does the child i thought. it wasn't Emily that stopped short.

an alley walled by buildings on three sides. this was not in the table of contents.

the house on the hill will be sold, the house you brought her through snow to. lying in sun on the carpet to cure her yellow, sucking white, and the deep content of night out in the country she was not to be brought up in. so there is the letting go of leaves of strawberry begonias, spider plant, the deck, the dogs . . . he wanted out so you moved.

this book, turning the pages tabled there, coupé Court(e). the book that Emily cannot read she is the title page for.

alone no solace, alone the symbiosis of two – pre-mirror, pre-frame. don't drop it: there is that fear you have, of not being able to carry her all alone.

the family is Emily but Emily is more.
Emily short with the short-sightedness of the small sleeps in her crib, blonde hair splayed in her court of little pigs (3) bears (3) the little train that could, dream the family dream of inheritance in her, in her irritants not the dream that could soothe her at all.

this was all about framing as a border frames the contents of the title page where rights are displayed. beyond design designation under the sign of famililacae: nothing so pure as a lily . . .

denying her her father he charged when you moved to the city where the difference three makes became apparent in the helping of friends. at the end of the alley sometimes you turn around.

(f.)Emily out of family. tabled.
in a trice (this is not nice Emilology) en trois coups de cuiller à pot stirred up in the social she comes out little dresses little rag doll tout Court(e) hands full of the train of them repeating tired so tired of the long sanctification in which she appears daddy's angel girl.

The difference three makes always this cry in the night as you return from your fear to find her calling daddy, name for the third person standing by who can pry her loose from the overwhelming two, tu. you teach her big girls don't nurse. let me hold it mama. the languaged mouth as one little pig went to market, one little first person one.

third person could be anyone when it comes to that.

the story says paternal-I,   don't rock the stable.

for the Word is His she will write as I distinct from mother-mine-o-lode, turning away in the script that writes her out of the reciprocal and into what she will become when narrative begins its triple beat about, about her/
accusative.

this is all about framing.

GLADYS HINDMARCH

Improsement 1

Beginning and beginning: writing is always (all ways) be(com)ing and be(ginn)ing in the wor(l)d. Once upon a time, she thought she'd write a beautiful book. She thought she was writing about here for (t)here. She thought, thinks almost everything was/is a possibility in writing. Here includes her as does hear which includes ear; she includes he as the (or thee) includes he. Letters and words are presents/present, presences. Sentences: shapes or structures which depend on who the writer is and how she feels when she writes which also depends on how much she loves sentences and what she's been doing with them recently.

Recently, she's been marking finals and critical essays. She doesn't ever think of writing a beautiful book or beginning a story. She marks down her time to keep her going. When she notices she's too slow, she walks the dog or washes the car so, when she returns, she can grade more quickly. She looks forward to minor amusements such as the student who wrote improsement meaning imprisonment and the one who wrote thoughs instead of those, but she had added a t for thoughts before she reread his sentence. One student, trying to get the title of an Ondaatje poem, wrote cinanum, cinimen, cannamen, cinnimen, cinniman, cinnamin. Another wrote, this exert from *In the Skin of a Lion* focuses on the work force. Exert force. Another said of bp nichol, he's talking about politics in general, that people must react, be aggressive, make changes, rather than stand back and watch as passifiers do. She imagined the whole Peace March, which was marching through Vancouver as she read that, sucking plastic pacifiers and thought that this student has no idea that pacifists make active choices.

Three years ago, she was in a composition class trying to explain, as one of her students put it, the mysteries of the semi-colon. She was joking away about independent and dependent clauses when a young man near the window said, I don't understand – what does the first cause have to do with the second? She looked over his shoulder and saw a male teacher walking towards what was supposed to be a temporary building named P. I'm glad I didn't sleep with you then, she thought. Oh no, she said laughing lightly, you're thinking of cause, but I mean (in a very teacherly voice) clause.

A clause has a subject and a verb that might be surrounded by a number of other words but, can, without these words, if it is independent, stand alone and make sense. Birds sing. Jack jumps. Jill wins. Each of those is a bare sentence with a subject – birds, Jack, Jill – and a verb. Each stands alone. Each is also an independent or main or principal clause. But look what happens if we add a word that makes them dependent or subordinate: when birds sing, if Jack jumps, because Jill wins. They don't stand alone anymore. Jack jumps over the candlestick – that stands alone and is what type of clause? Independent. Right. When Jack jumped over the candlestick

– does that stand alone? No. Right. It's what now? Dependent. Right. While, because, since, which, that, who, when, where, after, if – all sorts of words make independent clauses dependent or what is sometimes called subordinate. Excuse me, said a student, why can't they just give one name to these things? Because there isn't really a they, she said; I know it would be easier if all teachers used the same terminology, but we don't.

When the class was over, she went to her office. She thought about the teacher she had seen and how, in the context of a class, she hadn't missed a beat, but she had thought of that one night several years ago when she went out with him and how horrible she felt when he kissed her. He was between his first and second marriages then; she was still recovering from her first. He reminded her too much of her exhusband or, given the fact that she had truly enjoyed the evening, she was afraid because when she relaxed she wanted what was over and wasn't ready to begin again. Displaced loyalties. An urgent kiss. A pushing away. Nothing soft. A desperation. She wanted a man, but not that man. He wanted a woman, almost any woman. Maybe not. Maybe he really wanted her then. She'd never know. Just another mystery with a semicolon.

Within days, he visited her in her office. Semicolon. His second marriage was over. Semicolon. They talked. Semicolon. Can we talk again? Same time next week, she said. (One of the few things she hates about her work is how long it takes to arrange meetings of any sort, so if two people are available one week at a particular time then. . . .) The next work day, he came to her office door and said, what I really meant was, if I asked you out, would you go out with me? He was standing in the open doorway. She was sitting at her desk. Independent. In minutes, she was going to see the man she was then seeing but who was pissing her off with his self-centeredness as much as she loved his particular use of language, e.g. the lower intestines of Burnaby. Yes, yes I would.

Within weeks, she and he were in bed together. But we're so different, she'd say. They were different. They are different. They are also different than they were then different – then, back then, and then, three years ago. She discovered that he only kisses when he wants to make love. She loves making love, but she also likes to kiss kiss not butterfly kiss at other times. Compromise contains promise. Promise contains prose. Prose contains most of the letters of poetry, but means to turn forward, straightforward, the ordinary language of men in speaking and writing. To her, the turning forward is more the essence than the straightness (or men). To her, a sentence both improses and opens possibilities.

She loves turning, crookedness, circles, flexibility. Ability. The form of a sentence is so elastic that when she is not teaching others how to write sentences that are supposed to be straightforward she thinks she can do almost anything she wants within the confines of its structure. Sentences do make sense of the world. Ondaatje wrote *In the Skin of a Lion* in structures which, one of her students delighted in pointing out, are sometimes fragments, are sometimes run-on sentences, contain comma-splices etc. But, but, she said. Laurence uses fragments too, and there aren't any quotation marks, and she uses you when she doesn't mean the reader. Yet, yet, she said. Wah wrote whole paragraphs without punctuation in *Waiting for Saskatchewan*. Yes, she said. Wah's paragraphs cohere. Laurence's lack of quotation marks makes sense. Ondaatje's lines are written in the cleanest way they could possibly be. Naked prose. Speech rhythms. Everything fits. They begin and end in exactly the right place. What more is there?

Improsement 2

She sits at her computer on a grey August afternoon trying to think of some(any)thing to write, takes a sip of coffee out of a blue and grey mug, looks out through Japanese cherry tree branches to where the mountains usually are – nothing but mist. There's only a few days before the new term begins. Sounds like a sentence. Feels like a sentence: 120 or so new students. Some will be getting excited, exit, x it – in a newspaper the other day the word excites instead of exists caught her attention. Further down the page was exits instead of exists. She thought about spellcheckers, how they can't catch mistakes like that; she thought about saving the article and writing a letter to the editor, but she threw it out because she's on vacation and everytime she turns on TV or reads the paper there are misused apostrophes, it's or its' instead of its, subjects that don't agree with verbs etc – an unpaid language cop she is not.

When she was in grade five, she went to the Diamond Elementary School which had three outhouses at the foot of the field and a pot belly stove at the back of the classroom on which all the grade fives and sixes melted their rat-tail combs and plastic rulers. They had to write with straight pens on foolscap, a lined unsmooth and unbleached paper with flecks of brown pulp in it. Her fingers were always blue with washable ink. She made big blots. She jabbed holes in the paper. Her grade five teacher, Mr Wilson, told her many times that her work was too messy. She broke nibs so frequently that her grade six teacher, Mr Winters, told her once she had to try to write with just half of one. Impossible.

One day she spelled lawyer without the w and then put the layer in parentheses and spelled lawyer right. Mr Winter marked it wrong and, when she began to argue, he sent her out to the hallway where there was a red, fire EXIT sign. She worried and waited and began to cry. She tried to stop by pressing her fingers into her eyes. The tears rolled down her dirty arms, and whenever she opened her fingers she saw EXIT in red. She didn't want him to see her crying. Maybe she should run away or go home. She waited. She heard his feet walking down the aisle along the coal-oiled floor.

Finally, he opened the door. Mr Winter did not carry the strap. He did not look mad. He quietly explained that she was supposed to cross mistakes clearly with one or even more neat lines – exactly what Mr Wilson told the class not to do – and that lawyer was wrong no matter how much "fuss" she made. He was accusing her of deliberately crying? She cried more. He ordered her to go to washroom, meaning the outhouse, and not come back until she was "better." Writing now (words simply appear on screen), she sees that messy foolscap and muddy yard and remembers the smell of the girls' outhouse at the Diamond Elementary School where she threw that spelling test away.

X it: in London, at Dorothy Somerset House, people can look up records of births, marriages, and deaths. When she was in England, she went there, at her mother's request, to look up some information on her father's grandmother. Within less than twenty minutes, she had located her greatgrandmother's marriage certificate, not a xerox copy but the actual certificate, signed with a large X. The lines were extremely zigzaggy, much like those a two or three year old creates. She felt strangely connected with this greatgrandmother she had never seen nor heard anything about. She imagined she had large hands and wore a long dress and had not held a pen until her wedding day. Perhaps she had had to focus really hard to get the two wiggly lines to intersect which they did way off center. She imagined her, excited, exiting the church on a hill which overlooked a coal mining town in the north of England: moments ago, she was single, but now with that X, married.

Improsement 3

May 1, 1948. I thought I would write you sooner but you know how you think you will write tomorrow and by the time it is tomorrow you leave it to the next day. Yes, she knows that feeling and so do many other writers know that feeling, but she didn't know she knew it then when she was eight years old and living at the Diamond, named the Diamond because two sets of railway tracks – one for logging, one owned by the Esquimalt & Nanaimo Railway Company – crossed. She reads the letter that she wrote to her cousin that already shows her voice forming, her style, and contains concrete details of her family's day such as, Leni bought a watering can and now that we are home she is watering the garden. Her mother kept it along with another:

Dear Mom

There was'nt enuogh grain to feed any of the chickens I thought that daddy or you could feed them. But since it is my day I will give who ever feeds the chickens a dime. ~~I will take a banana from the warming closet.~~ I am going to Laye's and will be back soon.

Love
Gladys

Those sentences improse/open particulars for her. She smells wet chicken coops in February and sees a 1920s enamel electric stove (bought by her grandfather in Nanaimo), shaped like old wood stoves with a warming cupboard on top of the oven and a shelf above the elements. It had high curved legs: Leni used to crawl underneath the stove and hide. The warming cupboard was only warm when the oven was on for an hour, so that's where her mother hid the bananas which were something very special in the 1940s and may have cost as much then as they do now in the 90s. Did she put the banana back because she had already had her share? Did she think her parents would be mad at her because they forgot to buy grain? She remembers a path through the Douglas Firs, a shortcut to Layle's house, and almost chokes at the feathery-shitty-dusty closeness of chicken coops she hated cleaning or even entering. She always felt relief when she didn't have to scare hens off nests so she could collect eggs. She hated plucking dead chickens. But she loved little chicks and the feel of a warm egg in her palm, especially in February. The sentences and words in these notes improse/open memories for her: warm eggs from the Diamond on a winter afternoon.

LIONEL KEARNS

The Arrow of Time

This poem is the arrow of time whose outward flight
follows the full cosmic curve back to its unique point
of origin, as you observe the reversal of universal
expansion, and all its astonishing serial corollaries:
divers shooting feet first out of the frothing water,
trees collapsing into buried nuts that burst through
the earth's crust and jump to branches of other trees,
coffins, freshly disinterred, giving up their recently
constituted contents amid lugubrious ceremonials
of church and funeral parlor, before the ride in reverse
to the hospital where bedside technology animates
the dreary corpse surrounded by progressively
less distraught family members. Oh you witness this
feeble individual grow from initial decrepitude
through health to vigorous youth and on towards
perfection and innocence of a tiny baby, which
at that auspicious moment forcefully installs itself
in its loving mother's living body, and there dissolves
in wondrous biological union until all that remains
is the spitting of its last cell and the extraction,
through the father's penis, of the essential sperm
which is absorbed into his body and then that mother
and that father in their turns, shrinking towards
union with their parents, and they towards their parents
and on until all of humanity is drawn down into the one
old African Eve growing younger with the rest of creation
as individuals shed distinctiveness and mutations
fall away and species merge in the stream line
of converging chromosomes, and life devolves
into that single original cell awash and dissolving
in the steaming broth of primordial ocean,
the elements shining pure in the heat of concentration,
as planets spiral towards their stars swirling into centers
of imploding nebulae as everything folds in
upon its own intensity, and matter cracks
to give up its last, simplest constituents of deep energy,
the totality of universe falling together in unmeasurable
density and coherence in one ultimate infinitesimal point
of singularity.

DAVID CULL

Three Songs for Taofi

dark eyes in smiling features
    fit the loss

dark (I)s occluded

loose the fitting
shapes of sound –

skin brown
a circle of grass doors
around the fire

      you sing

      I'll follow

fire song
longing flesh surrounds

      hold you

      hold me

   raise inculcated
    potions of the new –

lips gather,   pace

the place allows

as many words
bare circumstance

      might fit

around an ocean view

a standing circle
fronds in flame

each door our mouths uncover
vibrates with a secret name

> skin calling
> stories of a grove
> prefigured –

>> wars and loves of children

>> playing waves on sand

>> tree, branch and leaf,
>>   incised by moonlight

Let it be!

sea tracing
edges of the earth

a village

> aureoles of juice
> define each body's
> island/
>   sun below.

Jaipur to Delhi

sadhu's eyrie
on the shoulder
of a twisted ridge of limestone

quarry at the butt-end
human ants with head-baskets –

be a while
before they reach him.

Jakarta Airport

terminal receiving line
the splendid 'long house'

    sprouting 'pergolas'
    where planes link up off angled walkways

    concrete 'log-beams,' high black roof
    caught here and there with gold paint filagree
    and precast plaster carvings over portals

fingers of a multi-arm myth –

inward traffic underneath
transit and joining passengers
now free to stroll above

regaled by all facilities

and if they'd somehow lose their scurrying
for food, drink, smoke
and objects of desire

the formal gardens
in between each arm

hold calm.

15 O'clock news:

New Zealand
Milk Worker's Union
action escalates

the milk of industry
gets dumped
in soak pits
dug with front-end loaders

      strikes, injunctions, bottom lines,
      and other modes of market economy data
      clog the holes and funnels of the human interface

the milk of human kindness
poured behind the shed,
rots, finally

groundwater and the streams that rise in it
are dangerous to drink for miles

the eyes of Asia watch
with curious attention

starving eyes in Africa,
not having access to a TV screen,
can only see it in the realm of mythic terrors

      generated by attention to the air and water
      and the seasons

      any careful man would keep a weather-eye on
      as the planet lurches
      under excess weight.

Generator screaming
convoluted psychic circuits
overload, or lose the way

between a private vision,
ruled by anger, ignorance, desire

and knowledge
that these fragile sacks of blood and pleasures
are as common as a speck of sand on one small beach

beside a night sky
full of splendour.

Port Hardy to Prince Rupert

this is the inside passage
as the fog burns off
you lift a camera or binoculars
and focus on the view –

a rocky foreshore
fir and cedar covered hills
three hump-backed whales

the ship slides past
a film of memory

all passengers may now record
positions on the channel
back and forth from here to formerly

some kind of instant brochure on the new

through a round gate facing Keefer St.

Dr. Sun Yat Sen Garden
spirits in the rocks
in form

go clockwise
round the area
in case some modicum of due respect
reveals a message

small left-turning circuit
near the entrance gate
defines the negative
at first glance
insignificant, stone fragments
dropped between the bamboo and the gravel,
afterthought, a sidetrack just to fill in space,

until you focus
on the dark doors
underneath each pile.

ROBERT HOGG

Extreme Positions

      (for bp

The lovely play language is .   The lay of the poem .
    The place maide .   The dropping or adding of a letter .
      Tension .   Love crosses all bodies
          of water   or of land

              vi
              o
              le
              (n)
              t

Love knows its own bounds
        but crosses these
                willingly
knows to stay
stray
        brings the point of light
right up to the eye
knows that all event
is also a screen
        retina
                page
where the hand trembles
to leave a mark in

                v
                i
                o
                l
                a
                t
                e

              space

so great the mind's
demand
that a map be drawn
lines be drawn
against chaos
but also
break the edge

Put an S on things. Put S in the world. Sing

                silent
                  p
                  a
                  c
            spell
            o   i
            u   g
            n   h
      words standing
                  a
                  l
                  o
                  n
            essential
free .   The lovely play   love is   a language made

                sign

(against unknowing

Becoming Night

(for Harry Flaig, artist

To tell the truth
when I look out my
west window I don't
see a snow clad
log cabin
its neat row of windows
amber against
gathering dusk

What I see is
a blank pane of glass
and beyond that a man
reflected in the glass

(though I believe the building's
out there
what's left of it

it was never a log
cabin with smoke
curling from its chimney
never exactly
sequestered
a branching tree
in the foreground
as you have chosen
to paint it
but it's true
it does lean over
as the barren
hickory bends to
prevailing winds

What I come back to
this snowfallen
December night

is not a decrepit
shed about to
collapse

nor indeed the
predictable portent
beyond the glass

What haunts me
simply
is the picture

you imagined
standing inside
the window as I

do now imagining
in early evening
a skilled brush

catching the subtle
greys and muted
blues of the winterscape

a yellow light
behind the windows
not so bright it couldn't

also be the setting
sun caught in
the southwest wall

it being that time
of day becoming
night

The Present

(with thanks to Harry & Bea

Let me come haltingly
face to face with the person
in the street the face
in my dream, whatever
rings clear or sounds
as true as this
Tibetan bell
moment beyond moment
rung with such
clarity to wake both
heart and mind
locked in one
step the soul
hungering, hovering
a mystical wave   air
moving   rhythm
repeated
memory of monks
in trance
ringing
hour upon hour
the worshippers
up the arduous
Mountain Path
to the shrine

Why do we seek
what is already
held in mind / hand
rocking the dorje
hour on hour
         sound
an eternal presence
ringing through every
stone on Himalayan
hills

      And there is no
falling no falling
away
      from the pure
sound the clear
water
      running
downhill
         in the mountains

      And I remember the spring
at Arunachula
the old men
bathing in the boiling sun
      and the stone so hot
to look into it
made you reel

Falling Through Space

What struck me
dumb in Escher's
art

was sound
uplifting
silence

taut
      bent

words
strung at curious
angles of intent

the whole
structure
about to fall
into new
sentence
walls

inhere
to an old
harmonics

of the heart
a new
syntax

the hand's
light
touch

a string's
vibration
resonant

measure
of time
spent

falling through space

caught &
held
in the eye's

start
a visioned
world

held so
momently
lines

run in all
directions
make it still

DAVID BROMIGE

Couplets

The time not spoken for
and the worry that nothing's late again.

This non-existent time
that wants you to watch.

To see you watch. The time
that hasn't existed.

The agenda realizes the hands
that, having written it, now hold it.

The time not spoken for
appointed to meet the silence.

The word death sprawled across
the word for being late. The time

non-existent since not spoken for
that wants to watch you see.

Hitch up that shift. That pony
to these shafts. Not light

but paint. The word spoken.
For, the experience. The port,

the restaurant they sat in,
the frontier. The ferry, late.

As usual. The child
that needed comforting.

The non-existent tugs
at vessel or sleeve.

The Edible World

1

Tourists
Wonder

their ideas
Idea

The huts, streets,
struts

hats, tattoos
like little socks

and stop a little
longer

Wistful
Grateful
to be not one of those

Hemmed, jammed

yet enabled
these ruins
kept up

the bells,
the flowers

the rats

The tourist's ponder
before the next

Cyclopean I
adorns the neck
stuck out for the instance

2

That the cardinal points
That the disposition of stars
That these systems of high pressure

accomodate

That one can be bent
into the straight

People catlike at the beach
register the next

The eased body
is its mind eased

Glancing up
off the cars
delivering and returning

the goods
destination
generated

Child in the wave
Watched by the parent

That nothing will occur
that hasn't yet

let go the string
when the balloon floats up

With each step down, the air grows cooler

This is the sense in which one has begun
before knowing it, to read the situation

if indeed it is a "situation" we "have" here

"I don't want to be psychopathologized"
"I don't want to be guilt-tripped"

"I would sooner analyze what occurred

before these stipulations
with their implicit analyses"

So he says we take on trust

what we know has a shape
that we owe to accident

to which one responds by shaping

The mounting fastness of parataxis

No matter, never mind that
the moment has or is its own dynamic

Fire from holes in the earth! Astounding

Hence the practice of amnesty
following such an event

"When I mutilated myself"

As the subject mutilated himself
this subliminal narrative voice took over

Let's view these agents as objects

"Irrational" "Distance" "of interest"
in the People's Theater Group

Or consider the person driving

at erratic speeds on the public highway
ennobled by constitutional guarantees

and the failure to indicate an imminent turn

"The heat was phenomenal" "Ennervating" *Nameable*
Do you view the line between love

and hate as "dotted" or better *dashed*
And the children who witness

as impressed by the chances taken

as the radio tells us hearts are breaking
"Self-dramatization at an early stage"

In physics, displacement

or the *quid pro quo* of common law
The sterile safety of all conclusions

The difficulty of all figures

intermits the wish to terminate
The bamboo through the concrete

"I feel you hate me lately"

Ten white counters, ten black
"Was that when we were making love"

When the subject knows its object
knows itself a like object

But because (of) our history

("I'm trying to think of everything"
"Well try to think of something")

Or nothing, treetops
or rooves in a light wind

and were you a bird or a slate

The parrot says "pieces of eight"
in the book that was hurled

at the self one was mutilating

TWO
Interviews

IRENE NIECHODA AND TIM HUNTER

A Tishstory

Introductory Note by Roy Miki

Back in October 1985 – what was the occasion for the re-union? Not twenty years since since its inaugural issue in September 1961, not twenty-five years, though nearly so. I recall that the years didn't round out then, but somehow the "idea" of a re-gathering sounded an appealing note. Charles Watts who works in the Contemporary Literature Collection in the library was the instigator and the plan was to organize an afternoon talk session at SFU. The call was issued to former *Tish* writers and a surprising number appeared. A reading was scheduled for the evening, at the Western Front.

The panel discussion was informal so that there would be, we hoped, some lively impromptu recollections and reflections. We began by asking each writer to speak for about five minutes on whatever aspect of *Tish* stood out in memory. These were followed by responses of the writers to each other, after which the audience was invited to ask questions. The section edited by Niechoda and Hunter is taken from the opening section of 5-minute statements (with some spontaneous interaction from some who could not help but react to what was being said).

For readers unfamiliar with the history of *Tish* in the 1960s, it may be useful to know that the writers on the panel were part of three phases of this Vancouver magazine. In its initial phase, from September 1961 to March 1963, it was run by an editorial collective consisting of Frank Davey, George Bowering, Fred Wah, David Dawson, Jamie Reid, the group of young writers gravitating towards UBC prof Warren Tallman, then a recent arrival from the US. The home of Warren and Ellen Tallman became a circle within which the Vancouver writers were to meet the American writers Robert Duncan, Charles Olson, Allen Ginsberg, Robert Creeley, Michael McClure, Jack Spicer et al. – the most influential voices of the generation described as the "new American poets." In the glamorous atmosphere of Duncan's stories of little mags, among them Cid Corman's *Origin*, *Black Mountain Review*, edited by Robert Creeley at Black Mountain College, Diane di Prima and LeRoy Jones' *The Floating Bear*, came the desire for a local mag with comparable energies. Nineteen monthly issues were published, until the summer of 1963 when the collective dispersed. Davey, Bowering, and Wah left Vancouver, and David Dawson remained as editor for five issues, published between August 1963 and June 1964. Lionel Kearns and Gladys Hindmarch were never officially acknowledged as members of the collective but they were certainly vital members of the working group. Dan McLeod (who would later begin the *Georgia Straight*) took over as editor for the second phase of *Tish* which included writers Peter Auxier, David Cull, Daphne Marlatt, Sam Perry, Gladys Hindmarch, Bobby Hogg. From issue 41 on, for five issues, the mag entered its third and final phase, ending in 1969 with 44 and

45, issued jokingly as D and E, signs that it had run its course. Soon after, Stan Persky and Dennis Wheeler, with the support of McLeod, began the *Writing* series, published as a supplement to the *Georgia Straight*. This tabloid mag, also known as the *George Straight Writing Supplement,* soon refocussed the poetic activities of the city – at which point *Tish* (as such) entered the gone world of literary history.

Warren Tallman: I'm writing a little introduction to this evening's reading by *Tish* writers, and I lit on a phrase: "How people come to possess their own imaginations." That seems to me to be what *Tish* was all about. I think of *Tish* actually as not the most important stage: it was the initial stage that was occupied by a collection of semi-delinquent young people, most of them small-town, and they drove cars a lot [laughter]. And when they got to Vancouver, they continued to drive cars a lot, and they weren't particularly *outstanding* students at the university, because they were so busy doing other things. But some force was in them which was creating a world in which they could possess their imaginations, and the device of it turned out to be poetry, in the broad sense, and some of them wrote prose, also. So it's really more an instance of how about a dozen or fifteen fairly goopy people [laughter], not really synched into the society very well, could manage – because there wasn't anything else around to do – to possess their own imaginations.

Now I think the subsequent story beyond *Tish* gets even more interesting because as a group, their communal sense was extraordinarily powerful. They obviously liked one another; they obviously lived on a great love-hate daily basis. You know: "I can't stand your poems, mine are better, all that is not *so.*" It was a very active communal thing. *Tish* wound down, the most active phase wound down, the summer of 1963. Everybody got a little tired. And it seemed as though it was over, but actually it was just beginning. A number of the main movers in *Tish* – and that would be Freddy Wah, George Bowering, and Frank Davey – particularly due to publications, went off to other places in Canada. But they continued the activity of the newsletter in its most effective sense in *Open Letter,* the magazine that Frank Davey has edited since 1966. And it is more long-lived, in continuity, than *Tish* was. And it has been a kind of a meeting place, and a gathering-in place, not only for the original *Tish* crowd, but for closely associated poets.

Roy Miki: Warren, George brought along his bound book of *Tish: 1-19*. After the July [1961] lectures that Duncan gave, this group got down to business. They had enough organization to say "We're going to put out a magazine once a month" – and it came out faithfully for nineteen issues, until March 1963. So there was an amazing amount of energy there, right?

WT: Yeah, well I think Roy is trying to get me back to the point of *Tish* [laughter]. Do I understand his devious mind? It is true that the *Tish* energy was phenomenal: it did come out once a month for nineteen consecutive months. I was only trying to point out the "beyond" stage. Where that energy went, once it was released.

RM: Warren, was there a pre-*Tish* stage? Was there a nucleus of writers before '61, or in the late 50s?

WT: There were "prominent" Canadian writers in town. Earle Birney was in town; Dorothy Livesay was on the scene; Phyllis Webb was partly on the scene, and partly not. But they were working in isolation. There was no coherent scene whatsoever, and the *Tish* group was working very much as a group, back and forth, day to day.

Gerry Gilbert: Warren? There was a coherent kind of downtown scene of artists and writers, an inner-city group that had gone on and grown up out of the traditional Vancouver scene.

WT: Right. What Gerry is talking about is what I call the "downtown poets." They were there. In fact the downtown poets and the *Tish* poets got in touch very fast.

Gladys Hindmarch: There was also about a year of Writers' Workshops, where people got together once every second week.

Frank Davey: I've got a photograph of you setting up a booth for the Writers' Workshop in 1959.

RM: I think Gladys' involvement in the Vancouver writing community predates *Tish* by about two or three years at least?

GH: If Warren's talking about poets that were already known, then yes indeed: that energy of the young people – they were not moving around a poet who was already known. But there were a number of us who met each other at a thing called Writers' Workshop, which was at a professor's [Tony Friedson's] place. We'd get together once every two weeks with a bunch of sake that Frank used to make. I thought it had been tested in the chemistry department at UBC, and was higher than normal wine in terms of alcoholic content. It looked like scotch, actually, a real *golden* sake. And he'd always bring a gallon or two of this –

George Bowering: Actually, it looked like Lake Okanagan [laughter] –

GH: And our stuff would be duplicated by this professor, and we liked this guy very much, because we didn't pay any attention to him. I mean, he was a marvellous guy: he provided a space, and whenever there was a vacuum in the conversation he had something to say. Say somebody read something that was quite horrible: Tony would jump in and say something for a minute and a half, and then we'd all shout at Tony that he was full of shit, and then we'd start talking about whatever it was. He was just great. It really set a ground [laughter]. It's at that place that a number of us met each other.

I guess a thing that *really* pulled it together was *The New American Poetry* book, which came out in 1960, but which people didn't really read in Vancouver until 1961. I remember getting that in the spring of '61. And through talking about that, Warren told me that Pauline Butling had written a very interesting essay on one of Robert Duncan's poems, and I read this essay; and then I read an essay by Fred Wah, which I think was on William Carlos Williams. Suddenly I wanted to meet these two people. Once that book came out and people were reading it, people who were in the Writers' Workshop – and in other circumstances like poetry classes, Warren's and Canadian Lit classes, and what not – got together at yet another professor's place, Elliott Gose's. We decided we would go through this *New American Poetry*, and try to make *some* sense, just some *little* sense, out of the essay "Projective Verse" by Charles Olson at the back. And I remember after about three Sundays in a row we finally decided that that was it, we couldn't get any further on that essay – could get *no* further, unless we had some outside help [laughs]. Not ourselves. It's at that point that we put together money, which I think only cost us five dollars each, to get Robert Duncan to come up and give a series of three lectures. And he came up by bus to do that for us. And from there a number of other names started to fill in that geography or map of the poetics of Vancouver.

FD: A lot of us were, as Warren said, coming from small towns, coming with a sense of being muzzled in that small town background, and seeing the university as a place where we would be able to find some way to become articulate. The recipe for the sake came from the Sumas Mountain area near Abbotsford [laughter].

GB: Where did it go? [laughter]. I hear the Vancouver police have it.

FD: So that when Robert Duncan came up and gave those lectures, there was, as Gladys indicated, about a two or three year history for some of us in moving toward being writers ourselves, in helping each other with criticism, or anger, or whatever else would serve as a catalyst. So the energy was there to move from Duncan's lectures to the publication of the first issue of *Tish*, roughly two months after those lectures. It took us a month to actually put it into production. He [Duncan] was there in late July, as I recall, and by middle of August, I was up in the Okanagan visiting George, tenting it in an Okanagan campsite, and typing the first issue of *Tish*, at one of those highly glossy, varnished, British Columbia picnic tables.

WT: Ask David [Dawson] what he was doing in Vancouver at that time, because he was a Vancouver poet.

GB: The only one besides Jamie [Reid].

RM: Jamie Reid and David Cull are not here. We have two *phases* of *Tish*, actually, sitting here. We've got the original collective of '61-'63. Then in the fall of '63 Daphne [Marlatt] and Dan [McLeod] and David [Dawson] – you stayed on in the second phase, with Peter Auxier, David Cull, and Gladys.

David Dawson: I was involved in the Writers' Workshop with Gladys. I met Lionel [Kearns] at the Writers' Workshop, I think, and Jamie [Reid]. That was in '59? '60? I guess 1960. And drank Frank's sake. I remember drinking Frank's sake, before I met Frank. I was very *sick* on Frank's sake before I met Frank [laughter]. And we terrorized – Warren was talking about delinquents – we terrorized faculty homes. I remember when a professor (who was I think, at one point, the head of the English Department at UBC) had invited the Writers' Workshop over, and we all got *terribly* drunk on Frank's sake, and Jamie levitated on the front lawn [laughter]. It was mad. It was really mad and exciting and exhausting the whole time. I'm trying to think about the continuity – where I *came* from. They were coming from other places and I was doing some just absolutely hideous, awful things – I mean *writing* [laughter] – many of which are in the first few *Tish*es. It was through Jamie that I got involved more directly with Frank and George. I was telling Gladys at lunch today that Jamie at one point said "We will meet at the Espresso House on Howe Street" – which I think is gone now – and he said "You will bring everything you have ever written, and I will look at it." So I said okay, and went down there, and I bought espresso all afternoon while he read everything, line by line, and said "This is great. This is *awful*. This is great. . . ." That was the beginning of it. He *dragged* me to meetings, and to Warren's place that summer, to the things with Duncan, and then it went from there.

GB: Hey – I've got *Tish* 1, 2, and 3 here. For ten bucks I won't read them out loud.

DD: Oohhhh. There are some *really* unbelievable things in the first three *Tish*es.

GB: That's what Warren was telling us gently – that *Tish* was not the most *important* step of the way [laughter]. And anybody that goes back and reads those poems would probably agree. I was *utterly shocked* – not really, 'cause I suspected it before – when I was reading *Tish: 1-19* this afternoon. I was shocked to find out that Fred Wah's poems were way better than mine [laughter].

RM: Keep going George.

GB: He wasn't better than I am, but the poems were way better than mine. I wasn't really going to say anything – that was more or less it.

It's really peculiar – I have large holes in my memory. I can't remember very much except the parts that I've been told by other people. The person who seems to have the best memory of what went on in that time, *if* it's true – that is to say it has the most *details* – is Fred Wah. But Warren saying "No, no, no, don't start a magazine!" – *that's* one part I remember [laughter]. Warren was saying "Whatever you do, don't start a magazine." Gladys has a great memory and she tells me, from time to time, what happened in those days. But I can't remember much about it. What was going on was a lot less interesting than the stories that were told about it.

And Warren's right: the fact that *Tish* magazine was happening is a lot more interesting than the poems that were written in it. Except – if you go and look at the *better* poems that were written by professional poets back east, they were poems that were way better than ours, but are nowhere near as interesting, because they're kind of pale copies of late-Georgian British poems. Or professor poems. And that was the policy on which we ran things in *Tish*. We used to startle, amaze, and anger people back east, by writing on our rejection slips "These poems that you have sent us are far superior to *anything* we are going to publish in the next issue" [laughter]. We believed it. That's true. I used to do that all the time.

Lionel Kearns: George, that's not true.

GB: Oh, sometimes we just said "pish," y'know. We used to state that policy to people all the time. We'd say "Well, this is not a grab-bag magazine." This is not *The Fiddlehead Review*, right? We were not like a lot of magazines that say "We haven't got any axe to grind. We're just going to publish the best of any kind of poetry we find." Which is really stupid, we thought. And I still do. We decided we wanted to *really promote* one certain kind of poetry, or angle of poetry, and we were *not* going to publish sonnets by Fred Cogswell. That was not going to happen. Quite often we would find poems that I think some of us agreed were better than—well, they were better than the poems I published in *Tish* 2, for instance. But we said "I'm sorry, but we're not in the market for the best poems. We have an attitude about poetry that we want to promote, that is different from the attitude that you find back east. Primarily. Or in other parts of Vancouver." I still believe that. I have *no use* for a magazine that just publishes a grab-bag of the best stuff they can get. Because it won't be any different from the seventy-five other magazines that are just there to get people published.

Daphne Marlatt: Well, the thing is that *Tish* wasn't just a poetry magazine. It was also a poetry magazine that published criticism. You guys were quite flagrant in your critical articles.

GB: Oh yeah. Like saying "John Milton was absolutely incorrect" [laughs]. Twenty-one-year-old guys saying "Wordsworth had the wrong idea entirely" [laughter]. But what Daphne says is important: it was called a "poetry newsletter," and by newsletter we meant largely a place for people to argue about poetics. Although we did put lots of news in: we gave news about new books that came out, and poetry readings that were going on, and stuff like that.

RM: In the late 70s, when I was going around trying to gather together tapes of readings in Vancouver, I finally got to Fred's house in the Kootenays. We were going through Fred's collection, and he had the *entire* collected tapes of the [1963] Vancouver poetry conference. He'd been sitting with them for close to twenty years. He told me the story of taping, in one of the sessions, and the speed wasn't correct, so he had to use his finger to maintain the right speed to keep a natural voice flow. He had to do it for the whole lecture [laughter]. I thought, this guy is sure devoted to the record of oral events. As it turned out, Fred had one of the best tape collections that we've ever managed to get. It was *rare* for people to be taping at that time. We couldn't get many tapes before 1961, in fact before Fred Wah started taping. So if Fred has that accurate memory, we should try to get him to talk about where he was coming from at that time.

Fred Wah: Well actually, the tape thing was really Warren's fault.

RM: Oh [laughing]. Everything was Warren's fault.

FW: Well, it really was. It was his idea to tape the '63 conference. Warren managed to get a brand new tape recorder – which broke down at the second session.

Ellen Tallman: These were *big* tape recorders.

FW: Yeah, this was a great big tape recorder. And it broke down. So I had to take up the slack for part of the time. That's how I got into taping, because Warren's tape recorder broke down and I had to pick it up.

It seems to me that one of the major things that I learned in my experience with *Tish* was through this technique that Warren had in the classroom, and outside the classroom, called resistance. Warren would always throw up these baffles. Even when he was teaching, he would throw up incredible interpretations of poems, so you'd have to fight back.

My memory of how I got involved with *Tish* was, I was in music – and perhaps that's why I can go at one and seven-eighths for forty minutes – and I'd been somewhat associated with Lionel Kearns in Nelson. Lionel and I were in a jazz group together. He was older, he'd come down to UBC and he was writing poetry, and I started writing poetry. I didn't know any poets – I was from Nelson, too. I didn't know anyone in Vancouver except other kids from Nelson. And I remember going to Lionel and saying "You write poetry and I write poetry, and you know some people who write poetry. We should start a magazine [laughter]. Why don't we get together." And Lionel said "You know who you need to talk to? George Bowering." And George Bowering was The Writer on campus. He wore capes, he wore a big hat [laughter], and he had set himself up as The Writer. He lived at a place around Seventh and Sasamat, up on the second floor; we had to get through his landlady first. And then we went up to this little garret-type room, and we talked to George, and he said "Well, you know, that's interesting that we should maybe get together. But we should go and see Warren Tallman." So we all got into one of our cars [laughter] and drove across town to see Warren. And Warren said "Yeah, that's really interesting, but you really shouldn't start a magazine yet. Just hold off. We've got to talk about this. Like, I know a lot of other writers, and we should get together and talk about it." So, in my memory anyway, Warren started setting up Sunday afternoon meetings, and we started talking. It was about the same time that *The New American Poetry* came out, too, and we focussed on that. We started reading some of our own poems at a certain point. We brought in Duncan and then as you say, the magazine got going. It was Warren's resistance, Warren's pedagogical device really was a key in, y'know, finishing it.

FD: The other side of this was that whenever you met Fred Wah, you said "Hello Fred," and he would reply "Let's start a magazine" [laughter].

WT: I have a different version of the *Tish* poets coming over to the house, and it goes approximately like this: I look out the front door, and uh-oh, somebody's coming. So I walk into the kitchen and I say, "Geez Ellen, here they come – what'll we do? [laughter]. And then Ellen says – and this is the greatest line of all: "Tell them that they've got to *say* something" [laughter]. And then I would very calmly walk into the living room and say, "Well now, what I think is, you should really *say* something". And really, it's all they've ever been doing ever since.

RM: I think we'll go over to Lionel.

FW: Lionel was the fringe factor of *Tish*. You've gotta know this: Lionel was offered an editorial position in our collective, and *turned us down*.

Voice: Hisssssss [laughter].

FW: And then he hung around the edges for those years, and he had his office right across from the *Tish* office, in one of the barracks that we had out at UBC, and he would always be poking his nose in and saying "Is that printer working yet?" [laughs].

GB: He was always using our *stuff* [laughter].

FW: I remember the first time Lionel really got involved with *Tish* was about a year after we were going. The Christmas issue was coming up. We hadn't missed the fourteenth of the month for over a whole year, and here we were all splitting for Christmas holidays. Who was gonna do *Tish*? Lionel was the only one. He was too poor to go anywhere, so he was staying in town. And Lionel said "I'd like to do an issue of *Tish*." So he put out all on his own the Christmas issue of *Tish*, I remember that. And I received a copy when I got home in Nelson, that you mailed to me.

LK: Gee, what I like about *Tish* is that its *legend* keeps on developing with the years.

GB: Yeah, well, Lionel was the only Catholic on the Vancouver scene.

LK: Oh, yeah! God, I had incense going all the time. A regular sacrament.

FD: I thought he gave up a position with the priesthood to become an editor.

LK: It was the same thing for a while. I had a sense that there were a lot of things happening in Vancouver before *Tish* came together, a particular stage in the development of what was going on there. There *was* a collective that was operating there for three years or so. I remember I came back from Mexico in 1959, and I took another – a third year, I think, at UBC. And there was a crazy guy in my Spanish class, who turned out to be George, and we got together in various ways, one of which was in the Writers' Workshop club. Very soon we saw that we had similar interests, and George said to me "You gotta meet Gladys Hindmarch." And we got together with Gladys, and she said "Oh, you're interested in Jack Kerouac – Warren Tallman has given a great talk on Kerouac." So I got connected with Warren. At one point I took Warren's poetry course. And in that course there was Gladys, and Frank, and bill bissett. And a lot of other people too. A lot of the writers on campus had seen Warren as being a very knowledgeable person, and a person in touch with a lot of interesting things that were going on. So, we tended to gather around him. That was at the time when Warren was inviting the San Francisco writers up, and so on. What I was most impressed with, in Warren's basement, when we were listening to Duncan, was the fact that Warren and Ellen owned an automatic washer. It was the first automatic washer that I'd ever seen a private citizen owning [laughter]. I'd seen them in laundromats, and I'd seen them in the ablution hut at Acadia camp, but I'd never known anybody that actually owned an automatic washer.

GB: But they're Americans, eh.

LK: That's right [laughter]. And I was flabbergasted. I thought, this is the way those professors live. He's a real city slicker.
Warren said that we lived very dangerously, and it is very true, we did. We had very fast lives in those days. I remember there was almost a whole generation of west coast writers that was almost wiped out because of being poisoned by Frank's sake.

GB: Also because of his driving at that time, right? [laughter].

LK: Fifteen or ten of the members of the club had to be taken to the General Hospital to have their stomachs pumped out. And that was the last time they discussed the Olson essay, too [laughter].

FD: It wasn't the sake!

Voice: What was it?

LK: It was the sake. It was terrible. What interests me, about *Tish*, now, and what interested me about *Tish* very early in the *Tish* history, was *Tish* as a medium. I declined to be an editor because I couldn't agree with the ideas that all my funny friends had about writing and poetry. And so I said "Well I can't back you guys up with all these crazy ideas that you have," so I stayed out of the editorialship of *Tish*. Then with the first and second issues I saw what an amazing *medium Tish* was. It was immediately successful, right from the very beginning. The idea of putting it out in a cheap edition, and not charging any money for it but sending it around to everybody that you wanted to read it, was a great idea. Suddenly, almost overnight, *Tish* made a big impression on the literary scene. Not in Vancouver, but nationally and internationally. At that point I said "Wow, I want to get in on this," and I think I did get into *Tish* 2 or at least *Tish* 3, and by that time I was a big supporter of what was going on.

WT: It was extremely important that *Tish* did *not* try to get subscribers. They made up their own list of subscribers, and *sent* the magazine to them. It was *active*, going out with a magazine, rather than seeking attention coming in on them. They went out after the attention. And they paid the postage themselves. They began to get responses from the people they sent it to.

LK: I think the abrasive editorialship of the magazine was very important, because the *Tish* people attacked all these establishment figures and irritated them. It was a kind of an irritant in the situation. And that got response, that was a good idea. But it worked in the context of the day, and the context of the day was a literary situation without very many literary magazines. Five years later, there were hundreds of literary magazines, and *Tish* would be lost, or a similar magazine would be lost.

GG: But there were literary magazines like *Floating Bear* all over that were very much like *Tish*.

LK: There had been a few, and in fact *Tish* was modelled to some extent on *Floating Bear*, and maybe *Combustion*, or something like that. That's true. But it was pre-Canada Council, that's another thing. All the Canada Council money to support magazines had not come in yet, and when you gave a reading, you didn't get paid for the reading. And there wasn't that great wealth of literary publications that we have now, so it did make its impact because it was singular in its own way.

FD: What Lionel, I think, is alluding to, and which was very important for *Tish*, was the sense that most of us had of being marginalized. I spoke about coming from a small town which was also Lionel's situation, and Gladys' situation, Fred's situation, and George's. I think we felt marginalized in a number of ways, having come from a small town, and being disadvantaged vis-à-vis, in our view, the students who had been educated in the city. Marginalized in terms of being young; marginalized also in terms of the educational or the academic or intellectual interests of the faculty at UBC. We definitely felt as if our own interests somehow were met, with the exception of Warren, unsympathetically. Which is why we abused the faculty houses. Marginalized by being Canadian in North America; marginalized by being west coast and British Columbian, in the Canadian context; marginalized by being interested in writing, and becoming more and more interested in language rather than in content, which was the dominant esthetic, it seemed to us, in the magazines that were most visible in Canada. And that sense of being marginalized, and the anger that that aroused in us, was I think a very important source of the abrasive energy that Lionel was talking about. And so that nasty edge, that irresponsible edge, that you see throughout *Tish*, I think it had very clear origins, and I think those origins turned out to be – with hindsight now – of enormous advantage.

FW: I remember looking at an issue of *Evidence* magazine at that time. I think George and maybe Lionel had gotten involved with *Evidence*, or had submitted some poetry, or had started getting some dialogue going with the editors of *Evidence*. And there was a letter to the editor in there – I think it was from Kenneth McRobbie – to the effect that "We in the east" – that is, in Montreal at that point – "aren't too interested in what's happening out west. We're more interested in what's going on with New York. That is, our axis is north-south." I remember I was outraged at seeing this, that they weren't interested in us, they weren't interested in what we had to say, or in our writing. And I know that for me that was one of the impetuses too.

ès

RM: The original *Tish* collective, I should point out, abandoned the project as they went to all these various places. Fred went to Albuquerque; and Frank you went to Victoria; George went to Calgary; and Lionel went to England; and David you stayed on; and Gladys stayed on. The second phase of *Tish* began in the fall of '63, just after the important UBC poetry conference in the summer of '63, where Duncan, Olson, Ginsberg, Creeley, Margaret Avison, Denise Levertov, and a few others came to Vancouver and had this very influential series of talks and readings. In the second phase Gladys and David stayed on, and then Dan McLeod and Daphne Marlatt joined the editorial collective. The post-*Tish* phase, when there are a lot of other literary magazines: Dan and Daphne could probably talk about that subsequent history of *Tish*.

DM: First of all we should mention Bob Hogg and Dave Cull, who also were part of that second wave. Bobby Hogg had already started another mimeo magazine, *Motion*, that was devoted to prose, that was to be a companion to *Tish*, and it ran about five issues?

Dan McLeod: In '62, I think. It came out before the nineteenth [issue of *Tish*] 'cause there are ads for it in the nineteenth.

DM: I just wanted to bring that up, because I think that was also an important little magazine, particularly for Gladys and myself who were both interested in prose, Gladys especially. It was an outlet that *Tish* itself didn't afford us. Jamie was also writing a lot of prose at that time. Then, I remember after the '63 conference we got together, as the sort of "junior set" [laughter] and said "My god, we have to bring out the first issue after the conference! What are we gonna do? How are we going to report on all of this!" Dan, we did some kind of collage of all of that, didn't we?

DMc: We requested everybody turn in their journals, remember that? And we went through and cut them up.

DM: That's right.

DMc: It was a *bizarre* thing full of descriptions of the socks that Duncan was wearing on a certain day – a wonderful record.

DD: I should set the record straight. The reason I was the point of continuity was not, as people may misinterpret it – the end of *Tish: 1-19* was a letter from both Frank and George about the end of this, and going on, and so on – *David Dawson* will be the continuity point. I think I was there simply because I was there. Not out of any particular editorial competence on my part. The energy level of the younger group, as I keep calling them – I was the little kid in the first group, so I was the same age as most of them in the second group – most of it was there. People were always coming to get me, and getting me to meetings so I could vote, or argue over what was going on in the subsequent issues.

DM: I'd like Dan to talk about this because I was in America a year, and then I went to Indiana, and I was still contributing from Indiana. But Dan you wrote me a long series of postcards, and that's how I kept in touch with what was going on. Do you want to carry on from there?

DMc: It's hard to describe where we were at at that particular time. We were not, for the most part, a bunch of graduate students with a single vision, or poetic vision apart from the mainstream, as it was before. And we weren't one of those magazines that's just trying to pick the best poems – the kind that George hates. But we were a bit of both of those things, and I guess I was the main continuity, myself and Peter Auxier, because we saw it through when others drifted away, or in and out. We weren't this tightly knit group of people. We just became a very few of us near the end, and we started to look beyond a magazine that communicated to 300 people on a mailing list, and to something bigger than that. And that's how the *Georgia Straight* sort of evolved.

LK: The 60s were opening up then too, and you were participating in all of that kind of energy, whereas *Tish* was kind of pre-60s. By the time you were into it, all the activity that one generally thinks about the 60s – the psychedelic movement, and –

DMc: Well, those things were there too. I remember, I think it was Olson carrying around *The Psychedelic Review*. And all those things were coming out at that time.

LK: You were also in close touch with Olson – you used to correspond with him regularly then.

DMc: Yeah, there were a lot of letters going back and forth with him. I remember he wanted me to be "Environmental Editor of *The Niagara Frontier Review*" or something [laughter]. Some of the letters that he'd send: "Oh, here's a letter from Olson" – it's quite obvious 'cause it was squirreled all over [laughs]. And I'd open it up, and there's nothing inside [laughter]. And I'd realize the letter is what he'd written on the back.

LK: He was one of the first people that talked about ecology, Olson, at that time. It's a pretty common word now, but it wasn't in those days.

DMc: Yeah. The column that he had suggested that I write was "Ecology and the Electronic Environment."

WT: I was mentioning earlier that most of the major *Tish* movers expanded literary activity beyond what *Tish* had been. I think Dan did that in a particular way, when he moved from those numbers in *Tish* where he was the main editor actually, into the early *Georgia Straight*, which was a much more public forum. There was a period when there was a *Georgia Straight* writing supplement, that Stan Persky and Dennis Wheeler were editing, and so it kept up during the 60s. It was keeping up an expanded literary activity which was available to a great many people in Vancouver because the *Georgia Straight*, for the kind of newspaper it was, achieved staggeringly large circulation for periods of time. A lot of people were reading the *Georgia Straight* in those days. But it's that same impulse, I think, in Dan that was so much a part of what *Tish* was, that it growed [laughs], just like Topsy.

RM: I wanted to get back to Daphne, and ask her if she could address some of the other issues that the magazine was dealing with – the poetics of that time, and what the magazine *Tish* was doing in relation to the development of *her* writing. That would maybe turn our attention away from just the details of the history towards the poetics that was the concern of the journal. I could ask Frank, but we'd have a thirty-minute dissertation. I've read things that Daphne's said about the emphasis on process, the emphasis on voice . . .

DM: You want to do it, Roy? [laughter]

RM: You were coming from North Vancouver, which is the woods –

DM: I know, I was coming from North Vancouver, and even further away than most of these guys were coming from. I was younger, and not as tuned-in to contemporary writing. My high school education was appalling – I don't think I even heard of T.S.Eliot.

GH: Neither did we.

DM: We didn't? Oh, all right [laughs]. I'd certainly never heard of William Carlos Williams, or Pound. However, I think we'd had one poem by Allen Ginsberg, which our English teacher couldn't make head or tail of, and sort of gave it to us as a curiosity. So, that was my introduction [laughs]. I felt fairly ambivalent when Frank was talking about marginalization: I felt even more marginalized. I was very interested in what was going on in the Writers' Workshops, and in *Tish*, but it was hard for me first of all to grasp all of what was going on, and I felt very much at a disadvantage at the Writers' Workshop meetings, because I was coming from so far afield. For instance, I can certainly agree with Warren's sense that everyone was hotrodding around. In fact at my first Writers' Workshop meeting, that seemed to be all that they were writing poems about – their cars [laughter]. Women and cars. But I got so fed up, I said to Frank, "I bet you don't even know *how* to write a sonnet." Which led Frank to prove to me that he did. At that point, I still thought of the sonnet as a good example of the well-made poem. I remember submitting to *Tish*, and being told that I was writing out of my imagination too much. This wasn't *real* stuff, y'know, this wasn't *experience*.

GB: You didn't have a car! [laughter]

DM: I certainly wasn't writing about what *men* were wearing, and how they looked as they walked around the campus [laughter]. Yeah, the poetics were obviously really crucial. I can remember a meeting of the Writers' Workshop in Frank's basement – I don't know at what point this was in the ongoing discussion of Olson's essay on "Projective Verse," but that was my first introduction to it. I remember all of us engaging in *wild* argument, and nobody really knowing what they were arguing about, or what their position really was. I remember feeling quite shocked that somebody as experienced as I thought Frank was didn't really know what he was talking about [laughter].

That whole business of the focus on process, the attention to language in very particular ways: I took a linguistics course from Ronald Baker, I think his name was, with Bobby Hogg, and Dave [Dawson], and Gladys. And we formed our own little study group so we could get through the exams. We considered it essential to take a linguistics course, to get into language in that way. I think that was probably a beginning for poets writing in Canada to feel that way about language. And I certainly remember when Creeley was at UBC teaching creative writing he gave us a lot of information about linguistics, and he stressed its importance. He was giving us excerpts from Whorf and all kinds of people.

The emphasis on writing out of your own place came very much from Olson. Getting into *this* locale, and writing out of *its* history and geography, as well as your own history in it, was very crucial to me, partly because as an immigrant I was coming from outside it anyway, and was fascinated, wanted to know a lot more about it. And this spurred my own interest in it. *Tish* often appeared with a map on the front, with a map of Vancouver, with Xs marking the houses where all of the contributing authors or the editors lived. That sense of claiming territory, that was very crucial. All the endless discussion about the line, and what the line was, and where the line ended, and how you manoeuvred a line break, was extremely important, and that was where I first began to listen to my own voice, and to the voices of other people speaking. Having spent years trying *not* to listen to my own voice, and trying to get rid of all the Britishisms in it, it was a real turn-around to realize that that was what I had to start listening to. That was first base.

RM: There have been many attacks on *Tish* – critics like Dudek, and I think Purdy mounted an attack, and also others like Milton Acorn. There are lots of critics and writers who didn't like *Tish*; they wanted *Tish* to go away. Somehow it was not only an affront to them, but I think it represented a whole different take on poetics in Canada. Things had been going in one direction in the east, and now there was this group of writers doing quite interesting things – powerfully interesting things – on the west coast, and dealing with the west coast as a particularized place. In Canada, the battle was between nationalism and regionalism. And the *Tish* poets were bringing in something called localism. I was going to ask Frank or George about that because they've gone on to write about a hundred and fifty essays on that topic [laughter].

FD: There are, in my mind, very different ways of looking at culture and looking at "nation." And from the very early times in *Tish*, maybe just before *Tish*, my sense has been that a nation or a culture is defined by its local components. That is, a culture is formed from the individual communities, and the people living in that community *up*, rather than determined centrally, with a singular, national culture disseminated downward, and accepted without question, uniformly, throughout a country. There has always been in Canada, I think, a sense of Ontario and Toronto as taste-setter or culture-setter for the English Canadian community. And I think that's one of the things that *Tish* ran into, and we were very much aware that we were running into that. It became a matter of sort of perverse pride with us, as well as belief, that one found one's energy and one's identity from the very specific grounds on which one lived. I believe Vancouver was on the masthead right from the beginning. Whatever our incoherence, we were sure about that, we were sure that it wasn't our personal selves that we were evidencing in this magazine. We weren't writing poetry to be some kind of subjective aggrandizement. We weren't writing poetry to make names for ourselves that were the same as those given to us at birth.

We were writing somehow not only out of the sense of community with ourselves, but out of a very particular geography and history that was in a sense a co-author of our works. *It* was making our writing possible. It deserved, on the masthead of the magazine, some acknowledgement of its role in the composition.

BRENDA CARR

Between Continuity and Difference:
An Interview with Daphne Marlatt

Brenda Carr: I like to think of your life/text in process as being like Adrienne Rich's – a dance between continuity and difference. Along these lines, is there a way in which the openness of the "Black Mountain" projective poetics that allowed for translation from an American to a Canadian *Tish* context, also allows for translation to the explicitly feminist context of your writing in the 1980s?

Daphne Marlatt: Part of the openness of that poetic had to do with being open to proprioception, to the bio-feedback of your body in the act of composition. That's what the breath-line is supposed to be based on. So that became a ground for me to shift into a feminist bringing of the body into the act of writing. When Cixous talks about the way a woman speaks in public, how she launches all of her body into the act of speaking, that resonated for me with Olson's sense of the body's rhythms in passionately engaged thought moving the breath line. But you can't make a simple transference. Woman's body has been so repressed in our culture – fetishized on the surface but repressed deeply in terms of our actual sexuality and the force of our desire. It has been a long journey for me to come into my body, to be centred in, the *subject* of, my desire and not the object of someone else's. To develop my own sense of the line or even of how i might move through syntax to speak my own being, i had to give up trying to imitate men. And of course in those days, the early 60s, when we had just discovered the New American writing and all my mentors and models were men, it was very easy to aspire to think like a man. After all, the writers we valued, the ones who seemed to have a large "take" on the world, a political edge combined with an historical-mythical, even spiritual breadth of vision, were all men: Duncan, Olson, Creeley, Snyder, Ginsberg, Williams, Pound. Where were the women? Well, there was H.D., there was Denise Levertov, Diane di Prima, Joanne Kyger – somehow their writing was regarded as secondary because it was too personal. Even when Levertov wrote about the Viet Nam War, it was "too personal" because she was "too angry," and that got in the way of the lyric. Being a woman writer seemed to mean being always on the periphery trying to emulate men, trying to emulate their "objectivity." So the question was, how did my being a woman make a difference in my writing? A difference not peripheral but central. And if we were going to start with the body, well, my body was certainly different from Charles Olson's. So there's the notion of body and body rhythms which, i think, have been strong in my work ever since *Rings*. But there's also how you position yourself in the world. To enter the world, I mean to really take it on conceptually and feel you have as valid an analysis of what you see going on around you as any man does, is a difficult thing for a woman, perhaps the most difficult leap to make as a woman writer. And I had the benefit of a poetic that, as you say, was open, that placed me, gender aside (well, there's the problem), in an open field of composition and, in terms of ethics, set me within an environment i was interwoven with and responsible to. I think the ecological aspect of this poetic is very strong. The twinning of the language field, how you move within it, and the environmental field, how you move within that, and what your response-ability is in each case—that was a very important contribution. Now we have this notion of eco-feminism and this sense that women take responsibility for what's happening in strip-mining, in the clear-cutting of forests, the polluting of our waters – this sense that women are no longer confined to the old archetypes of enclosure within a domestic space. And we're not only "urban guerillas," to use Nicole Brossard's term in another context, but forest guerrillas too, as the women who have gone to prison in B.C. recently to stop clear-cut logging have demonstrated. But this is happening because at last we see ourselves in responsible relation to what surrounds us, and we feel an urge to act or to write in that large relational context we're embedded in. I can see a distant link between that and the *Maximus Poems*, but it's taken many shifts and turns along the way. And that action by women is certainly not something Olson would have included in his universe. I mean the projective size of Maximus is definitely male.

BC: But you would be in some ways connecting up Olson's conception of the poem as open field with that relational poetic stance?

DM: Yes, but I think of that very much as Duncan's term too – the open field. When we talk about Black Mountain poetics, we always seem to talk about Olson and Creeley. And incidentally, it was Creeley who brought the sentence alive for me in prose, the way the movement of syntax reflects the movements of consciousness in the act of perception – a kind of reflexive action. Creeley's a remarkable prose writer. But it was Duncan's line that moved me. He was really the muse-figure or mentor who gave me permission to launch into the content of my first book, *Frames*. And being a gay writer, he also validated that claiming of sexuality that is not conventional heterosexuality. The other thing about Duncan is that he took me to H.D. and H.D. became a kind of guiding intelligence along my own path of discovery. Not so much the Imagist H.D. but the H.D. of *Trilogy* and of the prose. I read the Imagist H.D. first but the first book of hers I read that really spoke to me in the early 60s was *Bid Me To Live*. I don't remember now when I read *Trilogy* – it must have been some time in the mid-70s – but *Trilogy* opened up what a woman could do in the long poem, it just lifted the horizon line of what was possible. The way she weaves in history, culture, mythology, her own trepidations as a woman writer, her self-doubts, it was extraordinary and very moving for me to read. And then Duncan and his sense of the opening of the field: you could shift back and forth so radically between a large and very serious poetic vision and the colloquial, the profane, sexual joking. The fluidity of those levels of language, that was very important. Olson also does this in the overall context of his writing project, but he's less fluid in the immediate and he's more deliberate, more ponderous, he takes himself more seriously in the writing. Duncan's openness to the figures of the psyche, his sense of humour, those rhythms learned from Stein, all of these felt closer to me. But I suppose it wasn't until H.D. that I came across a *woman* whose work and whose concerns as a writer seemed so much in relation to my own, even though she lived in a different period and in other countries. That she was a poet who was equally interested in prose, that she'd had a strongly Christian upbringing and was engaged in working with that, that she'd been involved in her own process of discovery through therapy, that she was a lesbian and had an ongoing relationship with Bryher – that intrigued me, although at the time I was afraid to recognize my own leanings that way. But her insistence on the feminine in all her writing, her resistance to and her continuing dialogue with the men around her, particularly Pound. Her difficulty in extricating herself, even sending him, very late in her career, a poem and saying, "Well, it might give you some pleasure to tear this apart." Astonishing, but it echoes my own situation vis à vis the men in the *Tish* scene. I felt deeply involved with what they were all expounding, not only in terms of writing but in terms of ethics, a vision of how to live. You see, that was what was so amazing about that poetic – I was going to say it involved every aspect of your life, which is not true, certainly not as true as it is of feminism, which really does involve a total re-visioning of your life. But at that age, late teens and early twenties, the change in aesthetics and values was pretty profound for me.

BC: This leads me to think about the question of the way a woman writer situates herself in literary tradition, and perhaps I should say literary traditions. You were the only woman writer frequently cited and anthologized with the otherwise all male *Tish*-affiliated writers. As well, you've mentioned the literary patrimony fostered by the predominately male Black Mountain precursors who, in Olson's words, saw themselves as the "sons of Pound and Williams." As a young woman writer, you seem to be indicating by what you've been saying that there was a sense of internal conflict, perhaps similar to what Adrienne Rich defines as "an unconscious fragmentation of identity" between a sense of self as woman and poet. You're already speaking about finding a place in alternate traditions via Duncan.

DM: Definitely. Let me tell you about Denise Levertov. And it was through Duncan too that I got to know her work. Her presence at the 1963 conference at UBC was very important to me though I was very shy about approaching her – perhaps the people who personally mean the most to us are the ones we feel most shy with. Anyway, there she was, a woman poet who gave a marvellous reading, and that was the first time I ever saw a woman hold a whole audience with the magic of her voice. I remember going to lunch with her in the cafeteria and her openness towards me as a young woman poet, and her wanting, not just to talk about writing with me, but to talk about my life with me. I remember telling her something I was having trouble with, that one of the older writers in the department, a major figure in Canadian literature, had said to me, I suppose in a moment of his own despair, "What's the use of giving a woman an education? You'll just get married and stop writing." I was about to get married then. When I relayed this to Denise, she scoffed and said, "Why, that's ridiculous. Marriage doesn't have anything to do with whether you continue to write or not. Look at me." Well, that's a totally anecdotal answer to your question. I think the fragmentation was deeply unconscious at that age. I was still imbued with that tradition full of male models, and I didn't even realize consciously how much of a disparity there was, but I think probably that comment, which deeply shocked me, was the first recognition I had that women were not treated as equals to men in the seriousness of their engagement in writing. That's probably why I was so angry about it. I mean, I'm still angry about it, all these years later. Although they've been omitted from literary histories of that scene, there were other women involved in *Tish* and the Writer's Workshop then. Gladys Hindmarch was very present, and Pauline Butling was there, as well as Ginny Smith, Carol Johnson. And Maxine Gadd and Judy Copithorne were very active in the group around bill bissett and *Blew Ointment*. In fact, in the second phase of *Tish*, which nobody remembers, when a group of us who were younger took over the magazine after the others had left, there was more of a cross-over with the *Blew Ointment* group and we were publishing Maxine's poetry and Judy's. So I didn't feel, at the time, like I was the only one, though I did feel a certain resistance to the dominance of the men. It was the men who really defined the terms of the prevailing aesthetic at the writing workshops, which was really the collective activity behind *Tish*. It's only the filter of history that says that I'm the lone woman, and it overlooks the fact that Gladys, who was involved right from the beginning, has continued to write, continued to publish. Actually, my writing companionship with Fred and George and Gladys as well as with Maxine and Judy didn't really begin until after *Tish* was over and I had moved back to Vancouver. By then I had published two books and established myself as a writer. You see, in the *Tish* days there was quite a disparity in age. When I first met Frank, with whom I did have a sort of companionship for a while then, and Fred, George, Jamie, Lionel, I was only an undergraduate in my first year while they were all graduate students.

BC: You've already been pointing to the fact that the long poem is a very important genre for you, as it was for many of the other *Tish*-affiliated writers and their Black Mountain predecessors. In fact, your *Steveston* has been frequently compared with Olson's *Maximus Poems* and Williams' *Paterson*. Michael Bernstein, a theorist of the long poem, asserts that such works tell the "tale of the tribe." Is there a way in which your writing in its dance between long poem and autobiography, does not tell the tale of the tribe, but rather works to subvert the objective and "universal" (we could say, implicitly male) frames of the genre in terms of content, voice, and formal strategies?

DM: Well, first of all, who is the tribe? Louky Bersianik, in the paper she gave at the Women and Words Conference in 1983, did a brilliant critique of the masculinism of the anthropological assumptions bound up in the notion of tribe. The Steveston work that Robert [Minden] and I did involved coming to some understanding of that. In the beginning, when we were doing the aural history project with Maya [Koizumi] and Rex [Weyler], we all approached Steveston as a fishing community. Fishing is done by the men. Only gradually did it become apparent to some of us that we also needed to talk to the women – I mean, this was getting very one-sided. Later, when Robert and I were working on our own on *Steveston*, we talked about how Steveston's women seemed invisible and I realized that what I wanted to make surface through the obvious ring of that town's fishing activity were the women, the women you didn't see on the streets, you didn't see on the docks because they were at home, or they were in the cannery. In the hospital poem, which is based on an old photograph of the first community hospital in Steveston and is a poem about a woman either dying or giving birth, I began to realize that the movement of the river out towards the sea, where it disappears, was a movement into the invisible that had to do with birthing and dying, and that in fact the two were metaphors of each other. So that that which remained invisible and unspoken, women's part in the town, was also crucial – just as the movement of the river, which I was fascinated by and was trying to imitate in the rhythms of the poem, was not just background. Much later when I was working on *Touch to my Tongue* and heard the rhythms moving like the rhythms in *Steveston* I realized they were orgasmic. I think I got very close to realizing that in the hospital poem, but there was something in the way and that was the original concept of the project, that it was a fishing town, that it was the men's activity that was of interest. But throughout that book I think I was writing my way to a reversal of that focus, a sort of figure/ground reversal. This business of what becomes figure and what becomes ground is very fascinating to me. It's part of the ecological vision in *Steveston*, trying to shift that ground which is usually background for the figure so it becomes foreground. The shift in values that's involved is also what feminism is about. But to get back to your question about the autobiographical, yes, the voice in most of my work is subjective and individual rather than universal. It's marked by my gender as well as my history, class, national identity, race, all those things. *Steveston* has often been called a documentary but the writing doesn't assume that there is an unmediated objective position. I put myself in there, recording all the sexual baggage I carried as a woman on the dock. I suppose that continues in a different way in *How Hug a Stone* because I'm there as a woman in a foreign country which is not a foreign country. There's that twist running through it, that I'm claiming it and, at the same time, feeling very alienated from it, which is probably the classic emigrant position towards the country of origin. It's not really an origin in my case, it never was, though all the family stories pretended that it was, so i went back with that expectation. So there's this constant fracturing, just as there is in the mother/daughter duality, being both a daughter and a mother at the same time, the no-longer-English mother of a Canadian son who is fascinated by the foreignness of the English. A universal voice can't admit this kind of fracturing, or these kinds of differences. The universal wants to pretend difference doesn't exist.

BC: You've already indicated that Olson's projective poetics are rooted in his objectivist stance that proposes decentring the human subject and revaluing all the forms of life and experience. You really adapt this notion to the ecological vision that you've conceptualized in *Steveston* where you bring forward the image of the net or the web as a metaphor of this sense of interconnection between human life and all life forms in the environment. There seems to be a resonance between your ecological stance and your poetics, where you talk, for example in *What Matters*, about the "ecological movement of words." Has this vision of life and language that you were formulating in your early work been carried along and adapted to your present feminist poetics?

DM: Well, this brings up figure and ground in a different way. I think that where I was angry at the foregrounding of capitalist values and human life concerns at the expense of other forms of life, that anger then focussed on the foregrounding of patriarchal male values and concerns at the expense of female being and a female ethos that tends to be more relational and contextually aware. This shift meant that I was suddenly writing from the margin. As soon as you try to write from the margin versus the centre, so that the margin is seen from the centre of its own values, then you're open to the attack that you're simply trying to reverse the hierarchy and make this *the* centre. This is a trap of binary thinking, which is always hierarchical. It says there has to be an either/or and it can't get to that place of both/and. Cixous and Irigaray have written about this. The either/or seems to be actually embedded in the definitional activity of our language. As a poet, and even more intensively as a feminist writer, I am mostly having to resist that, to work against it. The question is, how to get to a multi-valency of meaning based on equivalency without losing meaning altogether? Meaning is so rooted in current usage, which itself is so freighted with patriarchal value. I can't ignore that, it's a given. But I can work to subvert it, to undermine it, and that's where all the different kinds of wordplay come into effect, from deconstructing words to inventing new ones, to using etymology as another variant on meaning. People seem to misunderstand my use of etymology and accuse it of being a validation of "the true literal meaning" of the word. That's very far from what I'm doing which is much more playful than that. It's a way of calling up an absolutely departed from or an ignored and forgotten meaning and recycling it as a variant slant on, a new fracture of, the current meaning, which after all still stands, though it's now no longer dominant. It's a form of polysemy.

BC: In recent writing, like *Touch to my Tongue*, you recycle the ecological imagery of *Steveston*, especially that of the Fraser River, so that it becomes an embodiment of your experience of woman-to-woman eroticism. It is possible to see this aspect of your work as sliding towards the patriarchal essentialist trap that reduces woman to body/sexuality, erases differences between women, conflates woman with nature, and ultimately leaves woman outside of culture and cultural production. In an interview with Janice Williamson, you indicate that you see your use of this imagery as a self-conscious recuperation, a gesture of double decolonization of what has been traditionally devalued as "feminine." Is this eco-feminist position still a necessary corrective in our world that is sometimes seen as "post-colonial" (and I might add "post-feminist")?

DM: Our world certainly isn't post-colonial or post-feminist. And presuming to speak from a "post" position just blinds us to the fact that things haven't really changed all that much. As for the essentialist position, the problem is that when women have been reduced in the dominant culture from being subjects in our own right to being objects of male desire, then it becomes necessary to try to "deculturate" ourselves in order to imagine what it could be like for us to be acculturated otherwise in a woman-affirmative culture. There are various images for this: the "wild zone," the "Amazon," and so on. What it comes down to in *Touch* is that I'm speaking from within a lesbian culture that is a sub-culture within the patriarchal culture we're all embroiled with. And lesbian culture tries to do something which, as Nicole Brossard has said, is unimaginable from within the dominant culture. We try to imagine the fullness of who we might be outside of patriarchal reference. Women have historically been defined in reference to men. So to imagine ourselves not in reference to them but in reference to ourselves, our own strengths, our own being, our own beauty, is almost unimaginable. It means seeing everything in a different light, it means seeing yourself in relation to what goes on around you in a new context. That contextual shift is dramatically different and it's hard to convey in the forms and language we have inherited, which are freighted so much the other way. To make present what has been erased – our bodies, our desire, our self-definition, and how that breaches the symbolic, our solidarity with other women at a level that can meet our differences, our reciprocity with other forms of life – so much that we are now trying to bring out of the unspeakable: this can only be seen as reductive if the large contextual shift it involves is ignored. Which means ignoring what we start off with, what Teresa de Lauretis, translating a term from the Italian feminists, calls "originary difference." To say that this leaves women outside of culture is to speak from within patriarchal ground, because it suggests that there is only one recognizable culture, the dominant patriarchal one, and it denies the radically new culture being born in that contextual shift. It's hard to recognize this culture because it isn't monolithic or singular. It's more like an area of response between different oppressed or minority cultures, and the women's movement is just beginning to work out the kind of response required in any truly reciprocal condition where the differences between women of colour and white women, and between lesbian women and heterosexual women, to name only two of a number of differences, make communication and trust very difficult.

BC: Self-consciously writing from the margins, claiming them, creating them as a "wild zone" where the differences resonate/vibrate between and among women and other oppressed groups, ultimately connects back to a reframing of Olson's notion of valuing the "local" in a feminist context.

DM: I do have my feet in the west coast. It was part of my original immigrant passion for the place, which I found validated in Olson's poetic. But feminism does reframe it. It's not such a big jump to see strip-mining, clear-cut logging, drift-netting all as forms of colonial domination. To see the connection between the exploitation of other species and the exploitation of women is not to reduce women to nature. That's exactly what patriarchal thought does. Seeing the ways in which we are connected to other forms of life, to other races, other classes, is to work against the domination of one over all the others. The vision feminism embodies, it seems to me, is relational, promoting an equivalency of needs, not the privileging of one set.

BC: "Salvage" is the title of a forthcoming work in which you recollect poems from the *Steveston* period and rewrite them. One of the meanings of the word "salvage" is "sophistical evasion." Is there a way in which an eco-feminist poetics as a gesture of "salvage" in language need not be contextualized within a rigid essentialist categorization of gender?

DM: Well, that meaning surprises me. I've been working on the sense of salvage as "something extracted (as from wreckage, ruins, or rubbish) as valuable," and it seems to me that this kind of salvaging involves revaluing in the way that we've just been talking about, re-visioning (I do use Adrienne Rich's term for it), and neither of those acts seems to participate in sophistry. In fact, they're essential for a woman's coming to speak out of her hitherto absent body, absent desire, and muted voice within a public context. To do this she has to valorize the ground out of which she speaks. Which means working for a really drastic change in our culture. Working for change is what makes feminism different from the postmodernism I learned from the *Tish* days. Even though there's a continuity with some of those strategies, I'm using them for different ends now. As Linda Hutcheon says in her article in *Tessera 7*, postmodernism, although it critiques the master narratives of our culture, the institutions and the codes, still ends up being complicit with them because it has no program for change. A program for change means valorizing a difference, and as soon as you valorize a difference you're moving out of postmodernist deconstruction into a position of, as she says, belief or trust in a certain meta-narrative. It's a difference at such a basic level that I think it's often been overlooked, but it's a difference that leads to a radical shift in world-view.

BC: I was thinking of "sophistical evasion" as playful possibility. What about the potential of salvage as a baffle, a feint, a dodge, a side-step game with cultural definitions? I am thinking of "s," the female protagonist of your *Character*, of Roland Barthes' notion of character in *S-Z*, where the character shows up in different guises/disguises at the multiple entrances and exits of the labyrinthine text. If the sophists were known for their "adroit, subtle and allegedly specious reasoning" (as in tending to deceive or mislead), this resonates with the playful evasion of the female subject of the feminist text, as well as with the playful dance, the shimmer of meanings of the text as subject, and links up too with the *ir*rational of your "Musing with Mothertongue" in subversion of Patriarchal Reason.

DM: What a wonderful inversion. Why *not* reclaim "sophistry" in order to take an alternate approach to representation? The "dodge" is what's required when we find ourselves up against our absence in patriarchal definition even as we assert our difference from it, not to mention our differences within it. And then there's "sapphistry" which might stand for another order of reason altogether.

GEOFFREY ZAMORA

Lionel Kearns Interview, January 4, 1990

Geoffrey Zamora: Let us begin with the most important question. Where has Lionel Kearns been these last years?

Lionel Kearns: What do you mean?

GZ: Well, I remember when you were current. Your work used to be in the magazines and you were giving readings and lectures around the country. I even remember seeing your name in the Times Literary Supplement. I heard Northrop Frye discussing your "Birth of God" poem on the CBC. But I never see your work around any more. What happened?

LK: Perhaps you are looking in the wrong places.

GZ: Well, I try to keep up with what is being published in Canada.

LK: Good luck.

GZ: So where should I be looking?

LK: OK, I understand what you are getting at. You are talking about the olden days, when we were young and naïve and poetry was going to change the world, and it made some kind of sense to send out poems to literary magazines, or to stand up and read them at coffee houses. That made sense then, but there is a very different context now.

GZ: Go on, I'm listening.

LK: Let me ask you a question. Do you still use a typewriter?

GZ: No, I use a word processor.

LK: That is the key to the difference. For most of us it is now the *screen* rather than the page that is the place where we focus and objectify our thoughts. Of course there are still literary fossils available in book form, and a number of collectors who still value books, but it is in the area of electronic media where the innovative literary events are occurring.

GZ: But television was around in the 60s, and there were screens in the theatres. In fact, I seem to remember that you were somehow connected with film in those days too.

LK: In 1965 Gerry Gilbert and I were in England working with Peter Watkins of his film, *The War Game*. Gordon Payne and Joe Fahrni were there too, and we were also participating in a very lively poetry scene that was devoted to "liberating the poem from the page." It was connected to the Kinetic Art movement, and also associated with a lot of Concrete and Sound Poetry activities, which at that time were fresh and fascinating.

GZ: Didn't you and Gordon Payne make a couple of animated film poems in the early 70s?

LK: Yes, but it was pretty tough going. We had to do it all by hand, making thousands of coloured plastic cells, which we manipulated and shot on the stand one frame at a time. It took months of slogging, and the end results were pretty rough compared with what we can do now with a desk top computer. The problem in those days was that it was difficult to work *as poets* in those media. The tools had not arrived.

GZ: So you saw some similarities between film and poetry?

LK: Of course. Both media use sound and images extended in time. The same editing processes of montage and continuity create the effects, and the reference is deepened by figures of metaphor and symbolism. But there are large differences as well.

GZ: What are they?

LK: Film, and cassette based video, are *linear*. You view it sequentially from the beginning, through the middle, to the end. And the audience just sits there and absorbs it. It's like a novel or a short story. A poem is much less linear, and it is interactive. The user can read it through or jump around and respond to all sorts of its patterns and interconnections. In fact, most traditional poetic devices are ways of layering more and more meaning into the language. The linear surface structure of a good poem is only a faction of what is available.

GZ: Sounds like a pretty interesting art form to me. So why aren't you working with poetry any more?

LK: I *am* working with it. But I have a wider definition of poetry than you seem to have. Poetry is literature (i.e. art made out of language) that focuses attention upon its form rather than merely upon its content. Poetry existed long before paper was available, and it is still a valid art form now that the screen has replaced the page as the most convenient place to objectify thought and explore ideas.

GZ: You mean more film and video poems, but now easier to produce?

LK: Well, perhaps. I am currently planning a poem for the big IMAX screen, but that is only a diversion. It is not the big public screens that are the important ones, but the small personal screens on your desk tops. It is there that the interactive performance occurs.

GZ: Interactive performance?

LK: Yes, the play of language, in all its magnificent extensions, including action, sound, colour, graphics, and voice, and most important the response of the poem to the reader. Have you never heard of hypertext?

GZ: Don't you mean response of the reader to the poem?

LK: Yes, that too, but we have always had that. What I am interested in is the response of the poem to the reader.

GZ: Do you really think that you will have readers for that kind of thing?

LK: Perhaps "reader" is not the most appropriate term. I sometimes say "user," but some of the connotations of that word throw people off. Perhaps we should say "audience," but that implies a group, whereas interactive computer poetry is a personal, individual activity that happens between you and your screen.

GZ: Well, I agree that the audience for this kind of thing will be limited.

LK: You are wrong. A recent computer poem of mine has reached a wider audience than anything that I have ever published before. It was distributed electronically on CompuServe, and so was available to any of their thousands of subscribers, many of whom downloaded it. It was then copied and passed around by computer users around the world. Now it is also available in a number of public domain collections that have come out on CD-ROM discs, and it is getting a lot of attention in the international press. Nothing like that happens when I publish a poem in a magazine or a book.

GZ: Did you ever imagine that your work would take this direction when you were part of the Tish group back in the early 60s?

LK: Yes, my work has been pointed in that direction for a long time. Do you remember my book *By the Light of the Silvery McLune: Media Parables, Poems, Signs,*

Gestures, and other Assaults on the Interface? It was a collection of poems influenced by the thought of Marshall McLuhan, who had given a series of lectures at UBC in 1964. I used McLuhan's ideas about media to explore and make statements about life, as it was occurring around me, and poetry. There was a poem in it, called "Kinetic Poem," that went something like this:

> "The poem is a machine," said that famous man, and so I'm building one.
> Or at least I'm having it built, because I want something big and impressive and automatic.
> You see, people will stand in front of it and insert money, dimes or quarters, depending upon the poem's locus.
> Yes the whole thing will clank and hum and light up and issue a string of words on colored ticker-tape.
> Or maybe the customers will wear ear-phones and turn small knobs so the experience will be more audile-tactile than old fashioned visual.
> In any case they will only get one line at a time,
> This being the most important feature of my design which is based on the principle that,
> In poetry, "one perception must immediately and directly lead to a further perception,"
> And therefore the audience will be compelled to feed in coin after coin.
>
> Now I admit that the prototype model that you see on display is something of a compromise, as it has a live poet concealed inside.
> But I assure you that this crudity will eventually be eliminated
> Because each machine, I mean each poem, is to be fully computerized
> And so able to stand on its own feet.

Readers at that time would recognize some spoofed phrases from William Carlos Williams and Charles Olson, who were, as you remember, popular poetry gurus of the day. But for all its irreverence, that poem predicts the kind of interactive poetry that I am involved with today.

GZ: Is there any other of your work in book form that relates to your computer poetry?

LK: Convergences, which came out from Coach House in 1984, was an attempt to bring together multiple stands of narrative, lyricism, history, fiction, and recursive self-reflection into a single unified work exploring the subjects of time and consciousness and text. With its various columns and type faces it accomplished on the page some of what is now possible on the screen. I am working on an electronic hypertextual version of *Convergences* at the moment.

GZ: When will it be finished?

LK: The problem with hypertext, at least from a compositional point of view, is that it is fractilian. Do you know what I mean?

GZ: No.

LK: In Mandlebrot's terms, the space between two points is contained, but infinite. A coastline expands as you measure it with finer and finer instruments. One's life is a fractile too, and so is *Convergences*. It just keeps expanding from the inside.

GZ: Unfortunately this interview, though most interesting, is not a fractile. We must end it here. Thank you for your co-operation.

LK: It was a pleasure.

THREE
Critical Essays

WARREN TALLMAN

A Brief Retro-Introduction to Tish

Thinking how to introduce the *Tish* Poets I, with characteristic modesty, realized how all but impossible such an attempt would be, particularly since introductions are supposed to be characterized by brevity, and how can anyone who is writing a first sentence of this length possibly be brief, especially when, though it may be the soul of wit, it isn't much fun. So, with that shy agility with which we Scorpios of the world solve such predicaments, I thought it would be more becoming of me to attempt no introduction at all, but instead join in as an equal-time *participant*, assuring myself that such is the right democratic thing to do. And, even though I'm actually twice-older than the other participants, I haven't insisted on two portions of equal time. In fact – the cowardice that goes with age – only a half-portion, 4 and 1/4 typed pages that is. And a short poem.

FALSE PROPOSITION #1
That the *Tish* poets originally were and still are a branch plant extension of poetics chauvinistically exported by American literary entrepreneurs Robin Blaser, Robert Creeley, Edward Dorn, Robert Duncan, Allen Ginsberg, Michael McClure, Charles Olson, Gary Snyder, Jack Spicer, and Philip Whalen.

CORRECTION: The *Tish* poets, fully supported by numerous friends of like inclination from blewointment press, Talonbooks, and *BC Monthly*, were, in polite guise, thoroughgoing literary delinquents who lifted everything they could lay hands on from their incredibly naïve American visitors for purposes of their own imaginations.

FALSE PROPOSITION #2
That being UBC students, thoroughly schooled in the negotiable value of English and Creative Writing BAs and MAs, the *Tish* editors were to a man to a woman – the distinction being hard to establish – a collection of supercilious academic wimps whose poetry, prose, and poetics have ever since been conspicuously likewise.

CORRECTION: Actually Gladys Hindmarch was a Vanc. island girl who thought Vancouver city was entirely too big. Daphne Marlatt, from Nowhere Malaysia, thought Vancouver and the way people talked around UBC entirely too strange. Angela Bowering, a Nanaimo girl, thought George Bowering was kinda cute. George Bowering, an Okanagan boy, thought Salt Lake City was the closest metropolis because his radio told him so. Freddy Wah and Pauline Butling were Kootenay kids who associated their ideas of romantic love with the gravel pit outside Nelson. Lionel Kearns was Nelson also, an incipient hockey hero who went to Vancouver and then he went wrong, and was the 1st to write impressive poems. Frank Davey and Bobby Hogg couldn't have been beyond the city limits of Abbotsford before arriving in Vancouver. Several of the others who *were* Vancouver kids, David Dawson, Jamie Reid, Dan McLeod, Peter Auxier, David Cull, thought UBC a rather quaint place to spend the daylight hours, and usually didn't. Collectively, they knew more about driving cars along small town one lane freeways than about the ins and outs of university literature courses. In sum, most of them were conspicuously delinquent students who persistently consorted with downtown types, pub-wise, leading to late-night car journeys across bridges and down back lanes in search of girl friends, boy friends, and the shape of their imaginations – as in poems.

FALSE PROPOSITION #3

That Warren Tallman, an energetic, highly intelligent, perceptive, persuasive, and supremely well-informed expatriate American UBC English prof led the *Tish* Poets by their trusting little hands down a garden path strewn with bottles of Carling's Black Label beer directly into realms of poetry with roses, roses, roses all the way.

CORRECTION: Malarkey. On campus Tallman, your typically panicky wimpy English prof spent his more effective hours hurrying over to Helen Sonthoff's and Jane Rule's house – Helen was chairman of the Vancouver Poetry Centre – and "Gee, Helen, what should we do now?" Helen always knew what and that's how all of those poets who came to town to liven the *Tish* poets' imaginations came to town . . . except when Ellen Tallman invited them. Typical weekend around the house at 2527 West 37th, the anxious wimp speaks "Oh my God Ellen, they're coming up the walk again . . . what shall I do now?" To which Ellen, with statuesque Berkeley indignation, "Tell them this time they'd better *say something*." The energetic, highly intelligent, perceptive, persuasive American expatriate professor strolls casually into the living room, wearing a fresh bottle of Carling Black Label beer on the five fingers of his right hand, the jewel effect, "Now today I think you'd better, well, you know, SAY SOMETHING." Of such stuff are influential professors made. Tallman's better classroom days were characterized by the baffling persistence and insistence with which he would turn back for the tenth or eleventh time to the first line of, say, "The Songs Of Maximus" to wonder for the twelfth time, "What on earth does Charles Olson have in mind in 'colored pictures / of all things to eat,' I mean how can you eat a colored picture?" It must be confrontation with such splendidly unwearying stupidity as this that causes poets, in sheer self defense, to create their own imaginations. Or learn, as Ellen put it, right on the money, to SAY SOMETHING. Which they did. And still do, even now, 25 years later along the pike.

FALSE PROPOSITION #4

That *Tish* was long ago, nowadays a literary curiosity, so why not let it rest in peace in pasture like Creeley's famous POOR. OLD. TIRED. HORSE. Or some long since discarded, broken down sad Cinderella of an automobile, rest in peace.

CORRECTION: As phenomenal a communal surge of energies as those first 19 consecutive appearances of Original *Tish* were, one would have thought the summer of '63 would mark an end point. There was the month long Götterdämmerung poetry klatsch when Margaret Avison, Robert Creeley, Robert Duncan, Allen Ginsberg, Denise Levertov, Charles Olson – the whale – and Philip Whalen – smiling Buddha – landed all over everyone with poetry in the morning, poetry in the afternoon, and poetry in the evening, after which all the parties began, Jamie and Carol Reid's immortal downtown pad. After which everyone involved was feeling understandably more than a little exhausted. With that weakening of the will to resist fate which such weariness brings on, George, Frank, and Fred decided to make honest women of . . . and did . . . and the honeymooners' strategy was GET OUT OF TOWN, as they did. Another major mover, Lionel Kearns, already married, set sail for England. Before long another, David Dawson, stepped sideways to Seattle. Another, Jamie Reid, followed in Mao's footsteps to Montreal and Toronto. Daphne Marlatt would leave for that lonesome year in Bloomington Indiana, keeping the faith in walkthrough closet writing room. Later, she and Gladys Hindmarch would put in that bitter year in Madison, Wisconsin.

All of which would seem to spell out *an end* to the *Tish* affair. But didn't. In New Mexico Fred would help edit *Sum* magazine, in Buffalo, *The Magazine of Further Studies*, and when he and Pauline came on back home to Nelson, *Scree* magazine. George edited *Imago* magazine and *Beaver Kosmos Folios*. Daphne helped edit *Periodics*, a prose venture. And all of these were a continuation, a flowering out, into all kinds of dooryards of the richness of communal imagination *Tish* had begun. I've saved the most important manifestation for last. With George and Fred as the steadiest contributing editors, Frank Davey began *Open Letter* in 1966 at Royal Roads in Victoria, and has continued it, almost 20 years now, in Toronto. So, for convenience let it stand for all the other ventures as evidence of some active secret of the imagination original *Tish* let loose in the world. And let Frank stand as a type of all the other *Tish* poets who were in on the secret, and have come to possess their imaginations.

Frank is a slender sort of runaway train or car who spends most of his time pretending he isn't such. Yet via his contributions to Original *Tish*, to original Royal Roads *Open Letter*, to subsequent Toronto *Open Letter*, to his active hand in Coach House Press activities, to his natural talent for provoking his enemies into furious counter-activities while collecting unexpected new road-running friends who go beep beep, beep – Nichol that is – into continuations of their own activities, he exemplifies in himself how much imagination when possessed can manage. And this is what his *Tish* compatriots have done and are still doing, each in her way, his way

– possession of the difficult kingdoms of the imagination. Some days I think Daphne is the most touching with her heroic dedication to her art in all kinds of dicey times and places. Some days I think Glady the most down-home, small town home town, west coast of the island. Some days I think George is most impressive in his accomplishments, BIG GEORGE. Other times it's Freddie and the Kootenays I'd like to be around. Some others, the reassurance of Lionel. On still others, so long *Tish*, I'm off to see billy bissett, Gerry Gilbert, and Roy Kiyooka – the three laureates of this city's innards. But at the moment I'm seeing Frank containing all these in what he has become, Hang a sign around his neck, reading, "this is the way *Tish* went."

Finally, I'm seeing all those cars, the one in his poems of his childhood, his dad's steady, stately chariot, Hi yo silver, away. George and Lionel coming over the Rockies – "listen, George" – the breathtaking free-form ways Fred and Pauline drive the local Nelson roads, and, now I remember, Lionel's "Family," I'll conclude with that.

Family

Angelo ducking his head
behind the dash
puffing to catch the flicker
of Ivo's lighter

Me beside them
in the front seat
watching the road
twist away to the left . . .

The car speeding
straight
on

end-over-end
       once slowly
    waiting for the
             and one
      and two rolls gently
and three and
          stop

We climbed up
from beach level
and the wreck

Noticing where the car
had crashed down
through the brush:

Small trees
sheared right off

A scrape
on the great douglas fir
by the side
of the road

Seven forty-five
P.M. —

Maria Ludavicci
her five brothers
and me

Struggling up
in the rain
onto the highway

Mrs. Ludavicci
at Benediction

Old Ludavicci
at home
drinking his wine
alone
in the big house

Lionel Kearns
1959-60

KEN NORRIS

How the Tish *Poets Came to Influence the Montreal Scene*

The history of the Véhicule poets has been told in various places (see, for example, my *The Little Magazine in Canada 1925-80* and Caroline Bayard's *The New Poetics in Canada and Quebec*). Suffice it to say that these seven poets all became associated with one another at the parallel gallery Véhicule Art, and that most of them published their early books with Véhicule Press circa 1975-80. They shared an interest in hip American poetry and in experimental European art movements. Within the parameters of the Canadian scene, the poetry that made the most sense to them was being published by the Coach House-Talonbooks nexus, which built upon the innovations of the *Tish* group.

The west coast *Tish* poets were not only an important aesthetic influence and reference point for the Véhicule poets of Montreal in the mid to late 70s, but for several members of the Véhicule crowd – Artie Gold, Tom Konyves, and John McAuley – George Bowering provided actual instruction in his years at Sir George Williams University (now Concordia). As it flowed eastward, the *Tish* influence provided a small group of Montreal poets with the means to see beyond Leonard Cohen and Irving Layton, something the Montreal poets of the 60s could *not* do.

I was a rather late arrival to the festivities. I moved back to Montreal in January of 1975 after spending two years in New York. It was early in 1975 that I got to know the various poets who shortly thereafter constellated into the Véhicule group. What I know of the years of George Bowering instruction I have been told by the various persons involved. After dropping out of the Colorado School of Mines, Artie Gold is rumoured to have one day dropped into a Bowering creative writing class and had his life forever changed. This would have been, I believe, in the last years of the 60s. Bowering exposed Artie and his friend Dwight Gardiner to the work of two American poets he was particularly interested in at the time, Jack Spicer and Frank O'Hara: the rest, as they say, is history. At the age of twenty Gold started to instantaneously produce some truly remarkable poetry. McAuley and Konyves, who would not start to publish work until some time later, registered various affinities and resistances. After George returned to the west (and started teaching at Simon Fraser) his springtime east coast readings in Montreal were a source of great joy to this group of poets. (I remember organizing one at McGill during the mid-70s, at a time when *A Short Sad Book* was still in notebook form).

Perhaps an important point to make is that Bowering and David McFadden (followed shortly thereafter by Lionel Kearns) were the first "established" poets to recognize the existence of the Véhicule poets in any kind of meaningful way. At the time Montreal was still recovering from its 60s hangover and any attention the Véhicule poets garnered in Montreal was usually negative. 60s holdovers David Solway and Michael Harris were at that time still working on their Layton and

Cohen impressions, which generally met with favorable results. Bowering and McFadden validated the existence of the Véhicule crowd by taking us seriously.

We were all very aware of the fact that the *Tish* poets had produced their own newsletter, had taken over the means of production. This set the example for us (somehow the Dudek/Contact Press example occurred to us later), and Stephen Morrissey's *what is* and John McAuley's *Maker*, both concrete newsletters, employed the *Tish* method of circulating to an exclusive mailing list. The official "organ" of the Véhicule poets, *Mouse Eggs*, adopted the in-group air of *Tish*. Its purpose was to give a public airing to the work of the Véhicule group. Rather than circulate by mailing list, it was sold exclusively (for 35 cents a copy) at The Word bookstore.

Looking back on the Véhicule years what I find so incredible is the number of things we had going at the same time. The Véhicule poets helped to run the art gallery, ran a battery of magazines (*what is*, *Maker*, *Mouse Eggs*, *CrossCountry*, *Hh*, *Every Man His Own Football*, and *The Montreal Journal of Poetics*), administered the reading series at the gallery, and edited books for Véhicule Press. Bowering, Kearns, and Marlatt were all brought in to give readings at various times. We were all enormous fans of George, and if you were to go back and read Véhicule poets' work from that period you would probably find traces of George everywhere. Lionel's impact was also quite immediate, particularly when it came to myself and Endre Farkas. The wonderful humanity of the work that was published in *Practicing Up to Be Human* was clear to us the first time we heard it, and exposure to Lionel's poetry certainly changed my own.

Our response to Daphne Marlatt's work was really quite curious, and again I best remember my own and Farkas' reaction. Daphne came to give a reading at Véhicule Art in, I believe, 1978, and I remember myself and Endre both quietly withdrawing from the gallery space and talking about how we couldn't get into what she was doing *at all*. At that time we just weren't ready for it. By 1980 we were both absolutely entranced by Daphne's writing. Poems like Endre's "Oral History" (in fact, most of his chapbook *From Here To Here*) and my own "Here/There" and "Rain" all emerged out of Daphne's method.

As a publishing house, Véhicule Press in the early days thought of itself as Montreal's Coach House Press in potential. (Since the rift in the early 80s that saw the Véhicule poets exit from Véhicule Press, the publishing house has gone in a completely different direction.) Claudia Lapp's first book, *Honey*, and my own *Vegetables* were almost spontaneously produced by the ambience of the gallery, the poets, and the fledgling press (being run as a cooperative print shop out of the back of the gallery) all sharing the same space together. Shortly thereafter an "official" editorial board was constituted, composed of Endre Farkas, Artie Gold, and myself. Up until that time books had been produced out of small parcels of cash and print shop labour. As the press began to announce itself with a greater flourish, we also decided to cut our teeth in terms of obtaining Canada Council money. Trying to secure a manuscript that would be guaranteed to be funded we turned to George Bowering; what resulted was *The Concrete Island*, the first bona fide, government-funded Véhicule Press title.

Even at the time it was not lost on me that Véhicule Press was establishing itself by publishing a book that was, in many ways, a put-down of Montreal. *The Concrete Island: Montreal Poems 1967-71*, contained what Bowering, even at that time, was calling "my last lyrics," stray poems that had been written in Montreal during the Sir George years. Bowering had entered his "symphonic period" (this was the time when he was composing *Genève* and *Autobiology*), and these poems were occasional squibs in which he was often knocking the east and longing for the west. It wasn't a great book, it might not even have been a good book, and we all had mixed feelings about it. We, too, had grave reservations about the mainstream Montreal poetry scene, but it was still our city he was knocking. In the end a few poems were excised and the book came out in an unusual, small format. But George *had* succeeded in securing for us that first alluring Canada Council cheque.

These are some sketchy reminiscences of an earlier time, when we were all much more willing to be influenced. The Véhicule poets stopped being an official group in the early 80s and, like the *Tish* poets, have all gone their separate ways while remembering to keep in touch. Most of us still write to George on a semi-regular basis and hear from Daphne and Lionel every now and again.

This piece by no means exhausts the subject, and if any of the others were writing this they would certainly be telling it differently. There are certainly plenty of other stories. For instance, Lionel Kearns once lent me his winter parka. This was on one of my trips to the South Seas. I'd stopped off in Vancouver for a few days, it was unseasonably cold, and I hadn't brought a jacket or anything so Lionel lent me his coat. I don't know exactly how tall Lionel is, but he is a big man. I am 5'5 1/2". David McFadden thought I looked very funny.

PAMELA BANTING

Translation A to Z: Notes on Daphne Marlatt's Ana Historic

More than ten years ago Robert Kroetsch asked a question, and it has been echoing in our ears ever since:

> *How do you grow a past/*
> to live in
>
>   the absence of silkworms
>   the absence of clay and wattles (whatever the hell
>   they are)
>   the absence of Lord Nelson
>   the absence of kings and queens
>   the absence of a bottle opener, and me with a vicious
>   attack of the 26-ounce flu . . .
>   the absence of a condom dispenser in the Lethbridge Hotel,
>   and me about to screw an old Blood whore.
>   I was in love . . . .
>   the absence of psychiatrists
>   the absence of sailing ships . . .
>   the absence of the Seine, the Rhine, the Danube, the Tiber
>   and the Thames. Shit, the Battle River ran dry one
>   fall. The Strauss boy could piss across it. He could
>   piss higher on a barn wall than any of us. He could
>   piss right clean over the principal's new car.
>   (*Seed Catalogue* 20-1)

The question was one of a series, including queries about how to grow, variously, a gardener, a garden, a prairie town, a lover, and a poet. In seeding these absences into presences, Kroetsch described what we as Canadian, more specifically Western Canadian, writers are or were up against. Even this brief excerpt from Kroetsch's list allows you to imagine though that the problem is even more complex for the woman writer, for whom many of these absences can never become presences, even by an act of positive negation. The questions Daphne Marlatt confronts in *Ana Historic* are essentially the same ones of how to grow a past, how to grow (in) a western city, how to grow a writer, a lover. Whereas Kroetsch germinates his text via the written document of the seed catalogue and the oral tradition, Marlatt takes on the problem of how to write a book about an historical woman, a contemporary woman, and the relationships among women, when the traces of women's history have been obliterated, and the official version, that is, men's history, is a narrative of subjection, exploitation and domination.

> Everything: an absence
>
> of satin sheets
> of embroidered pillow cases
> of tea towels and English china
> of silver serving spoons. (*Seed Catalogue* 20)

When *Seed Catalogue* was published, we all rejoiced. Yes, yes. That was it exactly. One of Kroetsch's answers to "the absence of books, journals, daily newspapers and every-/thing else but the *Free Press Prairie Farmer* and *The Western Producer*" was to rely on "a lot of A-1 Hard Northern bullshitters" (21), to resort, in other words, to the oral tradition – the tall tale, the joke, prairie pub conversation. However, like history, the oral tradition is also in large part a male inheritance. Vestiges of remembered speech between mothers and daughters often take the forms of proscriptions, warnings, taboos (keep your legs together, don't go into the bush, nice girls don't . . .), and the record of spoken or written words passing between female friends is very scant. When both speech and writing are coded as masculine then, how does the woman writer write a novel? How does she "step inside the picture and open it up" (*Ana Historic* 56).

In her essay "Musing with Mothertongue" Marlatt describes the woman writer's place as "that double edge where she has always lived, between the already spoken and the unspeakable, sense and non-sense." As Marlatt recognizes, writing from this double edge, "risking nonsense, chaotic language leafings, unspeakable breaches of usage, intuitive leaps" (*Touch to My Tongue* 48), both releases life in "old roots" and presents particular problems for the writer too. She points to misrepresentations of women's experience in a "patriarchally-loaded" mother tongue and to those absences within it of expressions describing women's power or such exclusively female experiences as breast-feeding a baby and lesbian lovemaking.

Furthermore, insofar as the mother tongue is a dialogue between mother and child, for example, it is also an unwritten language consisting of a general sonority and hieroglyphs of physical contact, warmth, the exchange of fluids, gesture, caretaking, and caress. Equally important, what has traditionally been called the mother tongue is actually the *father's* first language,[1] which often in the past has been reinforced by layering over it a "second" language (historically the learned Latin taught in residential schools for boys, the exile from the family and the translation exercises between these two languages further erasing or repressing the earlier semiotic exchanges with the mother). Even the very idea and name "mother tongue" imply a language which has been alienated, superceded or annulled by another.[2]

> Bring me the radish seeds,
> my mother whispered. (*Seed Catalogue* 14)

What Marlatt calls for is a rewriting of the whole idea of the mother tongue. The mother tongue we must now begin to learn to write and speak is *not* the same as our native language. It is an other mother tongue, not a new language outside patriarchal discourse but rather the "alterity that has always lain silent, unmarked and invisible within the mother tongue" (Gallop 317, 320). A (m)other tongue.

Ana Historic is the novel as translation. It is a translation of some of the missing details of the life of a Mrs. Richards, who emigrated to Burrard Inlet in the early days of the settlement to be the village school teacher, who subsequently married one Ben Springer, and then abruptly faded from the historical record. Her story is reconstructed from these scant historical fragments discovered by Annie, research assistant to her historian husband Richard, mother of two children, daughter of Ina, friend of Zoe. The novel interweaves Annie's reconstruction of a possible life for the unnamed Mrs. Richards (whom she names as Ana with one "n," thus marking her as a kind of cartouche between Annie and Ina) with the similarly unremarked life of Annie's mother, Ina, and recollections and recordings of Annie's own girlhood and present life. The juxtaposition of all these different life stories creates a non-linear, discontinuous, disrupted text:

> the smoky glass swan drifting in a pool of tears. les sylphides. the forlorn Soho flowergirl haunting the blue wall of the room i practised and practised in. music meant the moonlight sonata, meant someplace else, not history (i thought vaguely of the plaster busts lined up on Mrs. Pritchett's grand piano – Beethoven looking burgherish, Mozart looking slightly mad, they meant nothing to me), it wasn't the music i escaped to but the aura of tears, of blue walls, of infinite lemon layers of furniture polish. polish, everything said, in the grace is the promise. (that lie you spent hours perfecting.) i breathed it like incense after the hot betrayals of locker rooms, the ridicule of notes, of whispered gossip. my difference i was trying to erase. my English shoes and woolly vests. my very words. (22-3)

As the lives of all these different women and girls are written into narrative and history, so, without being altered or transformed in any way but simply through being quoted and collaged into this unfamiliar context, the archival documents which support official history undergo a process we might call a form of translation, since the documentary language becomes denatured, provoked to yield its ideological biases. The language of history breaks down into its components, namely, the language of nominalization, categorization, hierarchization, domination, colonization, subordination, and control:

> *'The red cedar, unequalled as a wood for shingles, comes next to the fir in importance. Because of its variety of shading, and the brilliant polish which it takes, it is prized for the interior finishing of houses. As the cedar lasts well underground it is used for telegraph poles and fence posts ... Well can this wood be called the settler's friend, for from it he can with simple tools, such*

as axe and saw, build his house, fence his farm, and make his furniture.'
(*Ana Historic* 19-20)

No. 1248 – **Hubbard Squash: "As mankind** seems to have a **particular fondness** for squash, **Nature** appears to have **especially** provided this **matchless** variety of **superlative flavor."** (*Seed Catalogue* 17)

Within this project of excavating, imagining, and inscribing a (m)other tongue, Marlatt's work is a simultaneous translation between language and the body, between the speakable and the unspeakable, between women's unrecorded speech and unwritten writing. In exploring the translative properties of the act of writing itself, she theorizes and invents this (m)other tongue. Translation for Marlatt is the means of moving between this as yet unmarked other tongue and her native language, Canadian English. Translation is essential in order to open up and convert a statement such as " 'first white child born on Burrard Inlet' " to something like "a woman's body in its intimacy, giving birth" (131) and to underscore that neither is the first *white* child the first child. The following passage occurs just after Mrs. Richards witnesses the birth: "mouth speaking flesh. she touches it to make it tell her present in this other language so difficult to translate. the difference" (126). This difficult, multiform translation is necessary because women's history, women's desire, and women's bodies are both unwritten and overwritten by men's history, desire, and bodies. And women's history is unwritten, according to Annie's friend Zoe, "because it runs through our bodies: we give birth to each other" (131).

Annie's mother, Ina, on the other hand, as a child virtually abandoned at an English boarding school while her parents pursued their privileged lifestyle in colonial India, becomes a victim partly of her own learned inability graduating to refusal to translate. I-na: I plus the negation of I. I/not-I. The mother who is not the mirror of the self. The mother as other, the mother as immigrant woman, discovers to her shock (emotional shock, eventually leading to the electrical kind) that her mother tongue (read father tongue), colonial British English, is not the same as the vernacular of British Columbia and attempts to recover her composure by trying to persuade her daughters to use the British terms instead of the Canadian – in other words, to preserve the source text and not to translate. Her response to her immigrant situation and to the circumscription of her life by the predefined roles of wife and mother in the forties and fifties is rigidly to preserve and perfect these roles through obsessive housecleaning – in other words, through compulsively miming, to the letter, the source of her victimization.

My own grandmother (an immigrant from England), speaking out of what would come to be diagnosed as her "madness," "sickness," "going out of her head" or "off the deep end," once said to one of her daughters, my mother, "Oh, you Canadians. You don't understand anything." Like Ina, Emily Davy was also sent off for a series of shock treatments, to have her symptoms as an immigrant woman translated literally into her treatment.

Near the end of *Ana Historic* when "Richard's Annie" has translated the name "Ana Richards" into narrative, she worries about her debt to the "characters" she has been working with. Zoe ridicules her: "truth, i suppose? fidelity? she sneers. as if you were *impersonating* them" (141). Zoe questions the prime values traditionally associated with a faithful translation. As a feminist compositional practice, translation does not work by matching meaning to meaning, the source text to a target text which can never be more than a pale imitation of the original. Feminist writing as translation is a faithless activity. Or, more accurately, it is faithless to transcendental abstractions such as truth, fidelity, imitation, woman, and other masculinist constructions which work to constitute the system of patriarchal discourse.

Just as Annie translates Mrs. Richard's buried life story into a novel, so Daphne Marlatt translates from a source language (the mother tongue as native language) which is never entirely pure or unitary into a target language (the (m)other tongue) which does not exist as a language separate unto itself either:

> i was slimming into another shape, finding a waist, gaining curves, attaining the sort of grace i was meant to have as a body marked *woman*'s. as if it were a brand name. . . . 'feminine' translated a score of different ways: doll, chick, baby, kitten. diminished to the tyranny of eyes: 'was he looking at me?' 'did you see how he looked at you?
>
> boy-crazy you said, shaking your head as we drove, walked, rode obsessed past street corners, sauntered past certain spots on the beach, our heads full of advertising images, converting all action into the passive: to be seen. (52)

That is to say, Marlatt explores writing as a process of translation into a language which only emerges in the act of translation. This translation is possible and necessary because, as Jane Gallop urges, "The question of language must be inserted as the wedge to break the hold of the figure of the mother [because patriarchal discourse structures the very ideas of 'mother' and 'woman']. *Ecriture féminine* must not be arrested by the plenitude of the mother tongue, but must try to be always and also an other tongue." The (m)other tongue is a composite that is no one's mother tongue and can only be comprehended in two languages at once (328-9). The (m)other tongue, then, is an interlanguage,[3] a language that emerges only in the process of second-language learning. It is a separate, yet intermediate, linguistic system situated between a source language and a target language and which results from a learner's attempted production of the target language. *Ana Historic* is translation A(nnie) to Z(oe).

Notes

[1] See, for example, Dennis Cooley's important essays in which "the vernacular" (another name for the mother tongue) is reserved exclusively for male "ear" poets: "It seems to me that what I am calling 'eye' poems tend to be written by women, and 'ear' poems to be written by men" ("Placing the Vernacular" 14). In a mere footnote I am bound to reduce the complexity of much of Cooley's argument. However, it must be pointed out that within its own terms Cooley's fundamental privileging of male poets' access to the vernacular "muse" is essentially a tautological argument. For the purposes of the present discussion, the problematical aspect of these two essays is not that Cooley privileges male poets' access to the vernacular (since that is true by definition) but rather that because he does not "hear" the (m)other tongue issuing from various female poets or, alternatively, because he does not hear the male vernacular in their voices, he places them on the side of what he calls "eye" poets, those whose poetry and poetics do not challenge and in fact uphold dominant power structures.

[2] As Kaja Silverman suggests, the term 'mother tongue' attributes to woman sole knowledge of that language within which lack can be experienced and known (20-1). Theorists of the process of the subject's entry into language routinely posit this entrance into signifying systems as a choice between meaning and life, between significance and insignificance. They are more than willing to surrender or abandon the presymbolic or semiotic in the Name of the Father (i.e., the symbolic, the native language). However, meaning is always already constituted in the sonorous envelope, the eye contact and the gestural hieroglyphs of the "mother tongue." Here the word "tongue" itself becomes inadequate as this domestic vernacular pervades the body as a whole and in fact blurs the boundaries between two bodies. Furthermore, this bond with the mother and with the feminine more generally need not, should not and in fact cannot be irretrievably renounced, forfeited or signed away in negotiating the social contract.

[3] See Gideon Toury on the concept of interlanguages.

Works Cited

Cooley, Dennis. "Placing the Vernacular: The Eye and the Ear in Saskatchewan Poetry" and "The Vernacular Muse in Prairie Poetry." In *The Vernacular Muse: The Eye and Ear in Contemporary Literature*. Winnipeg: Turnstone P, 1987. The latter essay was first printed in successive numbers of *Prairie Fire*.

Gallop, Jane. "Reading the Mother Tongue: Psychoanalytic Feminist Criticism." *Critical Inquiry* 13.2 (1987): 314-29.

Kroetsch, Robert. *Seed Catalogue*. Winnipeg: Turnstone P, 1979.

Marlatt, Daphne. "Musing with Mothertongue." *Touch to My Tongue*. Edmonton: Longspoon P, 1984. 43-49. Rpt. in *In the Feminine: Women and Words/Les Femmes et les Mots, Conference Proceedings 1983*. Ed. Ann Dybikowski, Victoria

Freeman, Daphne Marlatt, Barbara Pulling, Betsy Warland. Edmonton: Longspoon P, 1985. 171-4.

———. Ana Historic. Toronto:Coach House P, 1988.

Silverman, Kaja. *The Acoustic Mirror: The Female Voice in Psychoanalysis and Cinema*. Theories of Representation and Difference. Teresa de Lauretis, general ed. Bloomington and Indianapolis: Indiana UP, 1988.

Toury, Gideon. "Interlanguage and Its Manifestations in Translation." *In Search of a Theory of Translation*. Tel Aviv University: The Porter Institute for Poetics and Semiotics, 1980. 71-8.

E.D. BLODGETT

Frank Davey: Critic as Autobiographer

"the genuine reader is a self-reader, a self-subverter"
George Steiner

Liminary Note

Although Frank Davey is a remarkably explicit critic, the character of his critical interests do not appear to encourage him to explain the interrelation of his preoccupations and the project they shape. For Davey they form a whole. I, therefore, propose to consider them apart from one another, at least to the degree that this is possible. Discrete consideration will, of course, break up the "natural" flow of my remarks, but I agree with Davey that the structure of an essay is not natural in the first place. While most of my notes, finally, bear upon *Reading Canadian Reading*, its manifest reflection upon earlier work means that I will treat it as a kind of epitome that permits excursus.

1. "The orders of language" (Davey 1976a, 24)

Poets who are also critics make certain decisions, and not all of them are exercised by the *prima materia* of poetic craft. Poetry is primarily, as George Bowering has remarked with his apparent casualness, "a way with words." It is at once a manner with and toward words. It is where a poet begins and subsequently dwells. Davey as critic has never forgotten this. As a consequence, it may be asserted that for him the crafts of poetry and criticism are coterminous. Thus, in one his earliest reflections on *Tish* – and Davey's whole habitus as critic and poet is one of continuous reflection – he describes the highlights of the first nineteen issues as consisting "mostly of poems." After naming those he admires, he states that "[a]ll of these in some way – sound, structure, point of view – moved poetry to the kind of articulation of which we wanted to be capable" (Davey 1975, 10). Not until the next paragraph do we find what they articulate. The point of departure, then, is the way words fit together to make the poem. In a subsequent reflection, he remarks simply that "the writer is the custodian of the language and he has a responsibility to that language which requires him to make self-sacrifices if that is what is necessary for the language to be kept pure of imprecision and literary form to be kept free of conventionality and cliché" (Davey 1976b, 52). The echo of Mallarmé and Pound (Davey 1965, 71) is clear; the humility, clearer.

I have been drawing upon the "early" Davey, the Davey of "the black days on Black Mountain." That these days dominate the first decade, at least, of Davey's career is known and documented in many places. Nevertheless, the stance toward language, as a site in itself and the means by which a site is engendered, has not faded as the ineluctable and inescapable guide. It is, indeed, Davey's custodian. But what does "language" mean? In his recent work it no longer refers to the phenomenological understanding of it as understood in Charles Olson, for texts have no outside that might be called phenomena (Davey 1988a, 52). Language is not characterized by its ability to locate "the real" but by facilitating discussion of meanings that are a function of kinds of discourse. Language refers to itself and how it constructs. The articulation of such knowledge is the act by which Davey moves dialectically away from the implications of phenomenology. This is the burden of his reflection on his earlier study of Earle Birney, and especially his later work on Louis Dudek and Raymond Souster. Citing his commentary on Dudek's poetry, he observes that:

> I called these poems "rite poems, in which the poet commits himself to the poem without knowing the outcome . . . voyage poems into distant lands and distant possibilities . . . writing [as] an act of sympathetic magic" (79), but I left the belief on which the rite is based unnamed, as if I too saw it as "natural" or "objectively true." (Davey 1988a, 57)

Upon reconsideration, the "natural" is perceived as a construction. Olson's "composition by field," the principle of energy for *Tish*, is now understood as a position without self-awareness: the "magic," the "spell" that permits sympathy (feeling together) with language and place (cf. Davey 1965, 71) may be seen as a manifestation of contradictions in Dudek's text and, by implication, in Davey's, upon reflection, with respect to writing and culture.

The breaking of the spell is the work of Foucault and Althusser. For the constructed text and not merely "language" is a political field, "an immense system of codes continuously modified by the politics of human culture" (Davey 1988a, 107). One of the consequences of defining texts as constructed is that it shifts the reader away from a consumer stance. No text is neutral, uninterested, universal. It is, rather, the inscription of conflict (Davey 1988a, 28). Thus, the essay devoted to Pratt's *Brébeuf and his Brethren*, while constantly foregrounding the poem's language, does so in order to argue that the central opposition between *fort* and *forest* only appears to be binary. A closer reading suggests an indeterminacy that is to be found everywhere in the poem's semantic network. The significance of the indeterminacy permits the detection of "various competing ideologies": "the Counter-Reformation's conservative evangelical Catholicism, the Renaissance state's faith in bureaucracy, the North American Indian's belief in a natural world suffused with animate deities, the mid-twentieth-century Western belief in technology and progress" (Davey 1988a, 177). To argue that Davey merely uses language to identify central themes would be an error; for while these are indeed themes, they are also ideologies formed by the collusion of language and historical circumstance. The theme, at least in its untheorized state, belongs to a static criticism of imitation that Davey's reading excludes. But *Brébeuf* is capable of more: "its troubled vision of *fort* and *forest* is, despite its intertextual relationship with the *Jesuit Relations*, a Canadian one of 1941; it chooses that relationship, it re-writes those texts, it depicts its own particular Brébeuf and particular forests" (Davey 1988a, 177). By so doing, it anticipates the postmodern (re-writing) and suggests an access to phenomenology ("particular forests"), recalling Davey's early emphasis on "*particularism* and *localism*" (Davey 1976a, 23). It is a text, then, that explicitly inscribes a certain Marxism, as well as traces of a Davey elsewhere suppressed.

The postmodern is, of course, not suppressed, but itself rewritten. The postmodern of *From There to Here* is phenomenological, and echoes of the *Tish* statements are to be found again: "[T]he post-modernists seek to participate in anarchic cooperation with the elements of an environment in which no one element fully controls any other" (Davey 1974, 20). This statement is in turn a rewriting of an earlier reading of Olson:

> if a man exists in an "object-object" relationship with external nature, and if he admits the integrity and right to particularity of all members of external nature, then the only way in which this man can approach and know nature is by participating in an established "field" of objects. (Davey 1965, 71)

Nor does the Introduction to *From There to Here* hide its *Tish* roots, explicitly describing the postmodern as "this particularistic, phenomenological kind of writing" (22).

The function of postmodernism in *Reading* thematizes decentring and anti-humanism, familiar from *From There to Here*, and is also more explicit about the relation between "semiotics and politics" (116). Not surprisingly, postmodernism in Canada, at least, is marked by the particular, distinguishing it from the American and British variety (119). Hence, "[f]orm and language are again political" (120). "[C]entral authority," "the cultural relativity of language and perception," and "the epistemological grounds of power" are of necessity aspects of the postmodern (120). How they are more political in their use than in British and American postmodernism is not fully elaborated. Speaking only of Canada, Davey's practice is to privilege those writers who may be considered postmodern, and one might infer that it is because of their possibility as analogue to Davey's own writing. Let us consider Eli Mandel in this regard.

Mandel's life as Davey now reads it, in many respects at odds with the reading in *From There to Here*, is marked by a "de-placement" that bears upon the multiple relations of self and place and "how we envision these relationships, how we assign value in envisioning such relationships, and ultimately of how we perceive and constitute literary creation" (200). "De-placement" is an act of reading and of writing that takes the *place* away. On one level, it is the "pride of place" that is gone, indeed subverted in the rejection of "the hierarchical insistencies of formal rhetoric" (200). On another level, as successive versions and readings of "Minotaur Poems" argue, it would be wrong to assume that Mandel is a modernist, merely "lost in cosmopolitan literary fashion, lost in an alien mythology" (208). Rather, the sequence "encodes a sharp lexical struggle between margin and centre, between language as constructive act and language as hierarchical, referential and inherited" (211). A consequence is "that 'place' is rather strangely gained from the European father by a language that increasingly appears 'out of place' " (211). In language, then, one is always ambiguously "out of place." As Olson taught, it puts us in our place. As Foucault teaches, it tells us that our place is code, conflict, ideology. It is our place in that we are nowhere else.

2. Commodity Fetishism

Tish need not be read solely as a nexus of poetic thinking. Because of its mode of production (a Gestetner machine), it was characterized by its accessibility and inexpensiveness: "a local readership was the main goal" (Davey 1975, 97). It was no more and no less than "a poetry newsletter – Vancouver." As such, it was consistent with Davey's notion of place, community, and decentring. Its very materiality is a sign of its opposition to the stable, the homogenous, "the complete statement" (Davey 1974, 20-1). In its perfectly fortuitous fashion, it fell into being postmodern.

Tish, then, is marked by its refusal to be a commodity, especially in the sense of an object of exchange in Marx's sense (Tucker 320-1). Its format and mode of production themselves constitute a political statement. This is equally true for all Canadian literary magazines and the book trade in general. Author and audience, therefore, are a function of a text's production, both writer and reader bound together in the same enterprise. Consequences follow from such knowledge, and these are of interest in their relation to Davey's Canada. Because of Canada's economic and geographic position – always between the U.S. and Great Britain (France does not play a part in Davey's Canada) – "the petty-commodity mode of production [was and] remains the dominant form of literary production in English Canada." Furthermore, "[t]he audience inscribed in such texts . . . is a small, middle-class educated one, and very often with a regional or specifically ideological character" (Davey 1988a, 95). Canada, however, is powerfully within a North American economic sphere of influence which goes well beyond one aspect of the book trade. The "economy is . . . one of many interlocking manifestations of the liberal-humanist discourse, with its emphasis on precise and efficient reference, empirical description, and the interpellation of individuals as subjects, which western society has constructed and been constructed by for the past three or four centuries" (15). The problem, as Davey remarks frequently, begins with the Renaissance and should be understood as a problem of discourse ("reference," "description," "interpellation," "constructed"). The role, then, that educational institutions play in the act of construction (addressing the *écriture*) is crucial. Two discourses dominate in such education, namely, the freshman essay ("the discourse of unambiguous reference"), and, for the sake of our emotional satisfaction, "the discourse of fantasy-adventure, pulp fiction, television sit-coms" (16). We are trained in the usage of the text as commodity but not given access to the ideologies both discourses contain. For the function of the freshman essay implies "that the material world is objectively present, representable and manipulable by language, and that its efficient manipulation and consumption can lead to happiness" (16); the function of fantasy-adventure is to suggest that sooner or later a miracle will occur in the apparently objective world without our effort.

In many respects this argument has been developed before. Already in *From There to Here* he remarked: "The post-modern artist does not believe that he can absorb, structure, organize, and discourse definitively on the universe" (21). Such an artist refuses to be a consumer. Something occurs in Davey's thinking in the fifteen years between these two texts that distinguish their significance and that is the effort to eliminate the burden of phenomenology. This, I take it, is part of the point of the revisionism that is inscribed in the first four chapters of *Reading Canadian Reading*. One is prompted to ask, however, what became of "the universe" so easily referred to in the earlier work. While asserting that "I today stand fully behind the values explicitly declared by that introduction" (41), which are, at least, those of a militant postmodernism, the world outside discourse is not perceptible. "The world here [in Hodgin's *The Invention of the World*] is indeed to be invented, much like Nichol invents readings of his own writings" (117). Hence, the world as an epistemological and even ontological datum is open to question. Discussing Livesay's notion of the documentary, he observes: "[A] dialectic occurs here, but not so much between the 'objective facts' (presuming that there can be 'objective facts') and the subjective feelings of the poet as between the original texts and the new one" (133). One might, but I refrain from doing so, question the significance of "original" (it may have been an oversight), for speaking of subversion and transgression, he notes that they "may well be usual operations in writing and reading, in which case the question arises of whether, being so usual, such operations can occur, there being perhaps no thing or praxis to be transgressed against" (137).

Subversion of this kind is not a particularly difficult matter, and elsewhere Davey makes it clear that there are kinds of discourse that may be called official ("the western literary heritage") and authentic, and one of the functions of intertextual practice is to confront the two. The essay on Thomas and Atwood is designed expressly to indicate such operations. The problem left in a certain suspense is how literature mediates discursively with the *hors texte*. Davey's final argument with Olson is "that the relationship between the text and the phenomena that were alleged to precede it was undemonstrable" (52). There is no *hors texte*. The consequence is that the site of conflict – history, class relationships, economy, politics, sexuality – is a text of competing discourses.

As Hayden White reads Foucault,

> interpretation does not lead to the discovery of the relationship between the words in the text and the universe of things conceived to stand outside the text and to which the words of the text refer. It means, as Foucault has suggested as the key to the understanding of his method, "transcription" in such a way as to reveal the inner dynamics of the thought processes by which a given representation of the world in words is grounded in poesis. (258)

Why, then, the discussion of the book as commodity, the overture to Eagleton, the discussions of "late capitalist economy of North America and western Europe"

(Davey 1988a, 15)? As Fredric Jameson remarked some years ago, "it is a sobering and salutary experience for professional intellectuals to be reminded that the objects of their study and manipulation have a whole material infrastructure as well" (393). At the risk of sounding petulant, one wants to ask Frank, "What is the *matter*"? As John Frow puts it: "What is at issue here . . . is the ontological distinction between levels of the real and the forms of mediation between them" (37). His response, which follows closely upon that of Althusser, is that the argument of empiricism is too flawed to carry persuasive weight: "The decisive criterion of analysis can thus no longer be the relation between discourse and a reality which is external to it." At issue, then, are "the relations between discourse and *power*, the intrication of power in discourse" (57). As Frow goes on to argue, "[t]he discursive is a socially constructed reality which constructs the categories of the real and the symbolic and this distinction between them. It assigns structure to the real at the same time as it is a product and a moment of real structures" (58).

It is in such a context that the signal value of Davey's article, "Ideology and Visual Representation: Some Postcards From the Raj," may be understood. Here he argues that the sudden accessibility of the picture postcard in the late Victorian period and the use made of it guaranteed its function as a "fetishized object" (Davey 1988b, 48). Its discursive strategy followed "much nineteenth-century British fiction" (65) in that it supported the dominant ideology, suppressing the conflict implied in the colonization of India. Clearly, "real structures" operate in these images, constituting one of the several realities of the India depicted. Not only is the card a fetish in the Marxist sense (cf. White 185), but also "the Indian subjects here became reproducible commodities" (65). According to Davey, this was but an initial discursive strategy that prepared the so constituted subject for further "packaging," as one is tempted to say: "After the post card would come less subtle agents of homogenizing commercialism . . . nearly all of which have emphasized the visualities of empiricism and pragmatically assumed the commodity-status of knowledge" (65). As we are semiotically produced, so are we constituted.

3. Postmodernism or what matters?

It could not be said exactly that the postmodern preoccupies Davey. He does not theorize it; he asserts it, and he has done so since *Tish*. It forms a kind of substratum to all his thinking. It derives from Olson in particular, phenomenological fashion. Reflecting on Olson's presence in *Tish*, Davey cites Olson's perception (from "Against Wisdom as Such") of the poet: "[T]here are no symbols for him, there are only his own composed forms, and each one solely the issue of the time of the moment of its creation, not any ultimate except what he in his heat and that instant in its solidity yield" (Davey 1976a, 16-7). This refusal of reification is the "sign" beneath which the poet writes. While Olson is an origin of Davey's postmodernism, its subsequent development is shaped by Foucault and also Lyotard. What they assist him to eliminate from his thinking is the signified that remains in the final sentence in the passage from Olson: "That the poet cannot afford to traffick in any other 'sign' than his one, his self, the man or woman he is [sic]." Part of the point of the revised understanding of his reading of Birney is to clear it of Olson (27-30) and to take his subject to task for lapsing "into empiricist, humanist and organicist thinking. On numerous occasions *Earle Birney* invokes the principle of 'authenticity' as if some epistemological ground for the 'real' or the 'authentic' could be established" (Davey 1988a, 29).

No known ground may be posited outside the text. The overture to Foucault is evident here, not to speak of the Derrida who is never invoked. The postmodern enactment of *glissage* may also be observed, for not only is Earle Birney castigated – *Earle Birney* too is part of the problem. Davey unnamed becomes the signifier replacing the named Birney. What Davey, we are moved to ask, may be posited outside the text? In this manner Davey constructs himself as an intertextual sign that unobtrusively plays upon itself. As Aquin once reported, "le moi est un intertexte, la conscience du moi un commentaire desordonné – marginalia parfois indiscernable mais portant toujours formante, instauratrice" (271). One might argue that Davey has so "transcribed" his earlier phenomenology.

Let us return, however, to the ground that is of no matter but the text. "Ground" for Foucault is a discourse encoded in a certain way; thus, authority is relocated "as a function of discourse" (Foucault 127). The transcendent does not transcend the text unless it participates in the discourse of history (Davey 1988a, 54). We enter here the realm left vacant by the dissolution of the metanarrative (Lyotard 34-7) and are urged to ask what makes things matter? Are what we thought were things either things or matter? What is a commodity? I have recuperated the commodity, for its significance for Davey is governed by his discourse of postmodernism. While commodity exists for him as book and postcard, *inter alia*, it is evident their signal value lies in their possibilities as textual material: "The Indian subjects [in late Victorian postcards] here became reproducible commodities, pretexts . . . " (Davey 1988b, 65). The fetishized commodity is transcribed as sign in late capitalist society.

Arthur Kroker's reading of Baudrillard argues that "the logic of the sign" may be understood "as the emblematic expression in consumer culture of the commodity-form" (Kroker and Cook 179). As a consequence, "[i]n the *simulational* scheme of advanced capitalist society, use-value and exchange-value conflate into mirrored aspects of a single process of abstract, semiological reproduction: the classical poles of signifier and signified dilate into a single structural homology at the nucleus of the logic of the sign" (180). In such a world the commodity, then, implodes:

> use-value and exchange-value are stripped of their antinomic (and thus autonomous) status, and are transformed into endlessly refracted (and random) points in an aimless cycle of exchange which, being semiurgical and mirror-like, traces the path of disintegration and regression in contemporary experience. (180-1)

What, then, becomes of Marx who "wished to preserve a privileged space of freedom in concrete, living labour, in use-value with a vertical axis, in something *real*" (184)? Postmodernism, which may simply be another name (and lacking in a certain precision) for advanced capitalist economy and culture, through its continuous repositioning of an illusory referent, is sufficient as a delegitimizing discourse to produce the real (Marxian or not) "as a vast and seductive simulation" (186).

What, then, legitimizes the sign, the sign beneath which postmodernist discourse deploys itself? This is a question that Davey has chosen to leave "open." His use of discourse, however, suggests that he would not go as far as Baudrillard, despite the fact that the writing he privileges – " 'Canadian postmodern writing' " – "seems undismayed by cultural or literary disunity [and] seems diffident about its own authority." Furthermore, "[i]t usually sees mythology not as sacred inheritance but as arbitrary human construction" (Davey 1988a, 107). Hence, among central discursive conflicts that Davey identifies in such writing is that which is engaged between those metanarratives that descend from the Renaissance and the invented fictions that utter the authentic. The effect of the western literary tradition, especially the Bible and the mode of romance as theorized by Northrop Frye, is to destroy the authentic. The discursive conflict that may be discerned in such writers as Audrey Thomas and Margaret Atwood is designed, by means of its strategies of disjunction and multiplicity, to expose the constructed character and implied ideologies of the canon (165). The essay on Mandel argues similarly that the tradition hierarchizes the use of language, that the canon (and here, I would surmise, Davey alludes to Bakhtin) is an official text that represses the authentic.

"In Margaret Atwood's short stories," he observes, "there is a similarly [as in Thomas] recurrent separation between culturally 'received' stories and other potentially more authentic stories" (159). The subversion of the official in Hodgins is designed to show "characters deconstructing the myths which dispossess them of their lives" (197). This is a crucial point, for it forms the basis of the argument that Davey has steadily put forth since the days of *Tish*. What is interesting is the conflation of existential phenomenology with poststructuralism that forms, if I may anticipate, the character of Davey's nationalism. Thus the theme of authenticity is not merely a "trace" of earlier thinking that continues to preoccupy Davey's criticism, it is a foundation, and it conjoins him with "[l]es phénoménologues . . . et ceux [e.g. Olson] qui ont subi leur influence, [qui] ont tenté de lier à la théorie de l'existence une de l'être, de sauver parallèlement l'authenticité et la verité" (Mounier 133). If there is a difference, it is that for Davey the authentic is now but a construction of discourse. In this way he preserves his postmodernity and can combine it with his Althusserian Marxism.

For the postmodern in Canada, according to Davey, is postcolonial. It is opposed to the modern which is "typically viewed as an international movement, elitist, imperialist, 'totalizing,' willing to appropriate the local while being condescending toward its practice" (Davey 1988a, 119). It is a discursive practice with a political agenda. What, however, legitimizes a Marxist postmodernism in Davey's sense and inscribes it with the hegemony that he would see it possessed of? Is this not akin to the terrorizing that Davey, citing Lyotard, accuses canon-formation of doing (265)? Postmodern discourse only appears capable of making the possible possible, "by foregrounding the skeleton of layers" (McHale 39). It is, however, merely another discourse, as Marxism is. Both are language-games, at least within the postmodern frame-of-reference and cannot be legitimized, as science thought it could, on the basis of performativity (Lyotard 40-1).

4. The Subject

The initial essays of *Reading Canadian Reading* are marked by an apparent candour, employing the discourses of both confession and self-criticism. This is particularly true for the four essays that examine both the limitations of earlier books and the limitations of their reviewers. All the books, while engaging in theoretical issues, are studies of specific Canadian writers and, as he declares with respect to his study of Earle Birney, the series of which it is a part "expected a book that was as much about the author as about his texts" (21). How is the author to be addressed?

The book on Atwood, subtitled "a feminist poetics," because of the more theoretical expectations of the series in which it was published, allowed him to approach biography as more problematic than a simple equation of text as reflection of writer. In addressing her poetry, he refused to make use of "the modernist concept of *persona*" (72), for which certain critics took him to task. His analysis of poetic voice identifies three methods of approach: first, the naïve view that "I" refers to a " 'real' historic author"; second, the modernist view of the constructed persona; and third, discourse theory that argues that the lyric voice is a merely rhetorical utterance (72-3). The first two are dismissed summarily; so too is the latter, but only after some deliberation. Clearly the latter is a matter of some concern to Davey, for he is at pains to remain consistent with his own fidelity to discourse theory that does not permit intentionalist fallacies: "[N]o 'authentic' or 'sincere' utterance," no "essential 'I' " can be posited. The weakness of discourse theory in the analysis of Atwood's poetic is that it cannot account for efforts "to intervene – on *someone's* behalf – in human affairs" (74), that is, in the moments that appear "as constituting not an author's creation of a text (which it necessarily is) but an author's addressing of a reader" (74). Later, citing Todorov in turn citing Bakhtin, Davey suggests that at certain moments in analysis, the constraints of discourse theory may be overrided in favour of the notion of "the 'image of the author' " (75). This is a clever, indeed useful, argument, and it permits the reader to identify one voice among others in a particular way. Yet, as he remarks, "this is consistent with the approach of most discourse theorists" (75). Where it differs – or appears to differ – is that his strategy allows for the construction of a "sincere" or "non-literary" text. In this manner Davey remains faithful to poststructuralism, while at the same time clearing a space for something like an historical author that Barthes and Foucault have put under erasure.

Part of Davey's reservations in respect of discourse theory is that

> the "I" is under continuing construction and re-construction through its various actions and is visible only through them; if it does attempt to intervene [in history], it changes itself through the process of that intervention and is no longer available as the "I" that sought to intervene. (73)

This is a dilemma which resides, I think, at the core of Davey's enterprise. It is hard to accept the assumptions of poststructuralism and, at the same, intervene in history, and to intervene is precisely what Davey says he intends, especially at the beginning of the Atwood essay. He wanted "[t]o influence those [certain] readings and evaluations" (64). This suggests that the subject we have been seeking is in fact Davey, for it is difficult to escape the impact of the revaluation of an earlier "*Davey*" that takes place in these initial essays and that directs our thinking about the rest of the book. Indeed, at the very beginning of the book, when reflecting upon "Surviving the Paraphrase," and considering the dominance of thematic criticism at the time of that essay, he "wanted to argue that this was a narrow and sociological view of literature" (4). He then makes a critique of the essay and book of which it became the title, noting its limitations. One cannot miss the continual dialectic of Davey's examination of Davey. For the seasoned reader of Davey, this should come as no surprise. In his Introduction to *Tish 1-19* he may be seen performing a life-long task of revision, remarking upon the opening editorial as "[p]articularly embarrassing" in its "frivolity" (Davey 1975, 9), and going on to comment upon other distressing statements. The strategy is to present Davey as a text, and it appears an inescapable habit.

If we attend carefully his utterances in *Reading* (which is a word interchangeable with "writing"), it is evident that we cannot avoid reading Davey writing. Castigating his book on Dudek and Souster, he observes: "The problems in the Dudek chapters are largely extensions of the intentionalist and representational assumptions in *Earle Birney*" (51). Later in the same essay he declares: "Once these assumptions are questioned . . . [t]he focus of discussion ceases to be 'what is real?' and becomes 'what meanings are made possible by a particular choice of discourse?'" (53). In his essay, "Recent 'Prairie' Poetry," he states that "[t]he visibly constructed text not only contests that there can be any agreed-upon preexisting subject . . . but declines the task of constructing the illusion that there might be." Furthermore, "[t]he readership it implies is not one interested in the recovery, 'representing,' or honouring of a subject but in the processes of memory, the fabrication of history" (227). Davey's summary of Mandel's "Minotaur Poems" is that it "encodes a sharp lexical struggle between margin and centre, between language as constructive act and language as hierarchical, referential and inherited." Inasmuch as "the inherited loses its privilege" (211), it is evident what is valorized in the writing Davey reads. It is true, as Davey remarks, texts must be differentiated from authors; furthermore, "[t]he 'author' is only one of a text's authors, and is the very first of these to cease to contribute to its production of meaning" (32). The other, of course, is its reader(s), but the effect of this statement displaces the earlier Atwood that Davey identifies, she who "intervenes in history."

For a long time I considered a different epigraph for the paper. While George Steiner's comment "that the genuine reader is a self-reader, a self-subverter of acuity and nerve" (126), Bowering's "battling for the craft" (Davey 1974, 89) attracted me initially for it accurately gestures toward the polemical character of Davey's writing. I was also tempted by Davey's comment that "Gnarowski's rhetoric also works to valorize not the essays that follow but their author" (Davey 1988a, 252). In many ways, however, the reader of Davey is enjoined to replace the "author" by engaging in those writing strategies that produce significance. Hence, the irony of the word "author" in an epigraph introducing Davey could well be missed. More valid would have been Davey's re-reading of Davey's *Birney*: "I failed to point out that Birney, here, like Chaucer, presents himself as a field of competing discourses – discourses that reflect competing ideologies" (26). My reading of Davey writing cannot help but follow the same trajectory as this sentence, for Davey's continuous project is one of continuous self-interrogation that would pitilessly rid itself of self as referent. Thus the "real" is always approached gingerly, not to speak of history in which one would intervene, but he is aware, at the same time, that history is a fabrication, a text. John Frow wryly remarked about one of Fredric Jameson's arguments ("history is inaccessible to us except in textual form") that "[t]his is surely a case of having one's referent and eating it too" (38). Such strategies are necessary in Davey's enterprise as well, especially if one is at once writing and re-writing one's constitutive texts.

In this sense, Davey's polemic appears to be one of always giving up. Once he commented to an interviewer that his "meditations on loss . . . were the shipwreck poems. That testifies to my wish to evade, it's *there* – wish to evade personal experiences – but also testifies to my continual fascination with loss and my determination to work out, I suppose, some metaphysic of loss" (Davey 1978b, 53-4). Such a text is one that Davey would probably like to re-write now, particularly striking out the word "metaphysic." But the whole response, especially the statement that his meditations took a specific form, marks the centre of Davey's preoccupation as poet and critic: to find the meaning of the form. The effort of finding, even of identifying the loss in the process, the *différance* that is a function of the form and "the continual fascination with loss," becomes, then, a losing, and precisely at that moment when author surrenders to reader – or vice versa. In that surrender resides the subject, a discourse forever subject to its re-writing.

5. Canada: a coda

I cannot help but see "Canada" as coda, an ending, a surrender. Davey might argue that such a view does not follow from his reading. I think it does. I want to point out, however, that I do not share certain attacks that Davey has sustained from critics such as Robin Mathews, whose subtitle to his book *Canadian Literature: Surrender or Revolution* uses "surrender" in a manner that differs from mine. The case against is simply put: foreign influence constitutes contamination. Mathews charges Davey with neo-colonialism and a tendency toward assimilation and goes so far as to argue that the McGill movement follows in a direct course via Souster and Dudek to Davey and the *Tish* group. Worst of all: "The single characteristic that Tallman and the rest of the U.S. poetic missionaries shared was an almost total ignorance of Canada and the Canadian tradition" (156). Keith Richardson has also devoted a whole monograph of indictments against *Tish* that follow from the prompting of Mathews and need not be rehearsed here, especially inasmuch as Davey has ably defended himself on many occasions, each of which permitted a further elaboration of the subject.

In many respects, the arguments of Mathews and Richardson, not to speak of their predecessors, miss the central thrust of Davey's position. The dominant in Davey, as Mathews asserts, is not the "U.S./ novelty/ experiment/ individual/ cosmopolitan" (152) – terms which are easily capable of various definition – but rather how discursive practices constitute the language we use. Thus Canada is not a place, and even Mathews would concede this (as he does in his recent *Canadian Identity*), but an argument, a forum of competing ideologies. The ideology that is attributed to Davey in the earlier text is that of liberal humanism, the belief that the world is there for the sake of technological manipulation. In a certain way, in fact, Davey appears to embrace such an ideology – or at least one might so surmise from a reading of the Introduction to *From There to Here*. But it is one thing to assert that "the post-modernist ... works to assist the electronic media in the decentralization of human power ... and to make its already achieved decentralizations and anarchies visible" and quite another to claim that "[t]he post-modern artist does not believe that he can absorb, structure, organize, and discourse definitively on the universe" (Davey 1974, 21). The argument against liberal humanism, then, is one that chooses not to perceive technology as control, and the Canada that is read in *Reading Canadian Reading* is part of the Canada that Davey appears always to have been in the process of constituting, and part of his argument against a number of Canadian critics is their belief

> that the culture, like the patient, is a monolithic construct; that the culture, like the dreamer, is more significant than the images in which it is manifested; that literature, like the Freudian dream, is ultimately not productive of meaning but referential. (12)

In his reflection, then, upon *From There to Here* he makes three crucial points: first, that it consciously entered an ideological "field of conflict"; second, that it argued against "the centralized, Ontario-based, vision that has dominated Canadian criticism"; third, that it perceived language as play, rather than instrument (47). Taken together, it means "that each text, through the language structures by which it constitutes itself, serves some ideology" (47). Canada is discursive conflict.

I have not disguised my sympathy for Davey's position on "Canada," and it is what I was endeavouring to discuss in my Postscript to *Arché/Elegies* in which I spoke of Canada as a "sentence that cannot end, always condemned to seek itself without recognition, the sentence that laments its own losing" (62). It is in this sense, at least, that I agree with Davey that Canada, as a discursive process, is a continual giving up. It *is* nowhere in particular; its ontology is always under erasure. This, I take it, is what is meant when speaking of Hodgins that "Canadian culture [is] a culture here that should 'invent' rather than enact, that should seek vision rather than shelter within inherited forms" (Davey 1988a, 197). But invention has a price, and the price can be the loss of the referent. The expression in French-Canada for such a possibility is *se replier sur soi*, that movement by which one turns self-reflexively upon oneself. When the referent can only be perceived as a play of signifiers, one can begin to question the need to expose the conflict of ideologies, for they too become part of the ludic intent. But if Canada is a text whose textualization is realized only in a postmodern context, something will get lost in the zone of continual invention. The loss is the coda whose beginning constitutes an *aria da capo*.[1]

Notes

[1] In the passage to which I have already referred in Steiner, while discussing my search for an appropriate epigraph, he observes that the genuine reader "knows that he cannot escape comprehensively the playful circularity in which the signified signifies in turn, and so *ad infinitum* (Steiner 126). Davey writing Davey, then, cannot help but return continually to the origin he has constituted, but each time modifying the significance of the text as subject and, one is compelled to add, the subject as text.

Works Cited

Aquin, Hubert. *Blocs erratiques.* Montréal: Quinze, 1982.
Blodgett, E.D. *Arché/Elegies.* Edmonton: Longspoon P, 1983.
Davey, Frank, 1965. "Black Days on Black Mountain." *The Tamarack Review* (Spring): 62-71.
____.1974. *From There to Here: A Guide to English-Canadian Literature Since 1960.* Our Nature – Our Voices, vol. 2. Erin, Ont.: Press Porcépic.
____, ed.1975. *TISH No. 1-19.* Vancouver: Talonbooks.
____.1976a. Introduction. *The Writing Life: Historical and Critical Views of the Tish Movement.* Ed. C.H. Gervais. Coatsworth, Ont.: Black Moss P.
____.1976b. Interview. *White Pelican.* 5:2: 49-58.
____.1977. "TISH, B.C. and After." *Western Windows: A Comparative Anthology of Poetry in British Columbia.* Ed. Patricia B. Ellis. Vancouver: Commcept.
____.1988a. *Reading Canadian Reading.* Winnipeg: Turnstone P.
____.Spring 1988b. "Ideology and Visual Representation: Some Post Cards from the Raj." *Open Letter* 7th Ser. 1: 41-66.
Foucault, Michel. *Language, Counter-Memory, Practice.* Trans. Donald F. Bouchard and Sherry Simon. Ed. Donald F. Bouchard. Ithaca: Cornell UP, 1977.
Frow, John. *Marxism and Literary History.* Cambridge: Harvard UP, 1986.
Jameson, Fredric. *Marxism and Form.* Princeton: Princeton UP, 1971.
Kroker, Arthur and David Cook. *The Postmodern Scene: Excremental Culture and Hyper-Aesthetics.* Montréal: New World Perspectives, 1986.
Lyotard, Jean-François. *The Postmodern Condition: A Report on Knowledge.* Trans. Geoff Bennington and Brian Massumi. Theory and History of Literature, vol. 10. Minneapolis: U of Minnesota P, 1984.

Mathews, Robin. *Canadian Literature: Surrender or Revolution.* Toronto: Steel Rail, 1978.

———. *Canadian Identity: Major Forces Shaping a People.* Ottawa: Steel Rail, 1988.

McHale, Brian. *Postmodernist Fiction.* New York and London: Methuen, 1987.

Mounier, Emmanuel. *Introduction aux existentialismes.* Paris: Denoël, 1947.

Olson, Charles. *Human Universe and Other Essays.* Ed. Donald M. Allen. New York: Grove P, 1967.

Richardson, Keith. *Poetry and the Colonized Mind: Tish.* Oakville, Ottawa: Mosaic/Valley Editions, 1976.

Steiner, George. *Real Presences.* Chicago: U Chicago P, 1989.

Tucker, Robert C. *The Marx-Engels Reader.* 2nd ed. New York: Norton, 1978.

White, Hayden. *Tropics of Discourse: Essays in Cultural Criticism.* Baltimore and London: The Johns Hopkins UP, 1978.

LYNETTE HUNTER

War Poetry: Fears of Referentiality

Current Account

I have taught the poetry of Bowering and Marlatt, and to a lesser extent of Davey and Wah, in the UK since the mid-70s. From here, what has been compelling to watch is the way in which the initial attractions of the fear of referentiality in language, have become informed by the complications of a parallel fear of political referentiality. The two have pushed at each other and in the process established various agendas for literary criticism, theory and politics. A fear of the referential and a fear of politics are two of the main aspects relevant to a definition of postmodernism. Postmodernism provides a basis for the validation of late twentieth-century western capitalism with its so-called service society. At the same time it provides a basis for a critique of the modernism that underwrites that society. The curious doubleness of interest in the apolitical and the political leaves the works of these writers open to readings that engage with a variety of strategies for theorizing about/dealing with current contradictions in many western societies. More directly put, Canada is externally often constructed as an apolitical, apathetic, populist country, and this is frequently associated both positively and negatively in its literature with the strategies and techniques of postmodernism. What I'd like to explore is whether this is a helpful reconstruction and how the work of these writers relates to it.

    I realize also, in view of the severing ways that "postmodernism" is used, that some indication of how I approach the term is necessary. Roughly, I would propose that postmodernism has an analogous relation to poststructuralism, as modernism has to formalism and structuralism. I understand modernism to be/have been concerned at least in part to disrupt and strip off the habitually accepted images of social and cultural agreement, in order to uncover deep-rooted traditional patterns that it then redeployed in the interests of its own historical period into newly agreed upon and more immediately engaging images. Differently, postmodernism is/has been concerned to dislocate both the habitual image and the traditional pattern in order to indicate not only the ways in which they are structured, but also the activity that is necessary to agreeing and to engaging. On the one hand formalism looks for deep structures and structuralism finds their design, while on the other the vocabulary of poststructuralism focuses on aporia, the empty pockets of intended significance and memory loss, and asks how to communicate these forgotten margins and unrecounted presents.

    As many commentators have by now pointed out, a postmodernism that turns on the habitual image restricts itself to surfaces that appear to be ontologically free-floating and it invents games. This of course can appear to be a kind of mindless fun that gets people into lots of trouble because it does not appear to question the way in which the design is itself constructed. I emphasize "appear" because it seems to me that within a local and specific community this fun and games can have a radically unsettling action. But in order to engage with that action people do have to recognize the significance of the chosen image and context. Without context postmodernist strategies create a patina of mindless pluralism. There may not be an essential ontological origin, but there is an originating procedure or rhetoric, and it is with this activity and its validation that postmodernism can be engaged.

The two writers I'd like to focus on are Frank Davey and George Bowering; the internal tensions of the writing they produce are central to the postmodernist question: In a dislocated and fragmented world what validates action?

Appropriating the Carapace

Bowering constructed Davey as a leading post-thematic critic in the early 80s, and more recently Davey has been modelled into a scourge of thematic criticism on the basis of Barbara Godard's authorization of "Surviving the Paraphrase" (1976). What Davey suggests by the word "paraphrase" is an unreflexive thematics that takes cultural icons as givens. The article is specific enough to make a number of coherent readings about what Davey does not like, but we are left with the question of what he does want. Indeed much of his subsequent critical and editorial work has moved toward attempting definitions and strategies for alternative approaches that he perceives to be more valuable, and which provide points of departure for a commentary on postmodernism.

With a certain reluctance to concede a point to ontological actuality, it must be recognized that Frank Davey did not spring fully-formed out of "Surviving the Paraphrase." The intellectual curiosity is recorded in detail in *Tish*, in the several series of *Open Letter* and is anchored at moments in CanLit by *From There to Here*, *Surviving the Paraphrase*, and *Reading Canadian Reading*. Godard contextualizes "Surviving the Paraphrase" in terms of the western tradition of popular theory, and knocks up a kaleidoscope of opportunities for literary critical discussion in general. Davey takes a rather specific line through the offerings, that is charted with some clarity in his own response to Godard in the title essay of *Reading Canadian Reading*, in which he positions himself as concerned with "interest" and "contradiction" while being wary of pluralism. Yet his concluding "Preface" underwrites provisionality, not position. The tenuous line between provisionality and pluralism is, in itself, a thoroughly postmodern dilemma.

"Surviving the Paraphrase" is not a particularly sophisticated piece of criticism, but it is one that in the mid 70s brought widely used criteria to CanLit. It is a seedbed for Davey's concerns, but what is interesting is that the essay needed to be written at all, let alone that it should now be considered such a landmark. What the work does attempt is to uncover the ground, expose not only the taken for granted cultural icons but also the rooted desire of the critics for such icons, for such complexes of metaphor that achieve cultural stability because they underwrite ideological demands/concerns. In the essay the proposed alternatives to the thematic and sociological focus on "the form – style, structure, vocabulary, literary form, syntax – of the writing" (Davey 1983, 7), and generate a variety of criticisms: historical, analytical, generic, phenomenological, and archetypal. In *Reading Canadian Reading*, very much *"ReReading Writings of Readings of Canadian Writing (by Frank Davey),"* the direction of the alternatives is re-defined as ideological.

Now, what ideological readings are concerned with is finding the story: Not underwriting the story, but finding and analyzing it. "Surviving the Paraphrase" lies on the border between Davey's early approach to stories emerging somehow unprocessed from the real and his later stance which presents stories as a construction of societies, cultures and communities. While the earlier concern was with the ways in which the writer could re-present reality without being dishonestly referential, the later concern is with understanding the terms of that dishonesty.

What is common to each concern is the fear of referentiality and the power structures it implies: that words refer to objects, that symbols refer to fixed and definable cultural manifestations such as guilt or emotion, and that human beings can know and manipulate these connections with explicit rules about referentiality. Such structures underwrite a validation of mathematics, science and technology that has made possible the growth of industrial capitalism (see Hunter, 1991). The recognition of the limitations of such claims is a central feature of western humanism, and for various reasons primarily to do with the history of rhetoric, ever since the Renaissance poetics has been one of the primary sites for discussing the alternatives. These alternatives, however, have always been complicit in humanist ideology, and have usually diverted poetics into forms of heroism.

A contribution to an early issue of *Open Letter* indicates the extent of complicity, but more significantly, the emerging need to displace the assumption of a common cultural continuity. The writer notes that what is needed is a "Jessie Weston," a bibliographer, a fact-gatherer for Canada, so that Canadian writers can like Eliot write through "things that bear reality" of their own world: things such as "place names" and "tales of shipwreck": their own stories. This "reality" of place is, however, in the service of "epic . . . [which] has always been our final goal" (Davey 1966a, 17-8). In the following issue (March 1966), Daphne Marlatt immediately responds by pointing out that the heroic is egoistical and uninteresting, "The single point is the place" (7); and Davey, who has not yet learned to change his mind—something he does with the regularity of grace in recent years – ties himself up in a series of knots in order to appear to defend himself by agreeing (1966b, 7).

Later that year he elaborates, again in the pages of *Open Letter*, tying a rather more complicated knot in the name of the phenomenal world. He says that poetry testifies to

> what happens in that imaginary garden of the poet's mind when those real toads – the things, events, facts of the phenomenal world – hop their way into it. For things . . . take on significance only when they impinge upon

> consciousness, and it is in his fidelity to his own consciousness, in his ability to perceive objectively what this imaginary garden in his head does with the toads . . . that the poet encounters the real. The ego has little to do with this interaction . . . that the world of poetry is man-centred is not to say that it is ego-centred. (1966d, 24)

What is really in question is drawn more explicitly elsewhere in this issue of *Open Letter* when Davey criticizes the surrealist's words that "communicate only himself – and not the real world," that are "private (like Hitler's vision)" (8), not reality but a symptom of reality. This writer believes that he is objective in capital letters, "EVEN TO THE EXTENT OF SEEING MY OWN SUBJECTIVITY AS A COSMIC FACT" (8).

There are a few problems here: how do the toads hop into your head? who built the garden? what is ego if not consciousness? what is objectivity if not ego-centred? And there are a lot of open doors: significance is not fixed but arrived at in the act of becoming conscious; consciousness impinges upon the real; consciousness impinges as ego-centred: a private Hitler's vision dominates over and re-defines the real as self; consciousness impinges as man-centred. The claim for objectivity is a response common to many of the disempowered and nonpolitical, when faced with the breakdown of human control: they reach in a panic for a kind of materiality, for the cosmic fact of being. But as long as people hold on to this cosmic fact of being, they will continue to reinscribe the complications of heroism, which will reassert the problems of an essentialist, uniquely identified consciousness that retains the power to define, dominate and control its world. Furthermore, they will continue to need stories of identity, unique to self, nation, and region.

The writing in these early *Open Letter* issues is happy to discard those stories attached to nation and region but not to self, and is also apparently aware of this. Working out of readings of McLuhan that document a version of the breakdown of rationalism and romantic humanism, another piece from an early *Open Letter* castigates the tendency for Canadian critics to insist on the authority of the poet as writer (Davey 1968, 26). But against their "false image of the poet composing by imposing" (27), what is offered is the poet who "submits" to the "laws," "directions," and "disciplines" of the poem itself. The deferral of authority onto the "word" presents an attempt to de-centre power from private human beings; however somehow the "true" poet still has the unique ability to use his body as a physical medium for presenting the actual. This essentialist alternative is problematic, and the following two decades of Davey's critical writing locate that problematic as the central contradiction from which the writer derives a theory of a constructed subject that is quite different from the cosmic objectivity of being.

Modernism is, as Davey recognized, based on a tradition that validates reference, authorizes action by claiming essential authenticity. The moment you question that by discovering/desiring the need for a different tradition in a different culture, you upset the premise of essential authenticity. If you don't reclaim it you have to move on into other structures. Early western twentieth-century moves provided pragmatic private responses like suicide or solipsism, or club responses like nihilism, dada, surrealism: all increasingly more compromised approaches (that saved the body), but also all very individualistic and difficult to translate into community, although it could be argued that existentialism does exactly this. Chronologically parallel responses such as Marxism and psychoanalysis both permit a validation of action in terms of a constructed referential code and try to address the problems of groups defining society within non-traditional decentred power structures. Postmodernism can be read as a more recent response directed to addressing similar problems in terms of the individual attempting to define a self within such structures. What is interesting and problematic about postmodernism is that it allows for the formation of limited communities in order to encourage the idea of a local and participatory construction of individual subjects. At the same time it leaves those subjects vulnerable to broader economic and ideological effects.

From There to Here, Davey's 1974 review of recent Canadian writing, extends his quest for story into the political and arrives at postmodernism. Modernism is cast as "essentially an elitist, formalistic, anti-democratic, and anti-terrestrial movement" (19). It abandons both the material and processual worlds: what the writer refers to as the phenomenal and noumenal. In contrast, Canadian writing is held to recognize the discontinuous and post-logical operations of reality. It is phenomenological, unprocessed, pre-reflective: all criteria for the central topos of the body which has become so important for recent theoretical discourse; it turns to image and stimulus, not to idea. At the same time myth is held to be innate in the everyday.

Lacking any kind of theoretical base for materialism, the argument here clings on to the compromizes of objectivity by insisting on pre-reflective origins and innate mythologies. It is an argument that is reiterated in a roughly contemporaneous article on Gwendolyn MacEwen, in which Davey comments that her characters incarnate the imminent word. They involuntarily relive myth much as the characters in his own *King of Swords* do. But parallel to the comments on innate mythologies is an emergence of a political sensibility. *From There to Here* indicates an attempt at defining the pluralist politics of postmodernism, which have arisen from the decentralizing activities of technology and an enlargening power of the individual. Again from McLuhan, but here not ironically, the writer indicates analogies of form between politics and style, where he allies the business report with world-wide domination, and his own mythological patterns with individual recognitions of alternative structures. Yet in 1973 Davey had published *The Clallam*. *King of Swords* and *The Clallam* stand off against each other much as Davey's cultural commentary stands postmodernism off against a growing awareness of Marxist economics and the world-wide structure of capital.

Earlier twentieth-century movements within art/writing indicate similar responses to a growing politicization that often derives from changes in cultural position and educational background. As the politically marginalized sectors of society which have always had a written and oral verbal culture, moved into political enfranchisement there have been complications. The structure of poetics has been implicitly political since the Renaissance, but when faced with direct political involvement, the writer must deal with group rather than individual action. The problems that this may raise have become the topics for much twentieth-century writing as it has explored the conflict that has emerged between the writer, used to dealing with a personal poetic that deconstructs authority, and an enfranchised responsibility for engagement with that authority. The recently marginalized are often unaware or afraid of the possibilities for power; they are also often worried about compromise. It is only when it is recognized that the more insidious compromise lies in not taking up that power, that anything can change.

The comments in *From There to Here*, on technology and on the parallels between style and politics, indicate a tension between an increasing consciousness of broad political implications and a fear of jettisoning the unique self that western poetics have since the Renaissance posited in opposition to the faceless dehumanization of authoritative power structures. On the one hand the position denies the existence of the "totally integrated whole" of modernism, yet on the other it states that "The tightly controlled, formalistic, and elegant poem shares formal assumptions with a company directorship, while the loosely structured film or lifestyle shares assumptions with the commune" (14). Davey's postmodernism is at this time thoroughly tied into a form of Canadian nationalism that validates Canada in the name of the counter-culture, the (implicitly heroic) anti-hero. This counter, which was oppositional and therefore complicit in the structures it criticized, is later reconstructed in "Reading Canadian Reading," as a challenge to a dominant Canadian culture within the context of the early 70s. In either reading, the contradiction of the denial of essentialism running hand in hand with implicitly essentialist statements about form and politics underwrites a form of individualistic pluralism.

Fragments from the Front / Fragmental Attack / Frontal Fragments

There is an unusual opportunity for the reader to follow a movement from this complicated and superficially utopian frame for late twentieth-century artistic activity, from the isolation of postmodernism to a broader political perspective, in the series of seven runs of *Open Letter* which have been edited by Davey. What is of significance is the way that the pages of *Open Letter* move through linguistic and narrative experiment, to a multi-media environment that attempts to break down media divisions, to postmodernist excesses, to a sudden politicization in the early 80s, to an incorporation of theory. The politicization indicated from Davey's own writing, continues in the 70s with attempts to link the production of writing with materiality by constructing a theory of genre – writer/text/reader interaction – out of the criticism of thematic interpretation. It is a development that runs parallel with attempts to link the reproduction of writing with an economic materialism in a growing recognition of the historical conditions for the making and distribution of books. The developments signal two very different attempts to find a story adequate to the construction of the subject and its contingent materiality within ideology.

Davey's poetry, from *Edward and Patricia* to *The Louis Riel Organ & Piano Company*, and *Postcard Translations*, provides an alternative site for reading about these attempts.

"Reading Canadian Reading" reconstructs "Surviving the Paraphrase" as ideological and discourse-focused reading, in conflict with the consumerist concept of reading held out by thematic interpretation. Thematic readings are ignorant of ideology; they take theme and significance and meaning for granted as if they were innate. Thematic readings explicitly reject the theoretical, but in doing so enter a tautological world where the interpretation is validated by finding just what it writes into its assumptions. This process is the classic construction of post-Renaissance fantasy, based on an unreflective referentiality that attempts always to satisfy desire, even if that means the pre-definition of satisfiable desire (see Hunter 1989). The article goes on to criticize these readings not only for their literary referentiality but also for their unitary view of Canadian culture, their insistence on essential Canadian identity.

The commentary is particularly helpful on the topic of the commoditization of literature, both through theme and aesthetics, and their relation to the canon, in the article "Recontextualization in the Long Poem." On the one hand, "aesthetic commoditization occurs when a canonical text is no longer capable of producing meanings compatible with a society's dominant ideological formations"; on the other, "thematic commoditization is most likely to occur when a new or non-canonical text is perceived capable of producing meanings that aggrandize one or more of a society's dominant ideological formations" (127 n1). Yet here, in 1985, the commentary also goes on to give Steve McCaffery's work as an example of writing that "minimizes both aesthetic shape and denotative content to ensure that his text has values only as writing, that its 'truth' or meaning are inseparable from the play of its language" (127). In contrast to Dudek and Milton who "seek an encoded meaning," McCaffery seeks a "textually-produced" meaning.

The differentiation begs the question of how text alone produces meaning. Meaning derives from ideological training, through the media, education, domestic habit, all in recognition of significance. Textually produced meaning derives from encoding as much as thematic or aesthetic. However, elsewhere in the writings there are more instances of what the commentary may be getting at. Recalling the toads in the garden, the essay "The Language of the Contemporary Canadian Long Poem," in the collection *Surviving the Paraphrase*, speaks of the way that Canadian writing deconstructs the European myths necessary to modernism by substituting texts of "low cultural standing" (186). More importantly, there is no substituted transcendent, no "host" as in Duncan, nor even Spicer's angels and martians. Instead this transitional criticism posits writing which conflates the phenomenal with the noumenal, claims that the actual is real and ready to explode with "magic."

Technically, magic is fantasy based on extra-human authority somehow acquired by humans. It is the lurking underbelly of the essentialism predicated by cosmic being, and a retrograde step for a materialist because it is even more displaced from contingency than the innate.

This recognition of extra-human reality is in strict contradiction with contiguous statements that the "low" subtext is not a counterpoint but a challenge to reveal meaning; it is not making way for magic but for opposition. The contradiction is further reinforced with the comment that the "reality" of writing is a process that is not solitary, independent or adversarial, but a reliance on surprise from "outside" the poet's conscious self. Not yet having a way of speaking about the constructed self, the commentary is still tripping over ego.

Davey, and Bowering, both emerged into writing at the same time that the Canadian government began indirectly and directly to fund writing and publishing. Concurrently the costs of multiple print reproduction were becoming smaller with the advent of mimeographs and photocopying. Davey was quick to make use of the newly accessible media and makes a note in *From There to Here* on the way that "correspondence poetry" burgeoned during the 60s. His energetic editorial support for a series of projects from *Tish* to *Open Letter* to the computer-networked *Swift Current*, testifies to a continued awareness and clever use of the media. The comments in *From There to Here* on the appropriation of the media by national interests mark an early attempt at theorizing this awareness, which has recently emerged quite firmly in "Writers and Publishers in English-Canada" (in *Reading Canadian Reading*), and "Ideology and Visual Representation: Some Post Cards from the Raj" (1988). The studies of the interaction between literature/writing and economic materialism that result, indicate the immense significance of technological processes for an understanding of verbal communication. Here, however, technology is not described as something that underwrites pluralism, but something that makes possible the construction of isolated worlds necessary to political and ideological control. It is here that the pursuit of ideology has started to work into the network of social and political context which begins to describe the garden. And what is said about the economic garden and about the commoditization of the toads, is in radical contradiction to what is concurrently said about how they resist economics and ideology.

The commentary is unusually helpful about the commoditization/commodificaton of literature and criticism, but is continually straining within contradiction when it attempts to speak of the resistance to it. The recent outline of postmodernism in the Canadian context, "Some. (Canadian.) Postmodern. Texts." (*Reading Canadian Reading*), underlines the dichotomy. Reconstructing *From There to Here* as a text that described the sociological tendencies of postmodernism toward both totalization and decentralization, the extension of the commentary into postmodern literature moves topically, although not by name, from Saussure through Althusser to Habermas. In order to emphasize the construction rather than referential transmission and/or interpretation of texts, the essay outlines a background: Language is not an instrument but a system of continuously modified codes; humanity is not essentialist but constructed; there has been a fragmentation of public discourse so that there are no longer any authoritative voices for large communities of belief; hence the arbitrary can be a useful social construction. Writers such as bpNichol and Daphne Marlatt provide examples of language which has been treated as political and semiotic, not metaphysical; they are not concerned with external authority or the pain of its collapse, but with the construction of meaning.

This is a particularly helpful up front outline that invites engagement with a story about ideology and the constructed subject. But while it describes the positive values of postmodernism in terms of decentralization, it neglects to look at its totalizing effects: almost implying that postmodernism is in contradiction to totalizing, that totalizing is a remnant of modernism that postmodernism has dealt with. What it neglects is the garden, about whose construction Davey speaks quite differently in his work on the implications of the processes of print reproduction. The problem with the arbitrary is that it can use its arbitrariness to neglect the need for self-reflexivity or positioning. The writer is happy, in *Reading Canadian Reading*, to encourage the reader toward "reflective critical reading" for the identification of ideologies and interest, but is less open about helping the writer to position the stance of the text. The valorization of provisionality in the concluding "Preface" to *Reading Canadian Reading*, underwrites this potential for evasive action, as if Davey is still worried about taking specific political action in case it becomes totalizing.

Bowering: Appropriating the Body

Where Davey is acute on the identification of story and helpful with reading strategies, George Bowering's concern is continually to evade the story, and he is far more useful about what writers do than how stories emerge. Davey manages to sort through questions of consciousness and ego and move on to look at toads and gardens, at materiality and ideology, but Bowering really isn't interested in toads or gardens or, for that matter, in stories. What Bowering implicitly and continually returns to is consciousness and ego.

If fear of the referential in Davey's writing directs it into a study of where the stories come from and how they work, fear of the referential in Bowering's writing appears increasingly to have led him to attempt to reject story completely. In the former, what is indisputably there is culturally accepted myth whose artifice must be indicated. The rhetorical discussions of the strategies necessary to the construction and deconstruction of these commodities are written with the precise skill of a text that could as easily manipulate and appropriate as expose and indicate. What is just as indisputably there but far more difficult to speak of, is language: rhythm, rhyme, syntax, morpheme, line, and letter. Neither of these critics attempts to offer any rhetorical discussion of language that might, as in Nichol's work, indicate for it a semiotic basis. Yet while Davey produces awkward, contradictory, and hence helpful studies of the poetics, Bowering rejects this as yet another story and turns instead to enactments and descriptions of their production that have different contradictions and are valuable for entirely different reasons.

Bowering operates, superficially at least, as if consciousness were not problematic, as if the hero as ego can simply be dismissed. Davey's easy claim that the Canadian writing he cares for is processual and pre-reflective, which he later comes to recast, if failing to re-describe, as semiotic, is something that Bowering is living in the middle of and has no apparent need to foreground/discuss/artificialize. The result is quite curious. If process remains unforegrounded, if its artificiality is taken as a given/ground, if process simply "is," how can the reader learn to read? Bowering suggests that the words and letters will open up and tell us, that there's no need for the writer/writing consciousness to lead the reader since this would be manipulation (*Errata* 5). There are at least three readings that result. The first is an idealistic account dependent upon some transcendent authority informing the meaning of words – in other cultures this could happily be reconstructed as "magic" – but it is not an advisable mode for a highly technological society already sophisticated at masking its dependence on service/slave states. The second is a cynical suspicion that the writer is a precise manipulator covering all tracks of making. The third is a non-idealist account of the postmodern positive: that if we attempt to learn we end up imposing already-known structures on the material world and don't learn anything we didn't know already, and that if we try to let the words act without being specifically directed to this or that meaning then we might end up reading in a different way. However, the postmodern negative is that we simply will not know how to respond to the immediate demands upon choice and action.

How the West Was Won / Over

To raise questions of choice is once more to raise questions about the political. Unlike that of many writers of the 60s contributing to *Tish* and/or *Open Letter*, Bowering's early work often speaks openly about war, party lines, and national identity. Yet during exactly the same chronological period that Davey was finding ways to speak about politics, Bowering was finding ways to displace his political commentary. He was consistently criticized for the naïveté, crudeness, and directness of his political poetry (see Barbour), and it is extremely difficult to find a line for political commentary in the enfranchised but largely unpoliticized world of late twentieth-century capitalism. *At War with the U.S.*, one of the last openly political poems, is an extraordinary piece of war poetry, commenting implicitly on the internal Canadian conflict focused rather drastically on Quebec and the War Measures Act of 1970, but explicitly on the emptiness, futility and "few churrs" of the Viet Nam war. For whatever reason, possibly the ineffectiveness of individual protest during that war, possibly a transference from federal government actions toward Quebec on to the marginalized position of the west coast (with which, despite 80s' parody, the 70s' writing was obsessed), or whatever speculation, Bowering begins to shift toward less explicitly referential language and the need for writers first to effect change through the processes of writing.

Bowering's divergence from the referential into looking for contradictions within language itself can be placed in the context of the way he describes his attention to language. In *Errata* he notes that he needs and enjoys the easy, consolatory, comforting reading offered by many books (78), but that he takes writing itself as making a challenge, searching for contradiction. If we construct this back onto the political directions of his work, we can study his readings of others (criticism) as continual play with consolations, and the writing (poetry) as often going looking for resistances, ignoring story or context. The split that this suggests[1] emerges subsequent to *A Short Sad Book* (1977), which itself could fairly be called a scourge of thematic criticism and a scourge of politics as a specific party line; this concept of party-line politics indicates a definition of politics as referential that lingers behind Bowering's work of the following decade.

A Short Sad Book writes a fragmented discourse of dead ends and red herrings. The narrative voice, which is the only consistent line in the 56(-1) section work, sets out to put us off the track, to evade the hunter, the critic-detective looking for meaning. Taking up the national 1970s' obsession with the "Great Canadian Novel" that will speak for Canadian Identity, the voice opens with a catalogue of ideological markers – geography, history, myth, sport – all capable of providing thematic coherence. But, gradually insistent, comes the recognition that meaning is reserved for those in power. The text turns its attention to readings of other writing and speaks first of the split between the novelist who makes romance, makes the consolatory mountains for the reader to hide in, and the novel itself that is writing and process (80-1). Just so history is not the happened/written event, but making history: "history [is also] filled with mistakes & most of them are written by poetry" (103), because poetry constructs. "The novel can only sit back and try to understand" (103) and sometimes "go to war again" : as Bowering does here despite all.

The text is particularly interesting on the postmodern novel which forgets history and so history forgets you/it (107). Postmodernism offers a double-edged movement that at least residually allows for a writing that does not control publically recognized historical event, but conversely that movement away from control implies careful individual organization of the arbitrary: postmodern writing is a private puzzle. By contrast, Black Mountain writing is a mystery. But in either case there is no solution for Canadian Literature; it is neither puzzle nor mystery. To contribute to it we should be writing, not thinking. Once again there is the implication that to think is to fall into the referential, to think is to write "a mirror on the floor" (134), but to write is to construct (somehow) from the real, "as if it is there." The writer here puts the writing out with both. The Great Canadian Novel is neither a mystery story about a detective who confronts Tom Thompson in London, Ontario (the body at the bottom of the lake), nor is it the written currently departing utopian vision of Evangeline who leaves in good science fiction style, as does the writer, on the last page of the book, trailing surrealist clouds of oddly Kristevan feminism and mythic time. What the reader is left with is the book, no more no less. Only we are in fact left with a lot more because there were a few great similes along the way, and Bowering did go to war.

A simile works because it permits the reader to make comparisons with a known event or experience; it is roundly referential. And the procedure of *A Short Sad Book* is to dislocate that habitual tendency to the referential to which most readers move. In many ways, despite Bowering's own definition of the term, the book is an exemplary attempt at a postmodernist text. Come at from outside the community that supported its production, it reads as fragmented from the perspective of narrative, theme, grammar, and syntax. It can reduce the reader to playing games with numbers: of chapters (one missing), of pages in chapters (2 or 3); with structures: of character (how often do they appear, when do they appear first, are they encoded in the names of other characters), of plot (should we just rearrange the sections, is one story prioritized); and so on into other reaches of litcrit exercise. In other words it sets things up to get the reader to move the counters of literary expectation, but there is no particular end, no way of winning the game and reaching a conclusion or answer. Not only is this kind of strategy frustrating because it denies reference and the conventional satisfaction or fulfillment of desire, but it is profoundly abstracted from the actual world, from reality.

But, from within another context, the text is a tightly constructed catalogue of questions directed toward literary devices. It opens with a quotation from Alain Robbe-Grillet, which immediately provides an intertextual discourse with other strategies for dislocating readerly expectation in an attempt to artificialize the search for answers. Generically, the work takes the ideologically bound romance devices of the roman à clef, the detective story, and the science fiction plot, as the most fruitful place for disruption of narrative convention. The writing chooses to displace the cultural icons and images specific to works of literary criticism published in Canada during the immediately preceding decade. The writing offers a series of points of contact with narrative, generic, cultural, and other expectations which work intertextually rather than referentially because they ask both for the recognition of those links and for the dislocation of those links. But of course in each case the reader needs to be part of a particular literary/cultural community to appreciate the dislocation.

For that community the work is also a commentary on the marginalization of Western Canada, from the Ontarian centre: the story of an internal emigré. It talks about the limitations of Canadian nationalism and the frustration of regionalism. It provides an outline on publishers, writers and grant-giving systems, on the literary expectations of the educational system, during the 1970s in Canada. It is at times bitter and rude, patronizing and evasive especially when the writer allows himself to honour his own heroism: "You learn it in writing poetry you tell it in writing prose" (89), which returns us to the problem of the unproblematic conscious.

Embattled by Grace

Bowering's fear of the referential in language translates into a fear of the political referential, that turns *A Short Sad Book* into a tangle of conflict and opposition, without the necessary climax of a nice heterosexual book. The writing comes out the other side into a number of writings that implicitly admit the necessity for some semiotic in that they are, simply, easier to read, and that rehearse the topics of *A Short Sad Book* from a conversational stance that the writer develops in order to be able to justify "leading" the reader. In the process the writer attempts to net the political down under the immensely sophisticated and patterned constructions of language. The commentary is in a sense won over to the postmodernist artist who is described through Davey in *Craft Slices* as one who "does not believe that he can absorb, structure, organize and discourse definitively on the universe" (141). Bowering says that the best poets in Canada believe that:

> the animator of poetry is language. Not politics, not nationalism, not theme, not personality, not humanism, not real life, not the message, not self-expression, not confession, not the nobility of work, not the spirit of a region, not the Canadian Tradition – but language. The centre & the impetus, the world and the creator of poetry is language. (140)

And he goes on to describe these poets as children, without power over language, letting the language speak. While he here denies the mystical, he also evades the explicit idealism of the materiality of language operating without human control.

Unlike Davey who virtually begins with the deconstruction of the individual consciousness into the constructed subject which encourages him to concentrate on ideology and its relationship to the real (garden and toads), Bowering concentrates on existential control. Hence he has to distinguish between ego and consciousness but translates them into thinking and writing: respectively, language which is controlled by human beings (the unreflective garden of referentiality and content) and language which speaks through the human being (the unreflective toads appearing from the actual through verbal process). Bowering is always trying not to be "heroic," but to write where/what is within him that his heroism springs from. The poetry and much of the other writing is attempting to do without story or reference, which may be taken as an idealistic trust that we can read without story, or as a non-idealistic, materialist, meditative recognition, rooted in the local, struggling out of specific experience of repetition and contradiction. The latter is, in Bowering's poetry, a detailed act of provisionality, running alongside the possibility of pluralism, and particularly clearly enacted in *Burning Water* (Don Mills: Musson, 1980). Bowering's writings are both heroic and effacing of the hero. For all his rejection of politics and the knight who seeks the grail he is an errant writer, and as Marlatt also notes, arrant. The errant knight finds/completes the errand only by mistake, by erring, never by implication. But that the knight engages in the errand in the first place is an indication of arrogance and self.

The commentaries of *Errata* bend modernism and postmodernist theory as defined by Davey, toward the concept of potentially heroic self merely through the omission of any discussion of a constructed subject or consciousness. Modernist writing is set squarely in realism, and attempts a set of referential techniques. In contrast, postmodernist writing resists the referential and welcomes "stray" material (13). Reference and realism are made "purposive" by those people who do not recognise their accidental basis, and blindly accept the conventional as essential (93). So far, so good. But then we find that "stray" material is somehow a non-conventional revelation of reality, specific to the writer; the accidental is only apparent coincidence (6). The postmodernist writer is out to trick reality into revealing itself (19), to trick the idea into being so that it can then be dismantled, for the "art" is in the dismantling (55). It is as if the commentator on this activity fears the power of the conventional, of the ideological, of the symbolic order that defines consciousness, because once he acknowledges it he may lose articulacy, lose the ability to see and speak from strange places.

In *Errata* we find out most about the process of this postmodernist writing from the notes on intertextual reading that offer a commentary on the provisional rather than the pluralist activity of *A Short Sad Book* and several other writings. Rather than being a consoling recognition (78) that is a performance of re-reading (3), reading should work by breaking habits (10), by finding discontinuity. The reader should notice rather than buy/consume thought (18); thought should be discarded to allow for disunderstanding, dismantling, deprocessing (55). Intertextual reading here becomes analogous to articulating the world/reality. Reading, or tracking the real, is the writer's first action (91), yet the writer is able to read things "invisible to the rest of us" (91). There is some moment when the writer can evade the stories of ideology and see the real. And while in writing the craft may be visible, the referent remains invisible.

As a generic description for the necessary misrepresentation / apprehension of reality, the intertextual ties in well with many aspects put forward by other commentators concerned with the problems of reference. But Bowering presents it in *Errata* as a heroic or prophetic role carried out by "writer-poets." He says "Socially and politically I am a romantic leftist; but when it comes to the composition of literature I am an elitist" (22). Disregarding that "romantic leftist" can be glossed as "right-wing anarchist," what is interesting about the statement is that Bowering apparently thinks that the intertextual reader/writer from the real is part of a small group which is distinct from the popular desire for consumable re-readings.

There is a lurking implication that postmodernism can never become popular because, apparently, it is not consumable, specifically it is not referential. This openly evades the popular reception of postmodernism in pluralism, which is exactly referential.

Errata also offers the comment that literature has "a social responsibility. But it does not owe its forms to the state" (51). Well, no. Elsewhere this writer says that politics begins with language, and it does.[2] But to evade any clear choices in language in order to deny the power of the referential may generate not only a personal politics but also the pluralist. The distinct fear that the political positioning might entangle him into an ideology, a state story, seems to have enclosed the writer in an oppositional conflict of consolation and intertext centred in the individual which, as in *Kerrisdale Elegies* (Toronto: Coach House P, 1984), can only be lived with by continually trying to displace what is recognized as the self. Bowering's trust that there are some people who can read without any story should be interpreted either as a complete totality of blindness to convention, or as the non-idealistic, local, and long-term struggle through the disunderstanding of allegory that Davey puts forward as the positive material awareness of writers such as Nichol and Marlatt.

Just as Davey is concerned with toads and gardens, so Bowering is the gardener: indeed he makes play with "bowering" and gardens in *Errata*. He is inside the garden which is inside him: constantly handing over/offering over his body as pre-reflective and unprocessed/able. Davey offers the reader a constructed subject that is producing theorized commentary on where/what we have forgotten and marginalized in literary production. Bowering structures the literary production to invite recognition of the need continually to defer the stasis of that consciousness.

Provisioning the Army

Both writers are concerned with the essential and the referential, with dislocating it and moving it on. They are concerned with breaking down the patterns of language and literature that permit us to speak to each other in the encoded language of our society, because of their potentially totalizing effects. But in that breaking down they engage another set of strategies which are far more local and immediate. These strategies, built partly so that we may say to each other things that as members of the immediate community we need to say to each other, things that may not have been spoken before, can become both exclusive and appropriative. Postmodernist strategies are fragmenting/ary. From the outside they are perceived, as all new strategies are, as difficult to read and esoteric. From the inside they lead to challenge, they ask for engagement. All strategies begin work on a community level, with small groups of readers. They can become elitist if those people are in a position of power, in a position desired by others; or if those people gain power and become objects of desire (achieve fame). You could say that as larger groups of readers learn how to read, the strategy loses elitism and becomes popular, a movement that has happened with much other new writing. But postmodernism sets out to break that down, to maintain small groupings.

The maintenance of small groupings has in the west conventionally been favoured on the basis that only within small groups can you have an immediate address to the specific needs of the community, looking closely at the contingent, the material.[3] At the same time small groupings also permit the broader structure of current capitalism: small markets maintained by the satisfaction of discrete desires.[4] The larger the group the greater the financial reward but the more difficult to maintain satisfaction. Postmodernism is not operating to find a new, broad consensus, but to satisfy smaller immediate needs. This is important. You can argue that postmodernism works positively because only in small isolated groups do fundamental challenges to the dominant ideology get a chance to define themselves and emerge. But you can also argue that it works negatively both because in small isolated groups there is continual self-justification and validation, never any change impinging on the outside world, and because the isolation radically separates each group from an other. This separation enervates any attempt at dislocation on the part of a single group by leaving it apparently superficial and extraneous to the practical needs of the broader society.

The problem with postmodernism is that because it is after the radical disjuncture, there is no way for it to claim a common radical disjuncture, nor is there any clear methodology for how it is to construct after it has deconstructed. In the meantime it is extending the sanctioned strategy of working within isolated worlds, which encourages the neurotic worlds of desire serviced by discrete technologies that typify the power structures operated via rationalism on behalf of humanism in late twentieth-century capitalism. It is because of this radical complicity with the isolating and fragmenting structure from which the coherence of current technology and capitalism derives, that those advocating postmodernist strategies need rather more urgently to define their stance.

Reading the work of both these writers throws forward the problems of political empowerment. If you've ever been on the margins, you are always aware of how other people's positions of power oppress. If the marginalized gain access to power there is no point denying it and laying claim to pluralism. While I personally would rather that their provisional literary positions were more clearly presented, each writer provides a series of strategies appropriate for dealing with contemporary technological humanism: Davey offers succinct and enabling short-term strategies for deconstructing the ideology, and Bowering describes a long-term process for potential reconstruction, both of which can help in constructing valid actions in a fragmenting social order. Constructions of the Canadian postmodern, with its emphasis on process rather than product and apparent bias to the anti-referential and anti-political, can be diverted into an increasingly inadequate pluralism by the same interests that have diverted the materialist agenda of deconstruction in the Chinese box game. Both Bowering and Davey play into the hands of this diversion, but they also each offer ways of positioning ourselves politically by insisting on the provisional or the intertextual.

Notes

[1] A collection such as *Imaginary Hand* (Edmonton: NeWest, 1988) indicates the extent of this split.

[2] See the many commentaries in *Craft Slices* on this topic.

[3] This has been one of the primary arguments behind the privileging of the oral over the written, from Plato onwards; see L. Hunter, 1990.

[4] See L. Hunter, 1991.

Works Cited

Barbour, Douglas. *Open Letter*. 1st ser. 8 (November 1968): 21.
Bowering, George 1974. *At War with the U.S.* Vancouver: Talonbooks.
____.1977. *A Short Sad Book*. Vancouver: Talonbooks.
____.1985. *Craft Slices*. Toronto: Oberon P.

____.1988. *Errata*. Red Deer: Red Deer College P.
Davey, Frank 1966a. *Open Letter*. 1st ser. 1. 17-8.
____.1966b. *Open Letter*. 1st ser. 2 (March): 7.
____.1966c. *Open Letter*. 1st ser. 4 (March): 7-8.
____.1966d. *Open Letter*. 1st ser. 4. 24.
____.1968. "More Heat on Daedalus." *Open Letter*. 1st ser. 8 (November): 26-7.
____.1972. *King of Swords*. Vancouver: Talonbooks.
____.1973. *The Clallam*. Vancouver: Talonbooks.
____.1974. *From There to Here*. Erin, Ont.: Press Porcépic.
____.1983. *Surviving the Paraphrase*. Winnipeg: Turnstone P.
____.1984. *Edward and Patricia*. Toronto: Coach House P.
____.1985. *The Louis Riel Organ & Piano Co*. Winnipeg: Turnstone P.
____.1988. *Post Card Translations*. Toronto: Underwhich Editions.
____.1988. *Reading Canadian Reading*. Winnipeg: Turnstone P.
____.1988. "Ideology and Visual Representation: Some Post Cards from the Raj." *Open Letter*. 7th ser. 1 (Spring): 41-66.
Godard, Barbara. "Structuralism/Post-Structuralism: Language, Reality and Canadian Literature." In John Moss (ed.) *Future Indicative: Literary Theory and Canadian Literature*. Ottawa: University of Ottawa P, 1987: 25-51.
Hunter, Lynette 1989. *Modern Allegory and Fantasy*. London.
____.1990. "A Rhetoric of Mass Communication." *Written Communication Annual*.
____.1991. "A Rhetoric and Artificial Intelligence." In R. Roberts (ed.) *Rhetoric and the History of the Human Sciences*. Bristol: Bristol P.
Marlatt, Daphne. *Open Letter*. 1st ser. 2 (March 1966): 6.

JEFF DERKSEN

Torquing Time

Fred Wah's *Breathin' My Name with a Sigh* (1981)[1] remains an important book in the development and expansion of the poetics outlined by the *Tish* poets after they absorbed and modified them from New American poetics. These poetics were homogenized by their absorption into CanLit in its quest for a national identity constructed in opposition to a perceived American identity – issues of place and voice lost their active, investigative qualities and solidified into monologic poems that use a static landscape as self-sufficient naturalness or a bleak metaphor for the thematics of terror. Unfortunately, this type of poem still dominates the little magazines and anthologies of "new" writing to a certain extent. For Wah there are two important influences on these poetics of voice and place that distinguish his work from the rigidity that has resulted as these poetics passed into official verse culture: the concept of proprioception as outlined by Olson, and an intertwined sense of narrative.

Olson's idea of proprioception is based on movement and flux, "movement, at any cost." This is a movement of the body:

> the data of depth sensibility/ the 'body' of us as object which spontaneously or of its own order produces experience of, 'depth' Viz SENSIBILITY WITHIN THE ORGANISM BY MOVEMENT OF ITS OWN TISSUES ("Proprioception" 17)

The body here doesn't get satisfactorily described as socially constituted, but seems to be an object amongst other objects which can operate of "its own order." There is, however, an implied breakdown of the hierarchical subject/object split, a break out of the "western box." But included in this return to the physical body and the idea of being "true to one's self" there is attention to the effect of proprioception on language (or the effect of the body on thought and language). The breath line proposed by Olson is a device that arises out of this concern to manifest the sensibility of the organism in language. In Wah's work the *concept* of proprioception is formulated into a praxis where experience is *through* language with no separation of language from experience: language as the "body of us . . . which spontaneously or of its own order produces experience. . . ." The ability of language to be the act, to be the experience. I'm thinking here of a rapidity of thought evident in the poems and actualized by the syntactic turns and the heightened use of the elements of language.

> Are origins magnetic lines across an ocean

> Are origins magnetic lines across an ocean
> migrations of genetic spume or holes, dark
> mysteries within which I carry further into the World
> through blond and blue-eyed progeny father's fathers
> clan-name Wah from Canton east across the bridges
> still or could it all be lateral craving hinted
> in the bioplasmic cloud of simple other organism
>
> as close as out under the apple tree? (N. pag.)

This instantaneous quality of proprioception is, for Olson, grafted to narrative: the usual constraints of time on narrative are dissolved as it becomes proprioceptive. As he explains in "BBC Interview":

> One wants a narrative today to . . . strike like a piece of wood on a skin of a drum . . . or to be plucked like a string of any instrument. One does not want narrative to be anything but instantaneous in this sense. . . . In other words, the problem, the exciting thing about poetry in our century, is that you can get image and narrative both to wed each other again, so that you can get both extension and intensivity bound together. (80)

A proprioceptive narrative can lead the way, or provide an entry, to the poem as a direct experience – both for the writer in the act of writing and for the reader. Obviously this merging of the reader and the writer is not unique, but what strikes me in *Breathin' My Name with a Sigh* is that it is combined with the poetics of place and voice. There has been a tendency in these poetics to valorize the individual – particularly and usually a male – in history, and this is exaggerated by the domination of a "voice," which usually was the solidification of a poet's aesthetic gestures into recognizable style, over voices. So history, while not being linear in the usual sense, emanated from one source: the poet – how Olson is looked at as a "big" man. This notion is tied in with that of the one extending to the many (or that " 'ontogeny recapitulates phylogeny' " as Wah says in his preface), and has the danger of ignoring the contextual framing that occurs in reading, as well as ignoring the effect of social contexts on experience.

But in *Breathin' My Name with a Sigh*, there is no unified subject or fixed centre from which the landscape is viewed – the landscape is not static. An important shift occurs when the landscape is set in time by this extension and intensity of narrative. This enacts a radical multitemporality: images, details, phonetic clusters, and facts mix past and present in a matrix that is the contemporaneity of the poem. In discussing the work of Goethe, Bakhtin notes this saturation of place with time: "For him contemporaneity – both in nature and in human life – is revealed as an essential multitemporality . . ." and as a result "concrete visibility loses its static quality and fuses with time" (28, 29). For Wah, place is saturated with time and the "landscape" poems are not rigid imagistic gestures:

> the first bridge was in Trail
> and it crossed over the first river
> full of fish and it moved with weight
> not speed the first mountain
> a hill of sand and scrub brush
> Ernie's dog Mickey died
> it's where Donnie was born
> the Trail Smoke Eaters
> were the World Champions

The disruptive shifts in time enact a movement from a potentially static image to a landscape embedded with information – the landscape is saturated with lived history rather than operating within a thematic grid in which both nature and human life are subsumed to evidence of terror. In this grid the landscape stands in as a spring-loaded cipher for "larger" themes, or exists as pure image, condensed and docile but unable to enter a sociohistorical dialogue. Wah's engagement with the landscape and image occurs within a highly personal historical and social intercourse. The local then takes on a specificity that is both personal and historical: ontogeny does not simply recapitulate phylogeny, but the two intertwine in a torgued narrative time. The one does not act as a base model and extend into the many, but the one exists simultaneously with the many within a matrix.

> Not so much all of us dying
> or nobody else living or even one
> one shining master of light
> but a procession forth
> into I like the movement
> in our syntax goes
> something like a river Daphne
> so it's still "how" we do what
> and give a punch we hope words
> to take off on us dying to do that
> the best way we can.

And, although the poems are rooted in memory ("This is a book of remembering" Wah says in the preface), the multitemporality that the poems exist in asserts the moment. This is achieved through specific syntactic devices that force attention on the micro-elements of language (particularly the line and sound qualities). Narrative is generated by the syntactic turns and shifts in time – it is instantaneous the poem being a description of an *a priori* experience. As Barrett Watten says of Olson: ". . . the frantic movement from one thing to the next is identified in Olson's assertion of the moment as *the* value of his approach to the material. The hinge of the story becomes the story in its own right" (125). And in *Breathin' My Name with a Sigh*, there is the insistence on the poem as experience.

> No foolin I thought I was gonna die
> just about every day so much the mountains
> air clear blue sky & hum broke up
> as pieces each of themselves I was separate from
> larger than life the thought my face hands all
> action bigger my picture of head arms fingers sens
> ation at first something from mother my eyes
> at sleep birth
> swelld up like the stung finger head information
> creek the first time in McNaughton's
> January 1974 to know it's true even
> the enlargement now remember
> more?

Image and narrative are wed here in that they exist in the same time – the torguing of time creates a present that is the poem.

Wah's particular praxis that he has generated from these two concepts outlined by Olson provide an antidote to the kind of imagistic and temporal gridlock that the poetics of place and voice have often been reduced to. It also allows the poems to be much more *about* the nature of experience and to *provide* experience despite seeking the basis of identity. But because Wah situates a perceiving subject in a landscape that is set in time, the identity of this *one* is not a blueprint for the many. The project is not to define *an* identity that can then be projected across all social barriers (a kind of simplistic nationalism), but to track or map potential identities of a subject that is decentred by multitemporality. A projective verse that has reciprocity – what is projected from the subject is also projected back. That is the value of movement.

Note

[1] *Breathin' My Name with a Sigh* has appeared in several versions: the Coach House Press Manuscript Editions (1978 and 1979); the Talonbooks 1981 "third draft"; and in part in *Waiting for Saskatchewan* (Turnstone P, 1985). All poems quoted here are from the Talonbooks edition.

Works Cited

Bakhtin, M.M. "The *Bildungsroman* and Its Significance in the History of Realism (Toward a Historical Typology of the Novel)." *Speech Genres and Other Late Essays*. Trans. Vern W. McGee. Ed. Caryl Emerson and Michael Holquist. Austin: U of Texas P, 1986. 10-59.

Olson, Charles. "BBC Interview." *Muthologos*. Vol. 2. Bolinas: Four Seasons Foundation, 1979. 80-3.

———. "Proprioception." *Additional Prose*. Bolinas: Four Seasons Foundation, 1974. 17-35.

Wah, Fred. *Breathin' My Name with a Sigh*. Vancouver: Talonbooks, 1981.

Watten, Barrett. "Olson in Language." *Total Syntax*. Carbondale: Southern Illinois UP, 1985. 115-39.

SHARON THESEN

Writing the Continuing Story: Gladys Hindmarch's The Watery Part of the World

In Gladys Hindmarch's *The Peter Stories*, the husband really does put his wife (who "ran around quite a bit" [5]) in a pumpkin shell. The story makes the large gestures nursery rhymes make, those verses in which shadows and giants loom, clocks tick like doomsday machines, pies contain flocks of birds, and the wrong move could result in one's being cannibalized. *The Peter Stories* relocates these gestures and their unconscious relationships into a Modern Marriage in which the pumpkin shell is the life the woman has been enclosed by, the life that robs her of her spirit, and finally of the marriage itself, when the Pumpkin Eater/ husband meets Mary Contrary, a single woman who is lots more fun. This book, published in 1976 by Coach House Press, and *A Birth Account*, written in 1971 and also published in 1976 are, along with *The Watery Part of the World* (1988), the major texts of a writer whose reputation has persisted since her involvement with the *Tish* group. Of the women writers most often associated with the *Tish* group, Daphne Marlatt and Gladys Hindmarch made moves in writing that expanded language into areas of experience quite distinct from the minimalist experiments of writers like Frank Davey and George Bowering, who were exploring the mythpoetics of the vernacular. Theirs were the attentions to the big stories lurking in the shadows of the local and the particular. The other stories, the nursery rhymes, the childhood chronicles – all forms of a horror story – were at first the province of women writers, and along with Marlatt's, Hindmarch's writing explored the experience of childbirth, marriage, and sexuality in lines that were long, crowded, prosy. Lines that ran around quite a bit and wore "holey slips" and had "moley knees."

Both Hindmarch's and Marlatt's work of the late 1960s and early 1970s were pre-feminist/"theory" revelations of the life of the writing body: the glistening verbs of both *Rings* and *A Birth Account* are still new, fresh, and alive. While Marlatt has gone on continuously to explore the ramifications of her discoveries in writing, Hindmarch has returned to "The Boat Stories," begun in 1967 and edited and added to over the years finally to be published as a book of linked stories entitled *The Watery Part of the World*. The title comes from Melville, and suggests wateriness as a form of existence – sublunar, perhaps female, mysterious, deep, boundless – which Ishmael rather casually decides to "sail about a little and see." But there is nothing mysterious about Hindmarch's *Nootka*, an ordinary freighter, or its kitchen staff, whom the narrator, Jan, a university student, joins as a mess girl. The word "mess" takes on a certain vivid reality in the cramped quarters of the boat's kitchen (and it is a boat, not a ship) where Jan works alongside a couple of seasoned older women, Coco and Puppi. The scatalogical echoes of their names are answered by the names of some of the rest of the crew, which suggest body parts or kinesthesia of one sort or another: Beebo, Lefty, Chuckles, Buck, and Jock. Apart from the narrator, the only two crew members who have regular (though attenuated) names are the ones with whom Jan enjoys a mutual sexual attraction: Hal and Ken. In passages in which a number of these characters are present at once, the effect is clotted and rather unpleasant, as if one were inside a living hive of limbs and torsos and belt buckles and smiling teeth. Jan's experience of the crowdedness and lack of privacy on the boat? Or are the crew members of freighters condemned to limiting nicknames as a result of the work they do and the way they do it?

The writing in this book is markedly kinesthetic and onomatopoeic: busy women "screech" and "caw" (11); coffee break is "mugup" (17); in the kitchen there is pointing and tugging and pulling and snatching and leaning and clawing. The world of these "boat stories" is a world of doing and sensation that sometimes flows easily and efficiently among the phrases of direction:

> Two stew to follow, one bean up, the crow caws from the other side. Two stew, one bean, repeats Coco. I wait for Coco to dish out the beans before I ask where I can change: Puppi runs in, elbows Coco over, ladles soup into two bowls, then takes all three dishes out at once. Coco, where can I: see, she doesn't have to do that. (12)

and sometimes is stalled in awkwardness and inexperience. Jan is new at the job; she is young and attractive; she is a woman in a predominantly male working environment. In this tense and highly sexualized atmosphere, all actions are delineated with an attention to ergonomics. And because there is no solid ground on a boat, because everything is always adjusting to motion, the angles at which reality can be fixed for a moment or two are an essential and constant focus. In the flurry of breakfast orders, Jan has to move toward the stove, beyond the light, so she can "look up and see whoever it is because he's standing on the mess side of it and what with the angle and such I have to lean against the steel counter" (64). Hands reach down from the hatch into which Jan delivers cups of coffee, one at a time, one black, one white. To complaints that the scrambled eggs are taking too long, Puppi answers, "tell him *I am not the stove*" (65).

Those who are not the stove lift and wrap and grab and run. Plates are stacked at an angle, "one plate slightly left, one slightly right" (63), to dry. Puppi screeches and "squiggles" (65) her eyebrows, and Jan holds on to a half-peeled potato and looks at Chuckles, whose "thighs are only a few inches from Coco's uniformed bum" (64). In this frantic lopsidedness of doing, the writing persists, and never prettifies, never turns into a ballet what is not a ballet. Vomit must be cleaned from the deck and sometimes the toilet doesn't work and sometimes one's "tits" are grabbed and on one occasion Ken manages to slip into Jan's bed for a "quickie" (113), even though a "quickie" is the last thing Jan wants.

Even in the realm of the erotic, Jan imagines speed and slowness, coming and going. In one lovely passage in which the *Nootka* is approaching the port at Zeballos, she imagines being held on the edge of orgasm with Hal:

> The mudflats ahead on my right are full of driftlogs; yellow-green weeds press up between. I imagine Hal and I would be quite slow. I can't see a bed. I can't imagine a where. Our limbs kiss. Muscles full. . . . His whole body, like his black eyes, pulses in and out. Slow waves. I stop walking . . . and can feel the mountains, smell them, darkness sinking in from above, giving out from within. (89)

This is a writing in love with the literal, a truthfulness not so much of confession as of process, the articulation of the senses: smells, hunger, the satisfactions of the body, food and sex and sunshine and motion, the oases of small-town ports of call, the shifting orientation of boat on water, each clinging to each. In Jan's great moment of crisis about halfway through the journey/book/summer, she collapses crying in a shower stall. She thinks she should be swimming in the ocean, not "inside this piece of tin" (77) beneath the surface of the water. Layers of metal keep her from becoming "part of the ocean floor" (77) and she bemoans the fact that "[e]verything moves round and round on the surface" (78). She feels she must change. There is someone or something "out there" on the water that she wants to touch, but can't. The surfaces that the writing goes round and round on are also "surface": tactile, sensory; and so is the writing's sense of truth, i.e., truth is what happens. Jan's yearning for connection with something "out there" lends tension to the writing's insistence on what is "right here," including the kinetics of Jan's exit from the shower stall, weaned at last from the "empty nozzle" (78).

> Together my limbs pull the rest of me up, and the water coming down is warmer now, hits different edges of skin, hurts, is hot. I stand up into it. . . . Turn it off. Turn the tap off. Right arm/hand can't do it. Slips. Use both. I do. It stops. I stare at the empty nozzle a second, step away, out.
>
> Out of the blue coffin into a white metal room. (78)

Figurative language like "blue coffin" is rare in this book. Hindmarch lets actual experiencing stand for itself, even in a place where events might inspire metaphor. In the passage above, for example, the imagery of urination and the symbolic rejection of being pissed on, is, I think, unconscious in the writing, but "blue coffin" is not. Leaving the coffin means returning to life, or rather to living on this boat. It is not an image of rebirth (rebirth itself being symbolic).

This is not "meta-"anything writing; it is almost Sisyphean in its sense of dailiness, its response to its own demands for a particular kind of truthfulness. Hyperbole is utterly absent; instead, something like hyperbole is achieved through insistence on details. In one particularly painful (and comical) episode, a lifeboat drill, Jan and Puppi are ordered to lower a lifeboat but they cannot turn the handle of the crank that lets it down. Hindmarch captures the anxiety, the effort, the frustration and the embarrassment of the two women in a prose that spares no part of the process:

> Puppi springs onto the handle. It doesn't move. We stop. One, two, three, push, she mutters. We push and it won't budge. We try again. It won't move at all. Coco steps over to help us. She gets on the side I was on and prepares to pull. We bend our legs and push and pull. It won't budge. It won't budge at all. (106)

"We bend our legs and push and pull": at times Hindmarch's language seems to share the syntax and a fondness for the "simple" words of elementary school reading primers. And if it does share some aspects of that syntax, as well as the highlighted gestures of the nursery tales I mentioned earlier, I think it is to put us in that dreamlike space in which we are aware of every step, every action and its physical consequence, its ability to connect or not to connect. In the nursery tale, giants and deep holes await the unwary child; in the "watery part of the world" invisible shorelines and the future (love? no love?) await those who return from sea voyages. And in reading primers, the world is composed of people and animals and readers (who are being constantly enjoined to "see" something in the imperative mood) doing things. It is a world without emphasis, without subordination, a world of compounds.

While it is not quite a wariness Jan gains from her spell on the *Nootka*, it is a sense of containment, self-sufficiency, and control, as if the small efficient spaces inside the ship, and the immense flowing watery space outside it have made a pact, for the time being at least. This is a writing that inhabits a series of moments, almost as color inhabits the dots in a pointillist painting, as Pauline Butling has observed. One receives a strong sense of Jan as a figure standing up for herself in an unstable world, rejecting the siren song of a better job on a nicer Norwegian freighter, enduring her journey to its end. It is in her work and through her work that Jan distinguishes herself, and her working life aboard the Nootka is both an ironic comment on the tidy union rules that adorn various sections of the book as epigraphs, and an extension of their literalness, their attempt to describe work in such a way as to prevent exploitation of the worker. But it is precisely in Hindmarch's "description" of Jan's "job" that the very notion of a "job description" is demolished:

> What's the holdup? says Beebo, could you bring me a plate please? Sure, I say. That's not enough onion, says Lefty. I run back out, grab a plate for Beebo. Two sausage the works, says Puppi; two sausage, answers Coco. I take Beebo his plate and am slicing more onions when Jock comes in, but I finish first and take them out before . . . any more salad, me love, shouts Jock. What? (50)

Where Hindmarch's work in *The Watery Part of the World*, and more recently in "Improsement" (writing about being a writing and literature instructor at a community college), dovetails with the early interests of *Tish* is in its commitment to the local and the particular and its emphasis on language and place: topos, the here and now. This sensibility, fuelled in part by the poetic energies of Charles Olson and Jack Spicer via Warren Tallman at UBC went on to define a major poetics of the West

Coast in the 1970s which continues to evolve into and out of the writing of Fred Wah, Daphne Marlatt, George Bowering, and Gladys Hindmarch. Although Hindmarch has been the least prolific of these four, her work is nevertheless grounded in a sense of a continuing line, a serial "story" that language tells in all its exactitude and inexactitude. A sense of claustrophobia can sometimes overcome the reader of *The Watery Part of the World*, owing to its minuteness of vision and its relentless action inside a confined space, but the writing – and the landscape – opens up from time to time, often enough to allow us to catch our breath. With Jan, we can feel the relief of mountains and trees and solid ground. Even so, there is always somewhere else to go on to, and Jan returns from her journey dreaming of the wide world. "Hal," she says, "I think I'm going to ship out again" (143).

Works Cited

Butling, Pauline. "Gladys Hindmarch: Pointillist Prose." *Essays on Canadian Writing* 32 (Summer 1986): 70-91.

Hindmarch, Gladys. 1976. *The Peter Stories*. Toronto: Coach House P.

____. 1988. *The Watery Part of the World*. Vancouver & Toronto: Douglas & McIntyre.

JANICE WILLIAMSON

It gives me a great deal of pleasure to say yes: Writing/Reading Lesbian in Daphne Marlatt's Touch to My Tongue

> The desire for lyric: to shut down & modify the excessible
> Lyric noise (Not romance but the failure
> of the sign to mean, we're lost in it, not forest but the
> sign) or what the hell the lesbo-ex-machina:
> if the ending fails, send them to bed
> (Mouré 1989, 111)

"from *here to there*"

Touch to My Tongue includes five photographs by Cheryl Sourkes, as well as Marlatt's series of thirteen lesbian love poems and a lyrical essay on feminist poetics, "Musing with Mothertongue." The twin epigraphs in *Touch to My Tongue* are informed by issues of gender and writing rooted in Marlatt's writing history. They suggest how Marlatt's work continually turns on itself, extending thought and strategies of language through a diverse repertoire of influences. The first epigraph, a quotation from lesbian poet H.D.'s 1919 *Notes on Thought and Vision*, challenges a Cartesian order of things, making visible the specificity of the female body: "The brain and the womb are both centres of consciousness, equally important." And the second was written by Québec writer Louise Cotnoir: "*Une femme inscrite en exterritorialité du langage. Elle expose le sujet comme on s'expose à la mort. Car il est question qu'elle vive.*" These different and doubled epigraphs suggest how Marlatt has come to write at the intersection of two traditions in the bi-national Canada/Québec connections which circulate in some contemporary feminist writing.

If one element characterizes Marlatt's writing career, it is her ongoing intellectual engagement in various writing communities. From the 1963 Vancouver Poetry Conference on, her extensive work as an editor of *Tish*, *The Capilano Review*, *Island*, *Periodics*, and *Tessera*, has given her an eclectic intellectual and writerly context in which to develop her evolving poetics. H.D.'s name acknowledges a female modernist geneology which was marginally present in the almost exlusively male waves of *Tish* editors. That this group was dominated by a body of male writing and male bodies writing is suggested by the erasure of women's contributions from retrospective mythologies developing about *Tish*.[1] While the Black Mountain tradition influenced Marlatt, the implications of Olson's big breaths and giant proprioceptive body remain gender specific. Until the eighties, Marlatt's work was interpreted almost exclusively by male writers and critics.[2]

The progress of Marlatt's work can be read as both continuous and ruptured. Lorraine Weir makes a fierce plea for seeing Marlatt's development as unbroken:

To assume that pre-1984 is "lyrical" and ideologically neutral is to subscribe to the colonizing hypothesis of those who have attempted to typecast Marlatt as a "phenomenologist," and to relegate her to the role of bright observer of man's world (Weir 63 n6).

And, in her perceptive analysis of Marlatt's work, Brenda Carr encourages us to read the Steveston project extending from 1973 to Marlatt's recuperative new work, *Salvage*, as a textual practice of recovery, revision and renewal, a "feminine economy . . . [which refuses] to be the last word" (Carr 83).

In expanding our study beyond the body of the texts produced by Marlatt, we note a rupture and transformation in the critical community which engages with her work. In spite of her long-time woman-centered work, Marlatt had not called herself a feminist writer before 1980. Thus, Louise Cotnoir's epigraph to *Touch to My Tongue* recalls Hélène Cixous' comments on woman's relation to language and positions the reader at this turning point in Marlatt's writing which begins to self-consciously investigate theories of female-gendered writing. In this "écriture feminine," women writers "risk essentialism"[3] in order to articulate a different relation to authority and writing which privileges the unsaid and the "extra-territorial."[4] This epigraph also indicates another line of writing extending from Marlatt's early work translating Francis Ponge in her MA thesis; through her participation in an anglo-Canadian/Québec translation project extended in correspondence and initiated by Colin Browne; to the later "transformance" or translation exchanges between Marlatt and Nicole Brossard requested by Browne and Michel Gay.

While Marlatt had been reading Brossard, the two writers met for the first time at the York University 1981 Dialogue Conference which brought together anglophone-Canadian and Québec feminist writers and critics. Afterwards, Marlatt wrote to Barbara Godard, commenting on her position within the anglo-Canadian poetry community:

> feminist writing in English in Canada has been largely sociological & referential, hasn't involved much experimentation with language or structure (at least in poetry – that's not so true in fiction which has Audrey Thomas, Sharon Riis). the experimentation in poetry has been initiated by men, the Tish groupy [*sic*] in the West & the Four Horsemen, particularly Nichol & McCaffery, as well as Victor Coleman at CHP, in Ontario. their struggle to be heard is pretty much won, at least in certain quarters, & they're in danger of becoming the new establishment. i've been part of all that, in fact those men, along with Michael Ondaatje, have given me most encouragement & support over the years. which isn't something a feminist conference is likely to understand, but i think most women writers in English Canada have been isolated from each other & have found their encouragement & support coming from men writers – i think of the isolation of Phyllis Webb, Margaret Avison, Gwen MacEwen (?i've never even *seen* her). but things are changing & maybe we're at a crucial point in that change . . . [22 October 1981] (1989, 24).

It was here that the feminist innovative writing and theory journal *Tessera* began to take shape through conversations and letters between the original editors: Marlatt, Godard, Kathy Mezei, and Gail Scott. *Tessera* became part of a chorus of other feminist writing, publishing, and cultural initiatives which included: the 1983 Women and Words/Les femmes et les mots Conference, more public readings in feminist bookstores and women's spaces, women writers' workshops and retreats, women-only anthologies, feminist participation in government granting agencies, the extension of feminist publishing houses and periodicals, the development of feminist book distribution networks, and increasing interventions by feminists within the academy to identify sexist critical and institutional practices.[5] All of these activities enabled and were enabled by women like Marlatt who worked to make possible a feminist public sphere through editorial, organizational, teaching, and creative work.[6] A decade before, Marlatt's Steveston project from poem to oral history to radio documentary extended her community of readers from dedicated poets and literati to non-literary readers, from Japanese-Canadian community workers to government officials. With *Touch to My Tongue*, feminists, young and old, lesbian and otherwise, became eager readers of Marlatt's innovative writing. Although there is no public record, one also imagines that devoted but homophobic readers, surprised at this poetic coming out, abandoned her writing.[7]

"yes"

> For that which speaks wants at the same time to condemn the law that calls for its repression. That which is forbidden, desires, and that which desires, writes, propelled by the very law it transgresses. (Brossard in Gould 16)

While a connection between writing and the female body and representations of love between and among women must be spoken, the problem of how to write and speak them without falling into the same theoretical limitations which have censored these representations is a difficult one. Analyzing a heterosexual desiring economy, Kaja Silverman turns to *Tess of the d'Urbervilles*. "If Tess's body is produced within one symbolic order, other symbolic orders may very well produce different female bodies, and consequently different subjective possibilities" (28). Feminist and lesbian writers work to imagine alternative female bodies and subjectivities outside masculist, racist, and heterosexist domination. Marlatt's work challenges the cultural representations of woman as object, fetish, or mute territorialized nature. *Touch to My Tongue* can be read as an "answering touch" to a lesbian imaginary which enables Marlatt to conceive of women as desiring bodies, sisters, mothers, daughters, and lesbian lovers.

Unresolved issues are explored in Marlatt's text as strategies of writing. Her preoccupation with language is translated in her lesbian love poems into a self-reflexive exploration of a utopian "no place" space. It is in part because of its utopian character that this writing gestures toward an idealized ahistorical mythmaking about female sexuality in general, and lesbian sexuality more specifically. A countermovement between myth and history is unsurprising when we consider that within a heterosexual economy there is a "reluctance to add sex to history because we treasure sex as a retreat from time" (Snitow 10).

The erotic lesbian bodies which echo in Marlatt's sensual language become the site of not only a transhistorical ideal, but of history itself. For the text's mythopoeia is ruptured by different ideological positions in contemporary feminist theory. Some theorists would disavow the play of power between women, transforming lesbian sexuality into an idealist absolute. Others would simply reverse the hierarchy of heterosexuality versus lesbianism, fixing as "natural" what was earlier deemed "perverse."

In "yes," the third poem in *Touch to My Tongue*, language reveals itself as the bearer of social codes and structures in which the word "perverse" has come to organize heterosexist perceptions of lesbianism. The category of the perverse has a long and glorious history in the Judeo-Christian West from its association with sinful forms of sexual practice, to its use in the scientific literature on sexuality which began to be written in the late nineteenth century. In a homophobic culture, heterosexual prohibition becomes homoerotic suppression when the risks of self-revelation include shunning, humiliation, loss of employment, and violent attacks.[8]

In Marlatt's "yes," the "perverse" is recast in a different, affirmative place as the narrator repeats Molly Bloom's famous "yes," displacing it onto the terrain of lesbian desire. Here Gertrude Stein has announced, "It gives me a great deal of pleasure to say yes" (3). The narrator speaks of her own heterosexual history: "my fingers flutter to my ring, gone. only a white band the skin of years hidden under its reminder to myself of the self i was marrying – 'worthless woman, wilful girl' " (21). Then, shifting, she positions herself "standing athwart, objecting, 'so as to thwart or obstruct,' 'perversely.' no, so as to retain this small open space that was mine." Here, this moving "athwart" which means literally, "in opposition to the proper or expected course" is an affirmative deconstructive gesture. For by shifting beyond the boundaries of the oppositional codes of *good* heterosexual and *bad* lesbian, Marlatt's writing brings the reader into a place where desire does not constitute a fixed identity or essence, but is a movement – a "tidal place i knew as mine, know now is the place i find with you. not perverse but turned the *right* way around, redefined, it signals us beyond limits in a new tongue our connection runs along."

In an earlier series of poems, *here and there*, the speaker asks, "what draws, what moves us one way to return against the / procession?" Several lines later the writing tentatively responds, "light desire, from shine we are caught by. every / longing an atempt [*sic*] on the stars." Marlatt elaborates in a 1985 unpublished letter how this desire is rooted etymologically in "shine," "(what stars do) – desire, the movement that crosses distance?" This query moves desire beyond sexology's rigid oppositions and classifications of hetero-/homo-sexual. What matters in Marlatt's desire is between here and there, a recognition which crosses distances.

"it's Sappho . . . on the radio"

> Lesbian is the word/name a given woman chooses for her idea of herself, to represent her idea (representation) of herself. I am/you are/she is that place where wor(l)ds of meaning collide. (Meese 81)

When female pleasure is played on a cultural network which privileges male desire, lesbian desire is doubly prohibited. Sappho is only on record in lesbian archives. Marlatt's poems not only "come out" but also "go public" on the airwaves of lesbian eros which hum with rhythms of an alternative series of love poems from Sappho to Phyllis Webb's "Naked Poems" to Nicole Brossard's *Amantes* (*Lovhers*) and Adrienne Rich's "Twenty-One Love Poems." These writings refuse the canonical terms of "tradition," for the notion of a fixed lesbian essence or identity would deny the social historical dimension of sexuality itself. Lesbian historians and critics like Elizabeth Meese remind us that lesbian writing is not only constituted historically but also constitutive of what it means to write as a lesbian. Thus while one can trace certain social historical trends in the self-definition and writings of lesbianism, there are many differences in approaches. For instance, between Jane Rule and Nicole Brossard, formal and aesthetic differences can parallel different approaches to sexual identity and libidinal commitment. Daphne Marlatt's lesbian love poems do not stir up images of bad-sister butch/femme bar dykes which, during the 1950s, would have provided the lesbian reader with a recognizable code of signs. As in her novel *Ana Historic*, Marlatt's poems write lesbianism in a current of contemporary lesbian representations where sexuality is embedded in romantic friendship and relationship.[9]

Lesbian writing in Elizabeth Meese's essay becomes "lesbian : writing," a grammatical configuration which imagines lesbian as

> a contrastive shape in a shadow play, slightly formless, the edges blurred by the turns of the field, the sheets on which a drama is projected. The lesbian subject is not all I am and it is in all I am. (70)

The concern with frame and focalization central to lesbian writing is enacted in "Narrative Distance" by Suniti Namjoshi and Gillian Hanscombe which begins:

> Climb up here on this ready-made mountain,
> sit beside me, and watch the two women
> walking on the beach, observe their relation,
> mood and emotion, each connected to each.

From this vantage point the privileged couple have mastering eyes until the figures on the beach disappear and the two voyeurs "scramble down the slope, but there's nobody/there, just the two of us, anxious already"(12). The poem performs and then refuses the narrative improbability of reading the lesbian text as fixed or already written. The telescoping of those who watch with those who are watched indicates how lesbians come into being through self-representation in a cultural context which prefers their invisibility.

Marlatt's poems are in conversation with other lesbian writing, a conversation which offers an understanding of the multiple subject positions available to lesbians. The title itself directs us to two writers in particular: Betsy Warland and Luce Irigaray. French psychoanalyst Irigaray writes a textual exchange or double-voiced female monologue, "When Our Lips Speak Together," which like Marlatt's text insists on developing new female strategies of language and writing:

> If we keep on speaking sameness, if we speak to each other as men have been doing for centuries, as we have been taught to speak, we'll miss each other, fail ourselves. . . . Absent from ourselves: we'll be spoken machines, speaking machines. Enveloped in proper skins, but not our own. Withdrawn into proper names, violated by them. (205)

As though in response to Irigaray's urging, *Touch to My Tongue*'s dedication leads the reader "To Betsy," a name which signs a less distant textual body. Betsy Warland's volume, *Open is Broken* is reciprocally inscribed. Warland develops a more exclusive poetics of etymological rupture, a practice of "breaking words" which establishes links between lovers' bodies, love letters, and love poems – "between eroticism / etymology and tissue / text" (12). These connections sound within the poems as well as in their collaborative cross-genre performance dialogues of love letters and poems which accompanied the publication of their poems coast to Canadian coast. Unsurprisingly, mainstream literary periodicals reviewed the publication of the books as private reading events, while the public reading/ performances were enjoyed mainly by the feminist community and reviewed in feminist and lesbian periodicals (Nuse 1984/85; Parks 1984/85; Wright.)

In response to a question regarding whether the letters and poems are related in terms "of context or . . . translation," Marlatt responds:

> Well it's a little bit of both. The language in the letters is different, more mundane and less self-conscious than the poems. When I *say*, "I love you" it's not language conscious of itself, it's self conscious of this other self, body conscious of this other body, soul conscious of this other soul. And this language is subordinate to this feeling which roars through it. . . . The poems are saying both "I love you," and "This is what language can do in the service of love," in a language-conscious-of-itself way. (Williamson 1985, 25)

This textual practice is produced in an unauthorized "hidden ground" where Marlatt reconsiders the role of writer and reader. Woman is an "inhabitant of language, not master, not even mistress, [but . . .] on that double edge where she has always lived, between the already spoken and the unspeakable, sense and nonsense" (48). To write from this double edge is not simply to engage in a set of idealist word plays. For she continues: "putting the living body of language together means putting the world together, the world we live in: an act of composition, an act of birthing, us, uttered and outered there in it" (49). The writer is represented in an amphibious sensorious language: "water author sounding the dark edge of the words we come to, auger- ess, issa" (27). The reader is drawn from "author" to "augur- ess," an association that creates a kind of feminized translation of "author." Thus, the roots "garrire," to speak, and "augere," to increase, transform the activity of the "author," meaning "to originate," into a more organic less unitary notion of author as one who increases and "makes grow," or interprets as in "augury." It is up to the reader/critic to produce readings and make the connections between signs.[10]

The collection of poetic essay, prose poetry and photographs offer us a rich text/image fabric on which to work our reading. This fictive/theory cross genre writing is a practice shared by a number of contemporary lesbian writers whose theoretical texts provide a framing critical context. One could interpret this simply as a sign of contemporary textual self-reflexivity, however the recognition that lesbians write within a long homophobic cultural history provokes us to consider genre questions in relation to cultural context not formalist aesthetics. For theorist Elizabeth Meese, the epistolary genre offers her an amorous *rapport d'address* which allows her to think through the lesbian body in her "Theorizing Lesbian : Writing – A Love Letter." We consider Monique Wittig's fictional texts, themselves theoretical, in relation to her essays which provide a radical critique of the sex/gender system. Similarly, Gail Scott's "essays in progress," *Spaces Like Stairs*, talk back to her fictional texts in direct and indirect ways, alerting readers to lesbian questions less visible in the bisexuality of the novel *Heroine*. In *Furious*, Erin Mouré's prose section, "The Acts," reflects on and interrupts the poetry of "Pure Reason." Nicole Brossard's fiction-theory collapses the borders between the two genres making a lesbian space where "ALL FICTIVE ESCAPES ARE SO REAL" (Brossard 1989, 12). And Betsy Warland's *Proper Deafinitions: Collected Theorograms* combines prose and poetry about current feminist issues elaborating an "inhertextuality" (84) of connections between women.

Within *Touch to My Tongue*, a visual archeology of the lesbian imaginary can be found in the photographs by Cheryl Sourkes which accompany Marlatt's poems. Reproduced from a series called "Memory Room," the photographs are palimpsestic in form with negative images layered one on top of the other. In her published notes, Sourkes sees "these photographs as externalized memory rooms, each organized according to its own logic" (53). Reproductions of "current Vancouver images with the historic and the scholarly" include images of Chinese face reading, a pre-eleventh century woman's alchemical text, an Eleusinian womb-like maze, and the medieval figure of "gramatica." This collage of different visual signifying systems spatializes the female body within a representational frame of female iconography. Sourkes comments on the use of pictorial language in this work: "The admission of language into the image follows the first human marks from 100,000 years ago when writing and pictures were one" (53). It is significant that one of the representations of the female body in these photographs is a drawing of the medieval figure "gramatica," emblematic of "the study of literature and letters." Here the female figure becomes a kind of hieroglyph, or pictorial language which blurs the distinction between woman and writing.

Like the category "woman," the hieroglyph is defined by an internal contradiction. It is an enigma that possesses "an indecipherable though desireable otherness."[11] Paradoxically however, this writing in pictures is the most readable of languages. Because of the lack of distance between visual sign and referent, it is marked by a proximity which refuses the dominance of the controlling masculist gaze. The hieroglyph's contradictory identity as both enigmatic otherness and proximity is particularly significant in *Touch to My Tongue* where language calls through associative echoes.

"a rhapsody of translated senses"

Marlatt has noted how her writing develops autobiographically and documents her own "experience" as a western white woman in patriarchal culture. If we read this "experience" as a "process by which, for all social beings, subjectivity is constructed" (de Lauretis 1984, 159), we are better able to come to terms with Marlatt's focus on language. Writing about the novel, Julia Kristeva describes how the classical Menippean carnivalesque discourse "consists of communication between two spaces: that of the scene and that of the hieroglyph, that of representation *by* language, and that of experience *in* language"(85). Woman appears in *Touch to My Tongue* through a similar doubled strategy. For she is figured dialectically in the spatial representation of the body in the landscape and in the sonoral play or "experience" of language itself. While Kristeva would negate the importance of the gendered signature in her championing of the avant garde, Marlatt insists on the gendered specificity of language and writing in "Musing with Mothertongue": "if we are women poets, writers, speakers, we also take issue with the given, hearing the discrepancy between what our patriarchally-loaded language bears (can bear) of our experience and the difference from it our experience bears out – how it misrepresents, even miscarries, and so leaves unsaid what we actually experience" (47).

In a 1966 letter written to Frank Davey, Marlatt describes alliteration as "words on the move. A word on the move (named thing moves across the stage) changes its relationships with other things, other aspects of the scene. The dynamics of change echo in sound" (Davey). The relationship of sound to writing expands from this rhetorical strategy recalling Duncan to become Marlatt's embodied feminist poetics where "sound will initiate thought," a form of thought which is "erotic because it works by attraction," a language of touch where "words call each other up, evoke each other, provoke each other, nudge each other into utterance" (45). Reading the "experience of language" in *Touch to My Tongue* hinges on the ambiguity of its title. In what she once identified as Anaïs Nin's ability to write a "rhapsody of translated senses" (1972, 58), Marlatt creates an erotic synaesthesia where the body speaks a language fluid and uncontained. She discusses this relatedness in an interview:

> [the tongue] is the major organ which touches all the different parts of the mouth to make the different sounds – tongue as speech organ. Also, the tongue is a major organ in making love between women . . . an erotic organ. [There is an] intertwining of eroticism and speech – lovemaking as a form of organ speech, and poetry as a form of verbal speech. (Williamson 1985, 28)

Working through long prose lines of multi-directional linguistic associations, this female economy refuses the fixed identity of a dominating unitary discourse not only in the play of desire between the two women lovers within the text, but also within and between the intersubjective desire of Marlatt's writing and our reading. Along a horizontal axis, Marlatt explores the contiguous relations between etymology and foreign tongues: the Old Norse, French, and Indo-European roots of the English language. And along a vertical axis Marlatt's words play along through chains echoing signifiers from a familiar English lexicon.

In "coming up from underground," the lovers' desire is written in the ruptured transitions and translations in and among the words on the page, to mark out the lover's "healing":

> draw close, i am so glad to see you, bleak colour of your iris gone blue, that blue of a clear sky, *belo*, bright, Beltane, 'bright-fire.' draw me in, light a new flame after your sudden descent into the dark. draw me close so i see only light your eye a full moon rides. *bleikr* in the old tongue, shining, . . . white, radiant healing in various bright colours, *blanda*, to mingle and blend: the blaze of light we are, spiralling. (31)

Here her notes provide a key to the "powerful cluster of meanings and associations" (37) around the Indo-European *bhel-* which includes a connection with Beltane, the Celtic May Day when one imagines figures like Persephone rising each spring.

These signs of spiralling repetition and recovery are linked with feminist theorizing. The spiral plays an important role in the work of lesbian feminist theologian Mary Daly. Daly provided the epigraph to Marlatt's *What Matters* (1980) provoking Christina Cole to write: "The affinity between Marlatt and Daly exists because Marlatt's aims are those of Gyn/Ecology: 'dis-covering the sources of the Self's original movement' " (18). This quotation suggests how Daly's theorizing operates within categories many feminists are unsettling in their writing. Jane Gallop describes the limitations of those feminist arguments which reverse and recast patriarchal structures, reducing heterogeneity to "a unified, rigid representation" of women (Gallop 1982, 74). Roland Barthes provides a non-feminist but less teleological analysis of spiral symbolism which is the opposite of that of the circle; the circle is religious, theological; the spiral, a kind of circle distended to infinity, is dialectical: on the spiral things recur, but *at another level*: there is a return in difference, not in identity. . . . By repeating itself, it engenders a displacement. The same thing happens in poetic language . . . since the signs of this language are very limited in number and infinitely free to combine. (Barthes 1985, 218-9)

Nicole Brossard quotes Barthes in her analysis of a lesbian "spiral form [where] 'everything reappears as Fiction, that is, at each turn of the spirale' " (1989, 56). Brossard's graphic illustrations of "Aerial Vision" feminize and politicize the spiral to chart a journey from "[w]omen's invisibility" to "[n]ew perspectives: new configurations of woman-as-being-in-the-world of what's real, of reality, and of fiction" (1988, 116-7).

"New configurations" are achieved in Marlatt's spiralling play of identity and difference which operates between the English language, apparently transparent to the reader, and the disordering interruptions of the translated etymological chains of words. This doubleness is repeated in the narrative tension between historical and mythical time. A love story along the horizontal axis of the narrator's separation and longing traces a trip through the geographic distance between Canadian prairie and the west coast. This axis tilts vertical in the mythological echoes of the cyclic separation and recovery of Demeter and Persephone. A sensual excess, the narrator's provocative pleasure in language, connects these twinned narrative journeys.

"this place of contradiction"

> But we women listen so carefully to each other. The resurrection of the woman's body is of Kore, not the phallic king-dom. This affirmation is the true necessity. To inhabit freely the civic house of memory I am kept out of.
>
> Oh!
> (Mouré 1988, 91)

The title of the first poem sets the scene in "this place full of contradiction" (19). This is the space of lesbian desire where the narrator remarks, "it's Sappho I said, on the radio." Here the lesbian lovers are distanced by otherness in the confusion of ethnicity:

> a confusion of times if not of place, though you understood when i said no not the Danish Tearoom – the Indonesian or Indian, was in fact that place of warm walls [. . .] you wearing your irish drover's cap and waiting alive in the glow while i come up worrying danish and curry. (19)

This distance and difference is reinforced in the language of this poem which is divided in itself, and doubled in lexical repetition. The words "contradiction," "confusion," and a hyphenated "co-incidence" reinforce each other. Contradiction literally means "to speak on the opposite side." Confusion means "to pour against." And, coincidence in geometry is when "two locuses share a common point but do not coincide." While difference and separation are implicit in these words, they are simultaneously shattered in the poem. For the lovers share a kind of proximity that suggests fusion and loss of identity:

> i see your face because i don't see mine equally flush with being, co-incidence being together we meet in these far places we find in each other. (19)

Here in this female space, "negation does not exist, [. . .] consequently the terms of a contradiction, far from excluding one another, coexist and overlap" (Montrelay 894). The reader is confronted with a chain of signifiers which echo through the prose poem tracing a tension between narcissistic recognition, and the difference of the other.

This "co-incidence" of figures in lesbian writing surfaces in a number of other lesbian writers. Monique Wittig's *The Lesbian Body* performs orgasmic fusion in a dance between autonomy and surrender:

> . . . while you speak faster and faster clasping m/e *I* clasping you clasping each other with a marvellous strength, the sand is round our waists, at a given moment your skin splits from throat to pubis, m/ine in turn from below upwards, *I* spill m/yself into you, you mingle with m/e m/y mouth fastened on your mouth your neck squeezed by m/y arms . . . (51-2)

The first person is graphemically split to indicate the division, a division multiplied in the twists of exchange. The body exceeds itself, spilling beyond the limits of first and second person.

Erin Mouré accomplishes a similar loss of subject/object focus in "Rolling Motion."

> Your face in my neck &
> arms dwelling upward face
> in my soft leg open
> lifted upward airborne soft
> face into under into rolling
> over every upward motion
> (1988, 35)

Abandoning causal syntax, Mouré's looping phrases string together new rhetorical erotic possibilities which pre-position rather than position the lovers in relation to each other. The poem pushes the reader toward gestures and touches rather than the static shots of bodies glimpsed through the peephole of voyeuristic readerly conventions.

It is thus not surprising that in *Touch to My Tongue* the author turns to a twinned female narrative, the matrilineal myth of Demeter and Persephone to tell her lesbian love story and invent an embodied language. Marlatt's writing of the mother began in her early birth poems, *Rings* (1971), and continues through her more recent work including the ambivalent fictive portrait of the mother in *Ana Historic*. The resolution of a mother/daughter narrative of loss and recovery, central to feminist theorizing of female subjectivity, has a particular significance for Marlatt who has commented on her own ambivalence towards her mother:

> writing about her [Marlatt's mother] is my way of . . . getting to a place where I can feel some of that affection and empathy and understanding. It's a really different bond from the little girl's bond, because my understanding comes from empathizing with her experience as a mother, having had my own experience as a mother. And recognizing in myself the difficulties I had as an immigrant, and seeing how those were magnified for her. I can only realize what we had in common by also expressing where I felt she betrayed me as a mother, because she was in such deep psychological trouble. (Williamson 1989, 49)

The Demeter/Persephone mythical narrative space of continual return of daughter to mother offers Marlatt a textual field to write a different mother/daughter dynamic. As well, the myth is a feminist alternative to masculist Oedipal narratives. Marianne Hirsch describes the myth's narrative advantage for feminists:

> This mother-daughter narrative is resolved through continued *opposition*, *interruption*, and *contradiction*. As we follow Persephone's return to her mother for one part of the year and her repeated descent to marriage and the underworld for the rest, we have to revise our very notion of resolution. (35)

Within Marlatt's Demeter/Persephone story, contradictions emerge between distance and proximity; difference and sameness; autonomy and fusion; and the problematization of the category woman versus the search for a fixed identity "woman." These contradictions, set in motion and not fully resolved, have political implication for interpersonal relations between women, as well as in the way we speak and write about ourselves.

In *Steveston*, women are lost in the underworld of the sexist gaze, "caught, kore, in the black hole of your eye" (76). In *Touch to My Tongue*, the Persephone of "prairie" is similarly "caught in a whirlwind the underside churns up, the otherwise of where we are" (26). The kidnapper and god of the underworld, Hades, appears as "but only the latest technician in a long line of measurers." However the sensual economy of *Touch to My Tongue* escapes the specular order and violence of this masculist technician, for the figures of Demeter and Persephone inhabit not dry land, owned, along the highway, cleared for use, but that other, lowlying, moist and undefined, hidden ground, wild and running everywhere along the outer edges. (27)

It is on this site, an unauthorized space which is *not* property, that Marlatt describes woman's sexuality as an unmapped "hidden ground."

However the significance of this alternative site does not end with mere reversal. For the possibility of polarized terms dissolves in this "everywhere along the outer edges." The categories of mother and daughter are unbounded, "co-incident" with each other. Marlatt writes in "hidden ground":

lost, *losti*, lust-y one, who calls my untamed answering one to sally forth, finding alternate names, finding the child provoked, invoked, lost daughter, other mother and lover. (27)

This passage hides a private and autobiographical joke about alternate names for the author whose mother chose between Sally and Daphne in naming her. Thus Marlatt's project of "finding alternate names" inscribes a double signature in this text outside the Oedipal drama of rival sons and dead fathers. Beyond the intergenerational conflict authorized by "the law of the father," the double signature signifies a fluidity of feminist consciousness which "understands relationship and continuity" (Williamson 1985, 28), rather than domination and usurpation.

Marlatt's sexual economy answers Irigaray's elaboration of how woman

always remains several, but she is kept from dispersion because the other is already within her and is autoerotically familiar to her. Which is not to say that she appropriates the other for herself, that she reduces it to her own property. Ownership and property are doubtless quite foreign to the feminine. At least sexually. But not *nearness*. Nearness so pronounced that it makes all discrimination of identity, and thus all forms of property, impossible. (Irigaray, 31)

Daughter becomes Demeter, and mother, Persephone, as the fixed identities of two lovers slide. In the prose poem "kore," Demeter rising Hades-like out of her earth is transformed and translucent: "no one wears yellow like you excessive and radiant storehouse of sun, skin smooth as fruit but thin, leaking light" (23). In this erotic space, the first and second person pronoun are indeed thin skinned, slipping beyond their singular borders: "here i am you" the woman announces in a language where "you" becomes "*yu!* cry jubilant excess." Language makes the connection between the Indo-European root of the second person pronoun, and "yu," the Latin *jubilare*, "to raise a shout of joy." This blissful interpersonal fusion reminds us that "jouissance" is distinguished from the comfortable realm of pleasure and defined as "a loss of self, disruption of comfort, loss of control" which threatens ego boundaries (Gallop 1984, 114).

This ecstatic merging with the other takes on a more general *and* dangerous significance when in her notes to the same poem Marlatt's etymology takes her to the relation between "female," meaning "to suckle," in its "diversified" field of associations: "fetus, ([. . .] that which sucks), *fellatio* (sucking) and *felix* (fruitful, happy)" (36). "Female" in this linguistic space transgresses boundaries, as "excess," that is, the "overstepping of prescribed limits, the extravagant violation of the law." This is a language "out of place," ex-stasis, where oppositions between subject and object, surface and substance, body and writing dissolve.

The mother/daughter fusion of the Persephone narrative and the loss of identity implicit in this pre-Oedipal state is problematized and developed in the second poem of the series "houseless," where the narrator recounts the dark side of this love affair beginning "i'm afraid, you say, are you?" This is a different space of vulnerability and fear of separation. Here the relations of contradiction of the opening poem become relations of opposition. While the lover is most often represented as the daughter-returned, here she is distanced and made into a non-Western other, transfigured into the dark maternal figure, "mother of giving turned terrible mother, blood-sipper, sorrow Durga." This Hindu goddess incarnation is the terrifying representation of the female which has haunted so many male writers, a maternal figure who takes the reader out of the realm of an idealized fusion with the mother. The female psyche is "houseless," ego boundaries have crumbled and the nurturing Demeter is transformed into a phallic mother. This is the only moment in the long poem where this potential play of power between and among women is acknowledged. But isn't this negative aspect of fusion and being overwhelmed as threatening to the lesbian as it is within the heterosexual economy?

As the poem ends, the narrator redefines her relation to this maternal figure, translating fear of fusion into a more fluid relational subject position. Marlatt refuses the metaphor of "vessel" or the figuration of womb as enclosure and containment: "i can only be, no vessel but a movement running, out in the open, out in the dark and rising tide, in risk, knowing who i am with you – ."

"nine aflush"

> The body wanting to live, looks for a way to stretch. I don't have to go back to *once upon a time*; I simply look in our saliva for movement, desire's axis, which would have me speak of me, us, now. (Brossard 1988, 55)

According to Rosalind Coward, "Feminine positions are produced as responses to the pleasures offered to us; our subjectivity and identity are formed in the definitions of desire which encircle us" (114). In her opening poem, unraveling a numerical puzzle exposes the female pleasure of another text. Marlatt writes: "through your eyes i'm watching you talk of a different birth, blonde hair on my tongue, of numbers, nine aflush with cappuccino and brandy" (19). A reader familiar with the writing of Hélène Cixous recognizes in the phrase "nine aflush" a reference to the mythical bi-sexual Tiresias who having lived seven years as a woman and seven as a man declared, "'If sexual pleasure could be divided up into ten parts, nine of them would be the woman's'" (41-2).

In Marlatt's writing of this female pleasure and excess, her signifiers refuse to be pinned down. But a celebratory female desire has a history of eluding mastering pens. Readers of Western women's writing can look beyond the murky eighteenth-century corridors of Ann Radcliffe to find early representations of female desire. Gallop points out in her analysis of popular contemporary books about female sexuality, wickedly titled "Snatches of Conversation," that there is a "conviction that sense can be made from woman's eroticism, that light and order (male logic, discursive seriousness) can be brought to the murky tangles of the female genitalia/mind" (274).

With this in mind, a peculiar moment is uncovered in the introduction to *The Contemporary Canadian Poem Anthology* when editor George Bowering discusses Marlatt, one of the three women in his collection of twenty writers. He quotes Roland Barthes' familiar gender-blind eloquence, " 'Each poetic word is thus an unexpected object, a Pandora's box from which fly out all the potentialities of language'." Bowering expands on this metaphor: "The poets in this anthology tend to believe that discourse once open should remain open, like Pandora's heart to the world." What remains mysterious in Bowering's analysis is a romanticizing slippage, the substitution of the heart of Pandora for her notorious "box," root of "a multitude of evils and distempers." He cites Marlatt as exemplar of an open textual practice, "in fact, [she] seldom closes her parentheses, because the parenthetical has in short order become the main event" (2-3).

The parenthetical is indeed key to this reading of *Touch to My Tongue*. There is a puzzling moment in Ovid's story of Demeter and Persephone when an old woman, Baubô, tells an undisclosed joke and makes the mournful Demeter laugh. The translator to a pre-Ovidian version of the myth which appears in the *Homeric Hymns* reveals the secret joke and asks, "But who is Iambê, and why in the Orphic version is it not Iambê but the Eleusinian queen, Baubô, who induces the goddess to forget her sorrow and laugh by lifting her robe and exposing her pudenda?" (Athanassakis 76).

This exhibition of female genitalia was performed as part of the ancient rites of Eleusis celebrating the return of Persephone to Demeter. Film critic Peter Wollen suggests that Baubô offers "a way round the roadblock of the Medusa, a way to 'conceptualize' the female genitals outside the doublebind of castration, outside the phallocentric" (119). Here, Demeter's look and laughter affirms what it sees, while Freud's gaze at female genitalia hallucinates what it doesn't see, that is, the castrated penis. It is significant that Demeter's spirits are lifted by the sight of female genitalia. While Baubô doesn't appear in person in the writing of Marlatt's text, her performance is certainly evident metonymically as "pudenda" or "kiwi," as the other lips of *Touch to My Tongue*. As though thinking through the problematic Freudian castrated body, the only wounded female body in Marlatt's poems is the sick lover's "body traumatized" by abdominal surgery. In "healing," this wound is explicitly differentiated from female genitalia: "gauze, waiting for the two lips of your incision to knit, waiting for our mouths to close lip to other lip in the full spring of wet, revived, season plants come alive" (32).

"Not a Bad End"

As a child, Marlatt scribbled an alternate ending to Hans Christian Anderson's "The Snow Queen," "the basis" for *Frames: of a Story*. Anderson's fairy-tale text concludes, "There they sat, those two happy ones, grown-up and yet children – children in heart, while all around them glowed bright summer – warm glorious summer." In the thick pencilled script of a child, Marlatt's revisionary marginalia adds:

> And they got married, and lived happily ever
> bright, glorious afterwards, to the end of their
> summer .
> THE END

I note this juvenalia found in her Papers in The National Library, partially in the spirit of a light-hearted commentary on the sleuthing pleasures of literary archives. More seriously, the effect of this childhood overwriting is to affirm dominant culture's utopian narrative dream of heterosexuality and to indicate its power. However this closure is in fact partially subverted in Marlatt's graphic arrow and the fractured lines of her revision where the finite season "glorious – summer" interrupts the infinite expectations of "happily ever . . ." and "to the end of their. . . ."

Similarly, the ending to *Ana Historic* is both fixed and unfixed – fixed because it is an ending which locates itself in contradistinction to heterosexual narrative expectations, but entirely unfixed in that it begins again with the open-ended possibility of lesbian relationship which is celebrated in *Touch to My Tongue*. The representation of this "beginning again" in *Ana Historic* is in the form of a prose poem which makes the lovers' desire, the reader's:

> we give place, giving words, giving birth, to
> each other – she and me. you. hot skin writing
> skin. fluid edge, wick, wick. she draws me
> out. you she breathes, is where we meet.
> . . . it isn't dark but the luxury of being
> has woken you, the reach of your desire, reading
> us into the page ahead.

This "unwritten page" invites lesbian overwriting of a not yet imagined narrative. In the epigraph to this paper, Erin Mouré's ironic figure of the "lesbian ex machina" suggests the difficulty of writing lesbian love and avoiding the stereotypic and reductive. Marlatt's strategy writes the lesbian lover as a subject in the process of becoming, a space for reader and writer to affirm lesbian desire. As a result of this writerly orientation towards process, this lesbian figure is always multiple, achieved by "the reach of your desire."

Over the past few years of teaching lesbian writing to various English and Women's Studies classes, I've been astonished by the intelligence behind some students' resistance to the texts. When they begin to articulate their difficulties, significant revelations are at hand. For example in response to *Touch to My Tongue*, students have articulated their fear of "becoming lesbian if I let myself like the poems as much as I like them." This paradoxical response indicates the seductive power of the poetry to unsettle and defuse the culturally constructed prejudices and violence of heterosexism.

Other responses to Marlatt's lesbian writing are more complex to untangle. A recent critique by Lola Lemire Tostevin of Marlatt's "Not a Bad End" to *Ana Historic* conflates female desire with lesbian desire and describes it simply as "a writing of *jouissance* which cultivates, culminates in the pleasure principle and evokes the imaginative power of women writers" (38). Whose pleasure? one eagerly asks. Much lesbian writing invokes the female body, even if it is to deconstruct its gendered meanings, and it often concerns thinking through intimate care-giving relations with women, including, for many lesbians, the memory of the maternal as the site of primary affiliation – if only, as in the case of Nicole Brossard's *These Our Mothers*, to murder and write the womb (Brossard 21). While on the one hand, Tostevin assures the reader "lesbian-maternal texts are crucial in exploring the unrepresented, the unthought" (38), her critical investment in this statement is destabilized by what follows. She resists Marlatt's lesbian writing, and the tone of her critique intimates that in her eyes, Marlatt's text might be "prescriptive" or contaminated by "vulvalogocentrism." By refusing to recognize the strategic importance of some writing that might look like "vulvalogocentrism," a utopian feminine textual space, critics can easily preempt potentially important political and ethical imaginative spaces for lesbian readers and writers.[12]

Sue-Ellen Case notes that just as "feminism has moved to feminisms, . . . lesbian might move to lesbianS" (Case 13). This multiplicity of lesbian narratives is made complex in an interpretive extension of Audre Lorde's anti-racist feminist politics which rely, according to Teresa de Lauretis, not on the good will of liberal pluralism, but on "a conception of community . . . at once global and local – global in its inclusive and macro-political strategies, and local in its specific, micro-political practice" (de Lauretis 1990, 26).[13]

Just as our sexuality, lesbian or otherwise, is not natural or eternal, de Lauretis reminds us how our interpretive work is historically situated:

> representation is related to experience by codes that change historically and, significantly, reach in both directions: the writer struggles to inscribe experience in historically available forms of representation, the reader accedes to representation through her own historical and experiential context; each reading is a rewriting of the text, each writing a rereading of

(one's) experience. Each critic reads from a particular position, experiential but also historically available to her, and, moreover, a position chosen, or even politically assumed, from the spectrum of contemporary discourses on the relationship of feminism to lesbianism. (de Lauretis 1990, 23)

Having revised this essay from oral presentations to thesis to its publication here, it's easy to chart the changing limits of my own critical understanding which have been extended by the recent publication of several lesbian collections (see, for example, Jay and Stone). The increasing diversity of lesbian writing performs and challenges lesbian identities, making possible new lesbian reading and subject-positions. This political, ethical, and cultural project is accomplished not only by supporting the diverse writing practices which embody various lesbian histories, but through self-consciously developing critical and pedagogic practices which challenge the dominant culture's suppressive and silencing heterosexism. Marlatt's commitment to imagining "the page ahead" keeps us conscious of what is to be done.

Notes

I am grateful to Daphne Marlatt for permission to quote from her papers and for her spirited and generous conversations. My thanks to: Barbara Godard and Eli Mandel for introducing me to Marlatt's work; Pat Elliot and "The Bad Sisters," our feminist reading group which provided a supportive atmosphere of intellectual collectivity; Lorna Weir and Mariana Valverde who offered insightful commentary on lesbian issues; Evelyn Cobley and Shirley Neuman who made useful editorial suggestions on an earlier draft; the Humanities Division Special Collection, Simon Fraser University; and The National Library, especially Lorna Knight and Linda Hoad of the Literary Manuscripts Collection for their good-humoured assistance.

A version of this essay is part of my PhD dissertation "Citing Resistance: Vision, Space, Authority and Transgression in Canadian Women's Poetry" (York 1987). It developed from my original thesis proposal "A Feminist Poetics: The Embodied Language of Daphne Marlatt" (1984). Sections of this essay were presented: in "Amorous Sites: The Embodied Language and Double Signature in Daphne Marlatt's Lesbian Love Poems" at the Canadian Women's Studies Association and the Association of Canadian and Québec Literatures meetings, Montréal, June 1985; and in a reading of *Ana Historic*, "Hystorical Signs: Reading Daphne Marlatt's Writing *I*," at the University of Ottawa in 1987. The ACQL presentation happily developed a modest rabble-rousing reputation according to Dorothy Livesay who described it as having "utterly shattered some of the audience. Pulling out every sexual word about relationships between women in Marlatt's work" (Banting and Gunnars 13). The concept "writing/reading" originates in Brenda Carr's fine thesis.

¹ Pauline Butling's feminist critique in *Open Letter* (1990) of the BC Writers issue of the same periodical provides readers with a compensatory recuperation of women's contributions to *Tish*.

² The selected critical bibliography in editor Fred Wah's selection of Marlatt's writing *Net Work* (Vancouver: Talonbooks, 1980) lists only critical articles written by men. The first extended studies of Marlatt's work by women were published in 1985 (Cole and Godard).

³ An extended discussion of the problematic status of "essentialism" as a term used to dismiss certain feminist theorizing is developed in a special issue of *differences* 1.2 (1989). Diana Fuss (1989) attempts to develop a coincidence of opposites in her analysis of how "the tension produced by the essentialist/constructionist debate is responsible for some of feminist theory's greatest insights, that is, the very tension is constitutive of the field of feminist theory" (1).

⁴ French feminist Hélène Cixous originally spoke of the "exterritoriality of the feminine." The Cixous connection is traced by Josette Féral (53).

⁵ It should be noted that because women as a group are poor, some of these initiatives relied on government funding. As recent Mulroney government cutbacks to native and women's community and cultural organizations have indicated, these funding policies depend on the ideological good will of the state.

⁶ Rita Felski investigates what she calls "the feminist counter-public sphere" which "draws attention to the communicative networks, social institutions, and political and economic structures through which ideologies are produced and disseminated . . . (avoiding) the formalism and subjectivism of some feminist literary and cultural theory, which attempts to extrapolate grand political consequences from micrological textual excavations without any systematic account of the relationship between the two" (9).

⁷ This commentary is not intended to suggest that male critics/writers fled from Marlatt's lesbian work. However, all reviews of *Touch to My Tongue* but one were written by women, and a number were published in feminist or gay and lesbian periodicals (see Banting, Bennett, Dragland, Fitzgerald, Mouré, Nuse (1984/85), Parks, and Wright). On the other hand, Marlatt's most recent collaboration with Betsy Warland *Double Negative* has not been widely reviewed in Canadian periodicals, mainstream or otherwise. To my knowledge only feminist writers and critics Susan Knutson, Betsy Nuse (1988), and Carolyn Smart have reviewed the book, for American, lesbian feminist and local periodicals. Brenda Carr suggests this lack of national attention derives in part from the fact that collaborative work exceeds the autonomous authorial conventions which underpin literary studies.

⁸ While the topic of homophobia in the literary and academic community is too involved to develop in any depth here, it should be noted that a refereed Canadian poetry journal forwarded a reader's report to me which called the prose of this paper "soiled," a peculiar evaluative term contaminated by prudishness or heterosexism. Academics who introduce lesbian and gay material into their classrooms or who deliver conference papers on related topics are familiar with distancing responses in some listeners which range from aggressive resistance and harrassment to, in more

polite circles, dull glazed looks of incomprehension which one prefers to interpret as boredom.

9 Biddy Martin's historical analysis of lesbian identity politics informs this analysis and insists on the specificity and interrelationships of sexuality, gender, race, culture, and class: "lesbianism clearly does not figure as the exclusive ground of either identity or politics; however, it is neither divisible from nor subordinate to other identities" (94).

10 This organic quality of authorship extends to the critical community. Feminist literature and criticism is often bashed and battered by eager critics who see "feminist" as a reductive label. But feminist cultural criticism and the feminist movement have created a space for women to speak creatively and critically to each other. Over the past few years a number of excellent feminist PhD dissertations on Marlatt's work have enabled what one of the authors, Brenda Carr, calls "the spirit of feminist collaboration" (95). This creation of a feminist counter public sphere critiques the academy's competitive economy which depends upon authors as property relations. The radical implications of Marlatt's critical, creative, editorial, and pedagogic work to this new community is the subject of a longer study.

11 This relation between woman and hieroglyph is developed in Mary Ann Doane, "Film and the Masquerade: Theorising the Female Spectator," *Screen* 23.3-4 (1982): 74-87.

12 Thanks to Lorna Weir for alerting me to my own foreclosure of the lesbian imaginary in a discussion at the "Lesbian Culture" session with Daphne Marlatt, Betsy Warland, and Judy Springer at the Canadian Women's Studies Association meetings, University of Victoria, 26 May 1990. Pamela Banting analyses Tostevin's reading of Marlatt in terms of "translation poetics," the topic of her PhD dissertation, University of Alberta, 1990.

13 In foregrounding the "local," readers can map out critical routes from Marlatt's lesbian writing through the social history of lesbians in relation to the academy, state legislation, and community and cultural activism. (See for example: Lynne Fernie et al., eds. *Sight Specific: Lesbians and Representation*, and Stone, as well as articles on lesbian culture and politics in *Angles*, *Border/lines*, *Broadside* (which is no longer publishing), *Fireweed*, *Fuse*, *Kinesis*, and *Rites*. One can also trace how *Touch to My Tongue* connects with other collaborative work she has done. As well as the collaborative aspects of *The Story, She Said*, *How Hug a Stone*, and *Double Negative*, the National Library houses two unpublished collaborations with Penny Kemp and Roy Kiyooka. The visual elements of *Steveston*, *In the Month of Hungry Ghosts*, *How Hug a Stone*, and *Double Negative* invite comparative analyses with feminist visual artists who produce image/text work. In addition, Marlatt's own immigrant history and the "inside/outside reversals" she writes about in *Steveston* (1984, 92) link *Touch to My Tongue* with her travel narratives (*The Story, She Said*, *Zocalo*, *here & there*, *In the Month of Hungry Ghosts*, *How Hug a Stone*, and *Double Negative*), and the politics of the local landscapes inscribed in *Vancouver Poems*, *Our Lives*, and *Steveston*.

Works Cited

Athanassakis, Apoltolos N., trans. *The Homeric Hymns.* Baltimore: Johns Hopkins UP, 1976.
Banting, Pamela. "Powers of Seduction." Rev. of *Touch to My Tongue* and *Open Is Broken. Prairie Fire* 7.3 (1986): 148-52.
____, and Kristjana Gunnars. "Poetry Is For People: An Interview with Dorothy Livesay." *Prairie Fire* 7.3 (1986): 8-13.
Barthes, Roland. *Responsibility of Forms: Critical Essays on Music, Art and Representation.* New York: Hill and Wang, 1985.
____. *S/Z.* Trans. Richard Miller. New York: Hill and Wang, 1974.
Bennett, Donna. "Their Own Tongue." Rev. of *Touch to My Tongue, Open is Broken, Banff/Breaking, Animus. Canadian Literature* 107 (1985): 152-5.
Bowering, George. "Unexpected Objects." *The Contemporary Canadian Poem Anthology.* Vol. 1. Toronto: Coach House P, 1983. 1-3.
Brossard, Nicole. *The Aerial Letter.* Trans. Marlene Wildeman. Toronto: Women's Press, 1988.
____. *Lovhers.* Trans. Barbara Godard. Montreal: Guernica, 1986.
____. *Surfaces of Sense.* Trans. Fiona Strachan. Toronto: Coach House P, 1989.
____. *These Our Mothers: Or: The Disintegrating Chapter.* Trans. Barbara Godard. Coach House, 1983.
Butling, Pauline. "'Hall of Fame Blocks Women' Re/Righting Literary History: Women and BC Literary Magazines." *Open Letter* 7th ser. 8 (1990): 60-76.
Carr, Brenda. "Re-casting the Steveston Net: Re-calling the Invisible Women from the Margins." *Line* 13 (1989): 83-95.
____. "Daphne Marlatt's Salmon Texts – > Swimming/Jumping the Margins/Barriers," diss., U of Western Ontario, 1989.
Case, Sue-Ellen. *Performing Feminism: Feminist Critical Theory and Theatre.* Baltimore: Johns Hopkins UP, 1990.
Cixous, Hélène. "Castration or Decapitation?" Trans. Annette Kuhn. *Signs* 7.1 (1981): 41-55.
Cole, Christina. "Daphne Marlatt as Penelope, Weaver of Words: A Feminist Reading of *Steveston.*" *Open Letter* 6th ser. 1 (1985): 5-19.
Coward, Rosalind. *Female Desire: Woman's Sexuality Today.* London: Granada, 1984.
Davey, Frank. Letters. Humanities Division Special Collection, Simon Fraser University Library.
de Lauretis, Teresa. *Alice Doesn't: Feminism, Semiotics, Cinema.* Bloomington: Indiana UP, 1984.
____. "Sexual Indifference and Lesbian Representation." *Performing Feminisms: Feminist Critical Theory and Theatre.* Ed. Sue-Ellen Case. Baltimore: Johns Hopkins UP, 1990. 17-39.
Doane, Mary Ann. "Film and Masquerade: Theorizing the Female Spectator." *Screen* 23.3-4 (1982): 74-87.
Dragland, Stan. Rev. of *Touch to My Tongue. Journal of Canadian Poetry* (New Series) 1 (1986): 60-5.

Dybikowski, Ann et al. eds. *In the Feminine: Women and Words/Les Femmes et les Mots Conference Proceedings 1983.* Edmonton: Longspoon P, 1985.

Felski, Rita. *Beyond Feminist Aesthetics: Feminist Literature and Social Change.* Cambridge: Harvard UP, 1989.

Féral, Josette. "Towards a Theory of Displacement." Trans. Kristina Dragaitis. *SubStance* 32 (1981): 52-64.

Fernie, Lynne et al. eds. *Sight Specific: Lesbians and Representation.* Toronto: A Space, 1988.

Fitzgerald, Judith. "Women's vision comes of age." Rev. of *Touch to My Tongue* and *Open is Broken. The Toronto Star* 24 February 1985.

Fuss, Diana. *Essentially Speaking: Feminism, Nature and Difference.* New York: Routledge, 1989.

Gallop, Jane. "Beyond the *Jouissance* Principle." *Representations* 7 (1984): 110-5.

———. *The Daughter's Seduction: Feminism and Psychoanalysis.* Ithaca: Cornell UP, 1982.

———. "Snatches of Conversation." *Women and Language in Literature and Society.* Ed. McConnell-Ginet. New York: Praeger, 1980. 274-83.

Godard, Barbara. " 'Body I': Daphne Marlatt's Feminist Poetics." *American Review of Canadian Studies* 15.4 (1985): 481-96.

Gould, Karen. "The Censored Word and the Body Politic: Reconsidering the Fiction of Marie-Claire Blais." *Journal of Popular Culture* 15.3 (1981): 14-27.

Hirsch, Marianne. *The Mother/Daughter Plot: Narrative, Psychoanalysis, Feminism.* Bloomington: Indiana UP, 1989.

Irigaray, Luce. *This Sex Which Is Not One.* Trans. Catherine Porter. Ithaca: Cornell UP, 1985.

Jay, Karla and Joanne Glasgow. *Lesbian Texts and Contexts: Radical Revisions.* New York: New York UP, 1990.

Kristeva, Julia. *Desire in Language: A Semiotic Approach to Literature and Art.* Ed. Leon S. Roudiez. Trans. Thomas Gora, Alice Jardine, and Leon S. Roudiez. New York: Columbia UP, 1980.

Lemprière, Dr. J. "Pandora." *Lemprière's Classical Dictionary of Proper Names Mentioned in Ancient Authors.* 1788. London: Routledge and Kegan Paul, 1978.

Martin, Biddy. "Lesbian Identity and Autobiographical Difference[s]." *Life/Lines: Theorizing Women's Autobiography.* Ed. Bella Brodzki and Celeste Schenck. Ithaca: Cornell UP, 1988. 77-103.

Marlatt, Daphne. "Correspondences: Selected Letters." *Line* 13 (1989): 5-31.

———. "from somewhere." *here and there.* Lantzville: Island Writing Series, 1981.

———. Letter received by Janice Williamson. 22 July 1985.

———. *Selected Writing: Net Work.* Ed. Fred Wah. Vancouver: Talonbooks, 1980.

———. Rev. of Anais Nin, *Collages. Open Letter* 2nd ser. 2 (1972): 56-9.

———. *Steveston.* Vancouver: Talonbooks, 1974. Rpt. Edmonton; Longspoon P, 1984.

———. *Touch to My Tongue.* Edmonton: Longspoon P, 1984.

_____. *What Matters: Writing 1968-70.* Toronto: Coach House P, 1980.
Meese, Elizabeth. "Theorizing Lesbian : Writing – A Love Letter." *Lesbian Texts and Contexts.* Ed. Karla Jay and Joanne Glasgow. 70-87.
Montrelay, Michele. "Inquiry into Femininity." *m/f* 1 (1978): 83-102.
Mouré, Erin. *Furious.* Toronto: Anansi, 1988.
_____. *WSW (West South West).* Montreal: Véhicule, 1989.
Namjoshi, Suniti and Gillian Hanscombe. *Flesh and Paper.* Charlottetown: Ragweed P, 1986.
Nuse, Betsy. "The desert as lesbian landscape." Rev. of public reading of *Double Negative. Angles* (November, 1988): 16.
_____. "In Our Mother Tongue." *Broadside: A Feminist Review* 6.3 (December 1984/January 1985): 16.
Parks, Joy. "Magical erotica." *Rites* 1.7 (December 1984/January 1985): 19.
_____. "Breaking taboos." Rev. of *Touch to My Tongue* and *Open is Broken. Rites* 1.9 (1985).
_____. Rev. of *Touch to My Tongue* and *Open is Broken. Herizons* (March 1985): 44.
Silverman, Kaja. "History, Figuration and Female Subjectivity in Tess of the d'Urbervilles." *Novel* 18.1 (1984): 5-28.
Snitow, Ann, Christine Stansell, and Sharon Thompson. "Introduction." *Powers of Desire: The Politics of Sexuality.* New York: Monthly Review P, 1983.
Stein, Gertrude. *Lifting Belly.* Ed. Rebecca Mark. Tallahassee: Naiad, 1989.
Stone, Sharon Dale, ed. *Lesbians in Canada.* Toronto: Between the Lines, 1990.
Tostevin, Lola Lemire. "Daphne Marlatt: Writing in the Space That Is Her Mother's Face." *Line* 13, 1989: 32-9.
Warland, Betsy. *Open is Broken.* Edmonton: Longspoon P, 1984.
_____. *Proper Deafinitions: Collected Theorograms.* Vancouver: Press Gang, 1990.
Weir, Lorraine. "Daphne Marlatt's 'Ecology of Language.'" *Line* 13 (1989): 58-65.
Williamson, Janice. "Sounding a Difference: An Interview with Daphne Marlatt." *Line* 13 (1989): 47-56.
_____. "Speaking In and Of Each Other: An Interview with Daphne Marlatt and Betsy Warland." *Fuse* 8.5 (1985): 25-9.
Wittig, Monique. *The Lesbian Body.* Trans. David Le Vay. Boston: Beacon P, 1986.
Wright, Ellea. "Text and Tissue." Interview with Betsy Warland. *Broadside: A Feminist Review* 6.3 (December 1984/January 1985): 4-5.
Wollen, Peter. "Baubo." *subjects/objects* (1984): 119-23.

ED DYCK

Rhetoric and Poetry and Fred Wah

1. Rhetoric and Poetry

As Earle Birney once said, it's hard to separate myth and reality. If his point was that myth is itself a kind of reality, then his observation applies readily to the long and uneasy relationship between poetry and rhetoric. On the one hand, there is the tradition that poetry is not-rhetoric; another tradition suggests that poetry is a particular application of rhetoric; and the reality is that the intersection of poetry and rhetoric is neither empty nor total. This of course is not news – but the continuing prevalence of the belief that poetry is not rhetorical is hardly supported by the practice of poetry, both historically and in our time.

The relation between poetics and the poem is analogous to the relation between classical rhetoric and the oration: the former is, so to speak, the theory of the composition of the latter. If this sounds terribly prescriptive (and in the hands of the unskilled rhetor or poet it no doubt is) we might recall that for ancients art (theory, rhetoric, poetics) follows nature (practice, oration, poem), not the other way around. Lest the analogy be denied because of the difference between speaking and writing, Cicero reminds us that this separation too is theoretical not practical – "The pen is the best and most eminent author and teacher of eloquence, and rightly so" (*De Oratore* I.150).

The classical intersection between poetics and rhetoric, however, is more than an analogy. Aristotle's *Rhetoric* and *Poetics*, the arts of persuasion and mimesis, respectively, treat style as a common formal element in the production of discourse and epic. The rhetorical triad, ethos/logos/pathos (speaker/text/hearer), is not part of poetics; *a fortiori*, the theory of topoi, too, belongs only to rhetoric. The very basis of rhetorical persuasion (a topos is a simple formula – for example, "the greater and the lesser" – implicitly accepted by speaker and audience) would seem to be excluded from poetics on the grounds that it has nothing to do with mimesis.

But a funny thing happened on the way to the modern era. Style, as much as content (that is, manner, as much as matter), became subject to invention and grew to include matter as well as manner. Aristotle of course had said that the invention of good metaphors could not be taught, but the whole classical theory of style argued that style could. Kinds of style were related to the aims of rhetoric and to the rhetorical triad; the classical virtues of good style were identified; and ornaments were invented by reference to the lists of figures (Quintilian). By the time of Renaissance, poetics had become applied rhetoric: it retained its definition as a mimetic art; it adopted wholesale the aims of rhetoric and the theory of style; and it enlarged the lists of figures to include most of the classical topoi (Erasmus 1534 and Peacham 1577). For the Renaissance poet, style was *verborum et rerum*.

Still, the enterprise was bound to collapse, and collapse it did. Too many poets forgot to follow Peacham's injunction – "the onelye Ornamentes" are "wisdom and eloquence" together – and Locke's characterization of rhetoric as "that powerful instrument of error and deceit" (1690, X.34) applied as much to Renaissance poetry as to oratory. The straw that broke rhetoric's back, however, was not excess but rigidity: it could not accommodate a new poetic technique that emerged in the eighteenth and nineteenth centuries. The problem was not the *symbol qua* symbol: the writer who identified the symbol as the central poetic technique for his time based it squarely on the classical *pars pro toto* of synecdoche (Coleridge 1816). The problem was the symbol's link with the imagination. For Coleridge, the poet's (secondary) imagination creates symbols, the reader's imagination responds to symbols, and the poem is a symbolic construct (*Biographia Literaria*). But genius and taste, the exercise of symbolic imagination by poet and reader, just didn't seem to have much to do with synecdoche or rhetoric. The "duty and office of rhetoric," to recommend "reason" to the "imagination" (Bacon 535), was defeated by the Romantic promise of unity and transcendence by way of the imagination and the figure associated with it, the symbol.

The symbol went on to become absorbed into that centrepiece of poetics, the metaphor (Richards). Its association with unconscious processes (Coleridge) became an association with archetypes (Jung); its occasional iconicity prevented it from being treated as a linguistic sign (Saussure). And, despite some New Critical insights into the symbol's power to persuade (Wheelwright), it is still considered to be at best a "kind" of sign or a "mode" (Todorov, and Eco). And it continues to be confused with metaphor (Ricoeur).

Whatever the theoreticians have had to say, modern poetry has gone its symbolic (not metaphoric) way. The practice of Yeats, Eliot, Pound, Williams, Stevens, Olson, and so on, is evidently more symbolic than metaphoric, and the difference is easy to see in any given poem. When the vehicle and its tenor become unhinged, when the vehicle remains and the tenor disappears, then the boundary between metaphor and symbol has been crossed. The indeterminate signifier, in contemporary jargon, is the mark of the symbol: the symbol is a metaphor (vehicle) cut loose from fixity (its tenor). If this sounds suspiciously like Lacan, well it should: the symbol's association with the unconscious and the archetype parallels his association of the (unstable) signifier with unconscious processes and the emergence of repressed desires. Consider the *gyre*, the *great ball of crystal*, the *red wheelbarrow*, the *blue guitar*, and the *sea*!

Similarly, the rhetorical triad continues to be central to poetic practice. Speaker and hearer, writer and reader, are built into the language, are represented in the poem, are the locus of innumerable attempts at communication in poetry:

You! hypocrite lecteur! – mond semblable – mon frère!

What thou lovest well remains / the rest is dross.

> – Say it, no ideas but in things –

> They said, "You have a blue guitar,
> You do not play things as they are."

> I, Maximus, . . . tell you
> what is a lance . . . .

It is no secret that many readers of poetry recognize implicitly the role of the rhetorical triad – Jakobson's communication model, Barthes' crucifixion of the author and resurrection of the reader, Derrida's critique of the metaphysics of presence (ethos), Lacan's reading of Freud – the list goes on and on. All that's missing is the expletive word (*rhetoric*) that names what's present. Such reticence amounts to a terror of the word, a prissiness of idiom, rather like the pastor's insistence that his daughter has a "stomach" but no "belly." Rhetoric's presence is marked by (its name's) absence.

C.S. Peirce at the turn of the century had no such qualms. Rhetoric, he said, is that branch of semiotics whose function is to discover the processes by which "one sign gives birth to another, and especially one thought brings forth another" (2.229). And the *sign* (for example, any word) is a triple – representamen, object, interpretant (the word itself, its reference, and its meaning). Two aspects of the sign, its object (reference) and its interpretant (meaning), are *potential*: they grow by accretion, usage, and recursion. This potential measures the incompleteness, the instability, the unfixity, and the peculiar persuasive power of the word-as-symbol: the symbol, "growing" in the mind of the reader and writer of the poem, is part of the continuing production (endless play) of meaning(s).

Unlike Peirce, Charles Olson does suppress the expletive word: (1) "A poem is energy transferred from where the poet got it, by way of the poem itself, to . . . the reader" (1967, 16); (2) "Form is never more than an extension of content" (16); (3) "One perception must immediately and directly lead to a further perception" (17). Note the presence of the rhetorical triad with "energy" inserted into logos (1); a variation on the traditional relation between manner and matter (2); the hidden presence of the symbol within "perception" (3). As Olson (Maximus?) says, "I have had to learn the simplest things / last. Which made for difficulties" (*The Maximus Poems* n. pag.).

Poetry, then, cannot readily be separated from rhetoric. Each poem represents within itself some variation on the rhetorical triad; each poem invents its style from a living tradition of figuration; each poem argues by appealing to topoi old and new. The poem continues to engage the tradition of poetry and rhetoric of which it is a part, and the good poem will advance that tradition.

2. Fred Wah

It's a very long way from Aristotle to Fred Wah. But along that way stand the major influences on his practice as a poet: the Romantics, especially Coleridge (Bowering in Wah 1980, 12) and Keats (Wah 1985b, 214), and of course Charles Olson. In this tradition, as in Wah's poetry, is the trace of rhetoric. The relations among ethos, logos, and pathos constitute the basis of Fred Wah's poetic: narrator, text, and reader.

i. *Ethos: the self*

Wah is one of the most de-deconstructive poets writing in Canada today – which is to say that he takes his Derrida straight. Far from attempting to expunge presence from the text, Wah places a symbol of his presence at the very centre of that text. *Schwa* [ə] is precisely an instance of synecdoche, which as we have seen, is the rhetorical basis of Coleridge's definition of symbol, of Pierce's living sign, and of Olson's notion of perception. The "wholes" of which the symbol [ə] is or becomes a "part" are therefore various: the poet's own name; the poet's father; the poet's spiritual father; the poetics of the spiritual father; the breath itself; the sound of speech; and so on. To paraphrase Stephen Scobie, whose reading of Wah's *Breathin' My Name with a Sigh* (1981) I am here countering, "[i]t is not a letter but the absence of a letter" (62) *and the presence of Wah* that [ə] symbolizes. Thus:

> Breathin'
>
> My Name
>
> with a Sigh
>
> ə
>
> Fred Wah

(See also the unpaginated text, *passim*.)

To note that this technique is a representation (figuration) of ethos within the text is perhaps an understatement. The book might well have been titled "Breathin' My Name with a *Sign*." And the same representation reappears in *Music at the Heart of Thinking*:

> ([ə] Creekscape Looking Upstream)
>
> Fred Was. Fred War. Fred Wan. Fred Way.
> Fred Wash. Fred Wag. Fred Roy. Fred What.
> (*MHT* #55)

ii. *Logos: the topoi*

Definition: A topos is a (transitive) relation between two terms.

Examples: (1) "is greater than" (Aristotle); (2) metaphor, traditionally based on the topos "comparison" or "analogy," is the topos (vehicle, tenor) (Richards); (3) the symbol, traditionally based on synecdoche (part, whole), is an instance of the topos (signifier, signified).

If Bach is known today as a composer of canons, in his own time he was reviled for breaking the rules of canon. The point is that he knew the tradition intimately and enlarged it significantly. Fred Wah writes lyric poems in a radical rather than a conventional sense. Employing one of the oldest topoi known to poets, the topos that is the foundation of the lyric, (poetry, music), Wah substitutes the contemporary idiom of jazz to obtain a topos of both form and content in *Music at the Heart of Thinking*, illustrating precisely how the tradition can be made new (what, I ask, *is* the reference of Pound's *it*?!). Here is *MHT* #6 (I have *not* respected the line in the following reproduction of Wah's poem on the grounds that the prose poem really is a prose poem):

> Sentence the true morphology or shape of the mind including a complete thought forever little ridges little rhythms scoping out the total picture as a kind of automatic designing device or checklist anyone I've found in true thought goes for all solution to the end concatenates every component within the lines within the picture as a cry to represent going to it with the definite fascination of a game where the number of possibilities increases progressively with each additional bump Plato thought

I would call the figure of this poem a *tumble*. The poem is freely structured (the oxymoron is deliberate) – no punctuation, no line breaks, no sentence structures, apparently random associations. Yet the reader, tumbling through the poem, is in a controlled fall of words – sentence, morphology, shape, mind, thought, ridges, rhythms, picture, design, solution, end, concatenate, component, line, cry, represent, game, and so on – which lands him on earth with a bump ("Plato thought"). The poem's tumble is a free sentence; the shape of a mind thinking is the shape of jazz.

Wah's predilection for jazz is well known. His preface to *MHT* repeats some of his earlier associations of jazz with *ostranenie* (making strange) and *negative capability*, and extends these to the "practice [of] . . . tai chi while drunk." But a poet's pronouncements on his art are likely to lead his readers astray – especially if these pronouncements are taken at face value.

> Certainly the jazz model of a freely-moving line playing off of and against the bound chord progressions showed me the delight of distortion and surprise. (Wah 1985b, 214)

"Freely-moving," "playing," "delight," "distortion," and "surprise" evoke the *dis-order* strengthened by the associations in the earlier article and the later preface. In the same sentence, however, is the matter of "the jazz model," "the bound chord progressions," and, in the preface, the business of "a series of improvisations." That is, *dis-order* is unthinkable without *order*, on which it depends to establish itself as different and new. Even the drunken monk is "*im*balanced"; he does not "fall over" but "confuse[s his enemies] by his unpredictability."

If Wah's topos, the basis of his lyric art, is specifically (poetry, jazz), and if jazz is ordered dis-order, then the topos assumes the form (poetry, order/not-order). But this is an instance of a very old topos which Aristotle called "opposites" and which became a fundamental characteristic of Renaissance thought and poetry. Topoi of the form (A, B/not-B) include such figures as irony and paradox, figures which everyone will agree are part of poetry even in our beleaguered time. My freshman English students, for example, were quick to point out the irony of *MHT* #6: a second reading readily suggests that what Plato thought (B) (that is, what the poem [A] states and re-states) may not be what the poet thinks (not-B).

With paradox, however, we approach (although from a different direction altogether) the fashionable centre of contemporary (read postmodern) thought. The heritage of this figure includes its location within the topos "opposites," its relation to figures such as *aporia*, and its role in the problems of self-reference and *undecidability*. On the one hand, paradox leads directly to undecidability: there are statements in the restricted language of mathematical logic which are demonstrably neither provable nor disprovable (hence, paradoxical or undecidable), yet are intuitively true (hence, the logical system is incomplete) (Goedel's "Incompleteness Theorem"). It is a matter of fact that such statements are almost invariably self-referential (Brown; Martin). On the other hand, paradox leads directly to the mysteries of "truth" and its concomitants, especially "knowing" and "meaning." If this is the case for "restricted" languages such as mathematical logic, it is also the case for their enlargements such as "natural" English.

So paradox hovers wherever there is a binary of the form B/not-B. Consider the following poems from *MHT* (italics added):

Don't *think thinking* without *heart* (#1)

think notation *of the mind* ahead of the writing (#2)

once *thinking as feeling thought*
then becomes simple and there
crows fly in no pattern
through the fir and spruce . . . (from "Another MHT")

The first ten poems of the book are full of paradoxes: mind and body, stop and go, past and present, before and during and after. Each paradox, felt if not consciously recognized as such, contributes to the poems' effect on the reader, an effect of dislocation leading to undecidability. What keeps the lot (and the reader) from flying apart is that rhythm itself is proferred as the resolution of paradox. The apparent split between the objective (the poem) and the subjective (the experience) is healed in poem's cadence (Wah 1986, 114-15). This is rhetoric speaking through the music of thinking. Again, jazz.

Other sections of *MHT*, however, do not focus as intensely on paradox and consequently have rather different effects on the reader. Wah himself has attested to the centrality of *place* in his work (see Banting) first pointed out by Bowering (Wah 1981, 19-21). We may note that *place* translates *topos*, and that for Wah (as for his mentor Olson) place is a rhetorical device used to generate poems. Of course, literal references to place abound in the poems – whole books (for example, *Waiting for Saskatchewan*) are invented out of place. But the ultimate place for Wah is the language itself. Since language is "the true practice of thought," his topos is fitly (the rhetor would say decorously) identical with the mind – not the mind in *stasis*, but the mind in *process* (a process which, paradoxically but rightly, is full of "stops" or unstable moments of stasis). Thinking. Jazz.

A particular example of how this works (*MHT* #22):

> Always think thinking inside myself no place without death Kwakiutl song sings or watch sit scramble and catch last blue Pacific horizon no end to the complete thought transference of which the words "circling eyes" Mao knew this is the life writing questions even every rock etched in wonder sometimes the song feels like the master paradigm or river we return to with a sigh the archipelago syntagmed "empty from breathing" but the body as a place that is as a container has suddenness so the politics of dancing is a dead giveaway to the poet's "nothing will have taken place but the place."

The topos (poetry, place), given that place=topos, becomes (poetry, topos), an utterly self-referential statement that is literally present in the poem's last line. But the presence in the same poem of references to "real" place (including the body) saves the poem from mere tautology. The implication is rather that place is a paradox, is both reference and topos, and from that paradox the reader may recoil in dislocation as s/he is drawn to it in familiarity.

There are obviously other topoi in Wah's work, both familiar and strange, and one that deserves mention is repetition. "Repetition by nature desire and need becomes a relief or by jargon animals," says Wah (*MHT* #7). One can, of course, never mount the same animal twice, and so repetition is paradoxically also its Other, namely variation. This is to say that repetition is improvisation, which leads us back to the jazz of thinking. Repetition is related also to the production of meaning (that is, to signification) and therefore to the symbol.

In *Waiting for Saskatchewan*, a book which "repeats" parts of *Breathin' My Name with a Sigh* and reprints the very beautifully, privately printed *Grasp the Sparrow's Tail* (1982), the title poem innocently refers to the horse:

waiting for Saskatchewan to appear for me again over the edge horses led to
the huge sky the weight and colour of it over the mountains as if the mass
owed me. (3)

Later on, Wah offers up three "Horses": horse as a tai chi exercise ("Doing the horse" 25), "horse as father" and "as in any of us" (26), and horse as play ("Horsing around" 27). Horse as father and figure leads off the "Grasp the Sparrow's Tail" section of the book (31-56): "You never did the 'horse' like I do now," says the narrator, but the poem which follows shows the father doing the "horse" all his life. In the series called "Elite" (59-71), the narrator addresses the father in apostrophe: "Did you ever ride a horse?" (65), and we are back to innocent reference.

Perhaps it does not matter what we call Wah's use of *horse*, but the word (symbol, sign) runs like a current through the poems, erasing but never destroying its familiar symbolic value (Pegasus and poetry) as it accrues further signification. Repetition: desire, need, relief, jargon, animals. We might call this "doing the horse" of *horse*.

iii. *Pathos: the reader*

The reader is, in fact, inseparable from the narrator and the text, or, as the ancients would have said, logos presupposes ethos and pathos. For a topos to appear in and function persuasively through a text means that the narrator and the reader have both implicitly (unconsciously?) accepted the topos as a fit instrument of persuasion. Alternatively, the topoi define the reader as well as the narrator. The reader presupposed by and figured in Wah's poetry, therefore, is the reader who will be persuaded by topoi such as (poetry, jazz), (jazz, thought), (A, B/not-B), (poetry, place), and so on, as well as by their attendant figures (which are often inseparable from the topoi).

Similarly, the reader presupposed by and figured in these poems is one who will be persuaded by the ethos represented in the text. If the narrator's use of [∂] to represent himself leaves you cold, you won't like *Breathin' My Name with a Sigh*; if the narrator's "doing the horse" while *Waiting for Saskatchewan* seems irrelevant, you will dismount; if the musical signature and the citation of community (other authors, other texts) in the preface and poems of *Music at the Heart of Thinking* excludes you too emphatically, you won't enjoy the poems' tumbles. You won't, in short, be persuaded by what the poems say or by my admittedly rhetorical argument. Representation of ethos and pathos in logos doesn't always succeed. In rhetoric as in poetry. As in life.

Works Cited

Aristotle. *Rhetoric* and *Poetics*. Ed. Jonathan Barnes. *The Complete Works of Aristotle*. Revised Oxford Translation. 2 vols. Princeton: Princeton UP, 1984.

Bacon, Francis. *De Augmentis Scientarium*. Ed. John Robertson. *The Philosophical Works of Francis Bacon*. London: George Routledge and Sons, 1905.

Banting, Pamela. "An Interview with Fred Wah." *Brick* 27 (Spring 1986): 13-7.

Barthes, Roland. "The Death of the Author." *Image-Music-Text*. Trans. Stephen Heath. New York: Hill and Wang, 1977. 142-8.

Brown, Harold. "Self-Reference in Logic and *Mulligan Stew*." *Diogenes* 118 (Summer 1982): 121-42.

Cicero. *De Oratore*. Books 1 and 2. Revised ed. Trans. E.W. Sutton and H. Rackham. The Loeb Classical Library. Harvard UP, 1948.

Coleridge, S.T. *The Statesman's Manual* (1816). Ed. R.J. White. *Lay Sermons. The Collected Works of Samuel Taylor Coleridge*. Vol. 6. Princeton: Princeton UP, 1972. 1-114.

____. *Biographia Literaria*. Ed. John Beer. London: Dent, 1982.

Derrida, Jacques. *Of Grammatology*. Trans. Gayatri Chakravorty Spivak. Baltimore: Johns Hopkins UP, 1976.

Eco, Umberto. *Semiotics and the Philosophy of Language*. Indiana UP, 1984.

Erasmus, Desiderius. *De Copia*. Ed. C.R. Thompson. *Collected Works of Erasmus. Literary and Educational Writings 2*. U of Toronto P, 1978.

Goedel, Kurt. "Ueber formal unentscheidbare Saetze der *Principia Mathematica* und verwandter Systeme I." *Monatschrift der Mathematische Physik* 38 (1931): 173-98.

Lacan, Jacques. *Ecrits: A Selection*. Trans. A. Sheridan. London: Tavistock, 1977.

Locke, John. *An Essay Concerning Human Understanding (1690)*. Ed. Peter Nidditch. Oxford UP, 1975.

Martin, R.L., ed. *The Paradox of the Liar*. Yale UP, 1970.

Olson, Charles. *The Maximus Poems*. London: Cape Goliard P, 1960.

____. *Selected Writings*. Ed. Robert Creeley. New York: New Directions, 1967.

Peacham, Henry. *The Garden of Eloquence (1577)*. Meunston, England: The Scolar Press, 1971.

Peirce, C.S. *The Collected Papers of C.S. Peirce*. Vol. 2. Eds. Charles Hartshorne and Paul Weiss. Harvard UP, 1960.

Quintilian. *Institutio Oratoria*. 4 vols. Trans. H.E. Butler. The Loeb Classical Library. New York: G.P. Putnam and Sons, 1921-22.

Richards, I.A. *The Philosophy of Rhetoric*. Oxford UP, 1936.

Ricoeur, Paul. *The Rule of Metaphor*. Trans. R. Czerny. U of Toronto P, 1977.

Saussure, Ferdinand de. *Course in General Linguistics*. Trans. W. Baskin. New York: McGraw-Hill, 1966.

Scobie, Stephen. "Surviving the Paraph-raise." *Open Letter* 6th ser. 5/6 (Summer-Fall 1986): 49-68.

Todorov, Tzvetan. *Theories of the Symbol*. Trans. C. Porter. Cornell UP, 1982.

Wah, Fred. 1980. *Selected Poems*. Ed. George Bowering. Vancouver: Talonbooks.

____. 1981. *Breathin' My Name with a Sigh*. Vancouver: Talonbooks.

____. 1985a. *Waiting for Saskatchewan*. Winnipeg: Turnstone P.

____. 1985b. "Making Strange Poetics." *Open Letter* 6th ser.2/3 (Summer-Fall): 213-21.

____. 1986. "Subjective as Objective in the Lyric Poetry of Sharon Thesen." *Essays on Canadian Writing* 32: 114-21.

____. 1987. *Music at the Heart of Thinking*. Red Deer College P.

Wheelwright, Philip. *The Burning Fountain*. Rev. ed. Indiana UP, 1968.

LIANNE MOYES

Writing, the Uncanniest of Guests:
Daphne Marlatt's How Hug a Stone

In the recent issue of *Line* magazine devoted to the writing of Daphne Marlatt, several critics comment on the notion of origins implied by Marlatt's texts. Dennis Cooley argues: "Marlatt is aware of positions . . . that see language as constituting us. She has said so on more than one occasion. But in her writing she is drawn even more, I think, to quite a different sense of language. She forever searches for origins, beginnings, sources – always for realities that are prior to language" (72). Frank Davey identifies similar preoccupations in *How Hug a Stone*'s search for the mother:

> This woman is located in silence, "between the words" that elsewhere the scripting authorities of "father, teacher, doctor, dentist, priest" control. She is "source" (69), the one who writes "in monumental stones," "longstanding matter in the grass, settled hunks of mother crust," the "stone (mother)," "the old slow pulse beyond word" (75). (44)

And Lola Lemire Tostevin asserts that "If each of Marlatt's books is an additional ring in the progression of a dynamic circular chain that grows and moves from past to present, each book also conveys a nostalgia for a source, an origin" (35). As these critics suggest, some of Marlatt's most recent texts and many of her statements about her writing risk centring feminist debate in terms of traditional symbols of femininity. I would like to argue, however, that in *How Hug a Stone* origins are marked by the difference of writing, inscribed in the order of the "always already written." The text has a stake in exploring the largely unrepresented and perhaps unrepresentable *material* contingencies of beginnings. Many of the origins that regulate the play of differences in dominant discourse have referents in the female body; and the use of the female body as a prop both totalizes and elides the female subject. *How Hug a Stone* challenges this paradoxical totalization and elision not only by foregrounding the appropriate, synecdochal representation of the female body, but by producing a self-differentiated female subject.

As Cooley, Davey, and Tostevin point out, positing an origin establishes a locus of truth outside, or prior to, discourse. In Jacques Derrida's terms, "it has always been thought that the center, which is by definition unique, constituted that very thing within a structure which while governing the structure, escapes structurality" ("Structure, Sign, and Play" 279). So, although an origin would seem to hold the possibility of a space outside oppressive structures, it is nevertheless *part of* those structures. Rather than generating a structure, a centre is retroactively constructed by a structure to ground the play of differences and to lend closure. Drawing on this critique of origins, the critics mentioned above take the position that an origin does not exist as such, that an origin is "not a fixed locus but a function, a sort of nonlocus in which an infinite number of sign-substitutions came into play" ("Structure, Sign, and Play" 280). This decentring of origins is enabling for feminist thought, and, in the work of Luce Irigaray and others, there is ongoing consideration of the ways in which gender issues inflect the critique of origins. It is not enough, these feminists suggest, to critique the metaphysical principle of origin and remain indifferent to questions of gender. With this in mind, I will attend to the specific inscriptions of such terms as "mother" and "source" and to the particular terms of the speaker's "return" in *How Hug a Stone*.

a topographic mime

Before turning to Marlatt's text, it is useful to outline the ways in which Irigaray reframes the Derridean critique. In the "Plato's *Hystera*" section of *Speculum of the Other Woman*, Irigaray attends to the origins that regulate the reproduction of ideal forms in the Platonic theory of representation. The metaphor of the cave, she argues, provides the foundations of the theory. Yet as the *site* of representation, the walls onto which the shadows of ideal forms are cast, the cave is itself unrepresentable. It functions as an origin, a "fundamental ground" that is "paradoxically, *within* the structure and *outside* it" ("Structure, Sign, and Play" 279). For Irigaray as for Derrida, the centre cannot be privileged over that which inscribes and so repeats it. Irigaray's text is a *répétition* of the Platonic text in both senses of the word: a rehearsal and a reproduction. As such, it both precedes and exceeds the "original." On the level of the enunciation, the process of producing meaning, "Plato's *Hystera*" breaks down the origin-repetition distinction and allows repetition to proliferate *difference* rather than likeness. The text's "return" to Plato, then, confounds any attempt to recuperate an original act of mimesis:

> A *topographic mime*, but one whose process of repetition, reproduction, is always already multiply doubled up, divided, scaled down, demented, with no possible recourse to a first time, a first model. For if the cave is made in the image of the world, the world – as we shall see – is equally made in the image of the cave. In cave or "world" all is but the image of an image. For this cave is always already an attempt to re-present another cave, the *hystera*, the mold which silently dictates all replicas, all possible forms, all possible relation of forms and between forms, of any replica. (246)

By (mis)reading Plato's metaphor as a figure for both womb and representation, Irigaray's text emphasizes the intrication of representation and reproduction.

For Irigaray, the womb or *hystera* is not "outside" representation; it is never an undifferentiated locus of truth or essence. Rather, as the invisible screen onto which the visible is projected, it is both outside and inside representation. In an ironic miming of the position which the Platonic text offers her, Irigaray extends this analysis to the elided subjectivity of the woman-mother:

> She (is) pure mimicry. Which is always the case for inferior species, of course. Needed to define essences, her function requires that she herself have no definition. Neither will she have any distinct appearance. Invisible therefore. As the father is invisible? And the origin of the visible escapes representation. *She is in excess of any identification of presence.* The "beyond" of the mother, however, cannot be measured alongside that of the father. The two must be separated to avoid conflicts of pre-existence and a crisis of authority. (307, my emphasis)

Whereas Derrida posits a de-centred system, Irigaray insists that there is always already *more than one* origin, that there is an origin to which the system is always already blind. At the same time that the proliferating centre of Truth, Presence, Vision, Sun, God, Father regulates the reproduction of forms in Plato's text, the cave grounds the play of the entire "specular genealogy" (262). Both "origins" stand in an excessive or supplementary relation to the genealogical system, yet Derrida's de-centred structure, like Plato's centred structure, accounts for only one. And as long as this other "origin" remains unacknowledged, the woman-mother cannot stand on the ground of representation; she must constitute it.

Irigaray's critique of the theories of representation inaugurated by Plato's text turns on the issue of morphology – that is, the forms or meanings that male and female bodies acquire within representation. As the "unformed, 'amorphous' origin of all morphology" (265), the womb is not an ideal form to be reproduced mimetically but the empty space in which all other forms take shape. "Plato's *Hystera*" seeks to produce a different morphology; as Anna Munster suggests, "In a style which draws attention to the materiality of discourse, its sounds, its ambiguities, its traversal by desire, Irigaray plays with a different form of/for sexuality" (122). For example, the rhyming French words *antre* (cave) and *ventre* (womb) foreground the fact that the cave-womb connection operates within a system of differences. If Plato's *antre* can be read as a trace of *ventre*, then the apparently absent womb is always already a factor in the economy of meaning of Plato's parable. At the same time that Irigaray's text presents the womb as the corporeal referent of the cave metaphor, it presents reference as far more complex than the theory of mimesis would suggest. For example, it unveils the various substitutions and displacements in the Platonic text that elide the female subject: a synecdoche that takes a part for the whole, or rather a body part for the subject; a metaphor that substitutes the cave for this part; and another metaphor that displaces the terms entirely so that the cave stands for representation.

Irigaray's "Plato's *Hystera*," then, complicates the reading of *HHS* that takes the text to be a search for "origins, beginnings, sources . . . prior to language" (Cooley 72). Marlatt's text is attentive to the paradigms of representation and the gender-specific morphologies that locate the woman-mother in silence; but silence is not the only space that the text constructs for her. *HHS* returns, again and again, to the contradiction of *writing* in/from the position of "monumental stones" (75):

> . . . that is the limit of the old story, its ruined circle, that is not how it ended or we have forgotten parts, we have lost sense of the whole. left with a script that continues to write our parts in the passion we find ourselves enacting . . . . our "selves" our inheritance of words. wanting to make us new again: to speak what isn't spoken, even with the old words.
>
> although there are stories about her, versions of history that are versions of her, & though she comes in many guises she is not a person, she is what we come through to & what we come out of, ground & source. the space after the colon, the pause (between the words) of all possible relation. (73)

Taken out of context and "at its word," this excerpt seems to lament the loss of a "whole" story/representation of the woman-mother or to privilege the womb as a site of truth. I would argue, however, that here the woman-mother and the female body are differentiated because discursively mediated. The text rethinks silence in terms of discourse – in terms of "pauses," spaces, or differences, rather than positive terms or centres. Just as Plato's cave is a necessary but unrepresentable *part of* representation so also silence, empty space, temporal and spatial gaps are a necessary but unrepresentable part of verbal discourse. At the same time that the text works toward a decentring of structure, it maintains an analysis of the material contingencies of discourse. For example, the play on the word "parts" emphasizes that the signifier is always in excess of its signified. In the context of figures such as "*her tomb-body*" (72) in the previous poem, "parts" relates to the body as well as to representation; in this way, the text engages the problematic which Irigaray identifies in "Plato's *Hystera*." Further, by making the body-representation connection through "parts," a word that is metonymically related to both "body" and "representation," Marlatt's text points to the ways in which the female body grounds the privileged metaphors of the discourse of origins.

foreign members of the family

A number of the issues discussed in connection with Irigaray's text—the order of the always already written, the need for a gender-specific critique of origins, and the woman-mother as both absent and extra – can be traced through *HHS*'s play on the words "guest," "host," and "ghost." These and related words are collocated with topoi such as returning home, home ground, the earth, and the speaker's relation to mother and to child. Such topoi, it would seem, come dangerously close to re-inscribing the traditional domain of the feminine. Yet in the process of *re*-inscribing or repeating them, Marlatt's text, like Irigaray's, produces a margin of difference. Consider the following excerpt from "grounded in the family":

> i thought i was free, turning, wild at the bottom of the garden where the lady lies. stone white she hears our steps, faint brouhaha on the winds of the years,

> turbulent turning wing flutter, worm twist, back in our hands the beginning
> we took for the end. she is serene. she sees us, *ghos-ti-*, not ghostly nor free—
> reciprocally obliged. host & guest fixed in the one script, the prescribed line
> of relationship. (17-18)

The words "host" and "guest" share the etymological root "*ghos-ti-*," meaning stranger, enemy, guest, host – that is, someone with whom one has reciprocal duties of hospitality. What appears to be an oppositional difference, then, is more appropriately termed a *relational* difference. Nevertheless, "host" and "guest" sit uncomfortably together when one considers the duplicitous meanings of each. "Guest" has the sense of stranger – even enemy – parasite, and friendly visitor entertained at one's house. A "host" is a gathering for war, a heavenly multitude, an organism that affords lodgment to a parasite, as well as one who offers hospitality. These various meanings for both terms are everywhere co-present in *HHS*, thereby problematizing any attempt to choose one over the others in a given context.

The poem "grounded in the family" plays out the enmity and the hospitality, the familiar and the strange in the guest-host relation. In the excerpt above, the speaker describes her step-brother as "host" and the step-brother's mother as "she to whom we were hostage then, hostess & mother" (17). Further, the host lures the bodies of moths "heavy, beating against the walls," and "fix[es] them in their families . . . wing-pulled-open, pinned on a piece of cotton" (17). Read in relation to this metaphor for the violence of dominant family structures, the line "host & guest fixed in the one script, the prescribed line of relationship" seems more coercive and singular than polysemic. Yet it becomes more difficult to regulate the line's meaning if one recognizes in the words "script" and "prescribed" the Latin verb *scribere* (to write). The words "host & guest fixed in the one script" can be read as a comment on the undecidability of the script or written word, on the fact that one word can produce meanings that conventionally are mutually exclusive. In short, the potentially coercive singularity of "the one script" is undone by the text's attention to the way in which writing exceeds itself.

The reading of "the one script" is partly a function of the words that follow in the syntagmatic chain: "host & guest fixed in the one script, the prescribed line of relationship." In this context, "prescribed" modifies "one script." The verb "prescribe" means to write before, in the beginning, first, as well as to lay down as a rule, to order or direct, and to limit or confine. "Prescribed" can be read as that which is "*written* before" and this "always already written" has at least two meanings in the context of *HHS*. The first is that of a coercive patriarchal script, the meaning that perhaps is most readily available in the immediate context of the visit with the step-brother. The second meaning of "always already written" locates writing in/ as the "beginning." Here, writing is understood as a system of traces that signifies not through positive terms but through differences. The "origin" that is writing is "non-full, non-simple, structured and differentiating" (Derrida 1982, 11); it is *arche* (origin) without *telos* (end) or, in *HHS*'s terms, "the beginning we took for the end" (17). In fact, Derrida uses the word "origin" with the qualification that the word is no longer suitable:

> In attempting to put into question these traits of the provisional secondariness of the substitute [writing], one would come to see something like an originary *différance*; but one could no longer call it originary or final in the extent to which the values of origin, archi-, *telos, eskhaton*, etc. have always denoted presence – *ousia, parousia*. (Derrida 1982, 9)

To return to the line from Marlatt's text, the substitution of "always already written" for "prescribed" produces the reading "host & guest fixed in the one script, the [always already written] line of relationship." Irigaray's "Plato's *Hystera*" plays with a similar ambiguity when it describes the metaphor of the cave-womb as a "silent prescription for metaphysics" (243) – that is, an unrepresentable but always already written form which under-writes all other forms.

HHS points to yet another meaning for "prescribed" by foregrounding the prefix "pre-," the principal element that distinguishes "script" from "prescribed." If one places emphasis on the prefix and its temporal specificity, then "prescribed" has the sense of that which is pre-, or prior to, the written. This meaning seems to be in keeping with the classical view of writing as secondary to an originary speech and a lost plenitude of meaning. Substituting "prior to the written" for "prescribed" in Marlatt's text, however, produces the reading "host & guest fixed in the one script, the [prior to the written] line of relationship." The notion that the script is prior to the written implies that writing is preceded only by writing; no underlying principle outside the field of writing regulates the play of differences. This reading is supported by another series of words: "[to] be unnamed, walk unwritten, de-scripted, un-described" (35). Each word in this chain carries the mark of the words that precede and that follow. For example, the word "de-scripted" has the sense of both "*un*written" and "*de*scribed" – written or represented by words. "Un-de-scribed" further registers the ambivalence of the prefix "de-" and overdetermines meaning with a double negative. In this way, the sequence troubles the reading that suggests that the speaker longs to be free of the script. It also explores the paradoxical status of the female subject as unwritten without being prior to writing.

In both of the sequences discussed above, syntax works toward a general destabilization of the script; it operates according to a supplementary order of logic, accreting elements that are both "extra" and "missing." The addition of "prescribed" and "described," for example, marks the "script" as non-unitary and in need of modification. Further, the fact that the "script" is undone by a word related to it marks it as self-contradictory, both familiar and strange. This instability of meaning within families of words, an instability that is played out along the syntagmatic axis, signals the intrication of word relations and family relations, of enunciation and enounced. The "prescribed line of relationship," then, refers simultaneously to the speaker's sense of a fragmented genealogy, to the elaboration of the enunciation along the syntagmatic axis, and to the radical continuity of the guest-host relation.

ghost-writing

In the excerpt from "grounded in the family," the words "guest" and "host" are joined by a third, "*ghos-ti-*." In the sequence "she sees us, *ghos-ti-*, not ghostly nor free," "not ghostly" refers, among other things, to the fact that "*ghos-ti-*" is *not* the etymological root of "ghostly." The two terms are not, however, unrelated. Their phonic and graphic resemblance is strong enough to bear remark within the context of the poem; in fact, on the level of sound, the phoneme [l] is the only thing which distinguishes the two terms. "Not ghostly," then, can be read as a sign of the text's attention to the way in which phonemic difference produces meaningful distinctions. Tostevin has questioned the use of etymology in Marlatt's texts on the grounds that it places ultimate authority in the *etymon*, the true, original form or signification of a word (35). The *ghos-ti-*/ghostly example, however, shows that etymological roots do not have absolute jurisdiction over signification in HHS. Root words are rather a site for word-play, a way of disturbing the historical and institutional privileging of certain forms and meanings.

As if in defiance of its roots, "ghostly" makes a second appearance in connection with "guest" and "host":

> perched on the rocks, birdlike, picking over small life in tidal pools, dead crabs floating by, or live & gone from the hand, i see my ghostly child in him, not gone & not quite him, as she in me, mother, grandmother, grand, full grown we stand in, not for. that earth takes back what is given, *ghos-ti*, hostly & hostile at once. *guests will be provided with a hot water bottle*, immaculately shining bath, long boat, long barrow at the end of the day's rambles. (49)

Just as "*ghos-ti*" calls up "ghostly," "ghostly" calls up "hostly." In fact, the words "guest-ghost-host" form a chain in which "host" differs from "ghost" by virtue of the phoneme [g], and "ghost" differs from "guest" by virtue of the substitution of [o] for [E]. The relation between each link in the chain is characterized by both resemblance and difference, familiarity and strangeness. As Derrida argues, "every concept is inscribed in a chain or in a system within which it refers to the other, to other concepts, by means of the systematic play of differences" (Derrida 1982, 11). Both "*ghos-ti*" and "ghostly" operate as third terms that draw attention to this chain and disrupt any unequivocal reading of the guest-host binary; "*ghos-ti*" undoes the binary on the diachronic level and "ghostly" undoes it on the synchronic level. Both terms signal the difference within "guest" and "host," the shadow-presence of meanings that will not let the pair settle into a tidy opposition.

Like "guest" and "host," "ghost" is multiple within itself. It can be defined variously as the life principle or vital spark; a disembodied soul, especially in the soul of a dead person believed to be an inhabitant of the unseen world or to appear to the living in bodily likeness; a person; a corpse, a mark or visible sign left by something dead, lost, or no longer present; a faint shadowy outline or semblance, a trace; a false image. "Ghost" defies a number of the antinomies that structure

Western thought: death-life, body-soul, embodied-disembodied, visible-invisible, presence-absence, truth-falsity. Like the woman-mother in Irigaray's reading of Plato, "ghost" is in excess of dominant meanings. Further, the notion of ghost as trace, of trace as ghost, is suggestive for a consideration of writing in *HHS*. It suggests, for example, that the linguistic sign does not stand for a presence but rather marks something dead, lost, or no longer present. Or as Derrida writes: "each element appearing on the scene of presence, is related to something other than itself, thereby keeping within itself the mark of the past element, and already letting itself be vitiated by the mark of its relation to the future element" (Derrida 1982, 13).

This ghostly difference-within is foregrounded in Marlatt's text. The sequences "dead crabs floating by, or live & gone from the hand" and "that earth takes back what is given, *ghos-ti*, hostly and hostile at once" are generated through addition or doubling rather than through opposition. The earth, for example, takes *and* gives; it is marked by the contradictory coherence of *ghos-ti*. Further, the crabs are dead *or* live, live *and* gone. In this chiasmus, the addition of each element reframes the one previous in such a way that both and neither are true. Through a form of supplementary logic, death and life, presence and absence, friend and enemy are added to one another and replace one another instead of being opposed to one another. As Barbara Johnson explains:

> The logic of the supplement wrenches apart the neatness of the metaphysical binary oppositions. Instead of "A is opposed to B" we have "B is both added to A and replaces A." A and B are no longer opposed, nor are they equivalent. Indeed, they are no longer even equivalent to themselves. They are their own differance from themselves. (xiii)

These differential relations structure the text's presentation of family relations: "i see my ghostly child in him, not gone & not quite him, as she in me" (49). Each member of the family differs not only from other members but also within her/himself. The speaker sees in her child both herself and her difference from herself, and in herself, both her mother and her mother's self-difference.

In *HHS*, the mother is not a person as such; she is a subject written, a subject writing. Double within herself, the mother is one of the ghosts of the text. In fact, *HHS* is a "ghost story" of the mother in more than one sense. On the level of the enounced – that is, the events of the story – the mother haunts the speaker's return to England. And on the level of the enunciation – the process or production of the narrative – the mother can be traced in writing, in the contradictions of the mother writing the mother, and in the excess of signifiers such as "ghost." In the words of Marlatt's text, the mother is "*ubilaz*, exceeding the proper limit . . . for either the dead or the living" (68). Standing on the threshold of life and death, "blurring distinction between corpus & corpse" (72), she is a liminal figure, a figure situated between the poles of binary oppositions, a figure in both linguistic and corporeal terms. The mother is neither a lost presence for which the speaker longs nor a body outside discourse but a *mark* or *sign* left by something no longer present, the trace of "corpus" in "corpse."

The poem "driving Dartmoor hills" explores the link between mother and ghost through a play on the word "mare":

> "Old Uncle Tom Cobley & all" my uncle sings through open windows of his car escaping "all along, down along, out along lee," the old grey mare "a-making her will," these wilful tensions twisted in the blood familial. (33)

The uncle's song, "Widecombe Fair," presented only in fragments, tells the story of a man who lends his grey mare to a group of farmers who want to go to the fair. When the mare is not returned, the man climbs a hill and spies his mare "a-making her will." She dies, and legend has it that when the "wind whistles cold on the moor of a night," "Tom Pearse's old mare doth appear, gashly white" (de la Mare 72-74). As the poem "driving Dartmoor hills" unfolds, the "old grey mare" is refigured as "the shadow of the wild grey *mère*," as "lost, on the night-mare," as "the shadow, märe, moon sea," and as "the moor . . . where you come to get lost, the mysterious moor with its mire at Fox Tor, with its ghosts." By attending to the differential play of sound and graphic marks, the text resists a stable meaning for "mare"; "mare" signifies variously a female horse, a spirit supposed to cause nightmares, and shadows on the moon that Galileo read as bodies of water. The text allows vowel sounds to drift, thereby adding "*mère*" (mother), "mire," and "moor," with its connotations of darkness, to the "mare" constellation. And linking this constellation to the guest-ghost-host relation is the shadow presence of the mother.

Freud's haunted house

The fascination with ghosts in *HHS* points toward an important Freudian intertext. In an essay entitled "The Critic as Host," J. Hillis Miller reads the doubleness of the guest-host relation through the *uncanny*:

> The uncanny antithetical relation exists not only between pairs of words in this system, host and parasite, host and guest, but within each word in itself. It reforms itself in each polar opposite when that opposite is separated out. This subverts or nullifies the apparently unequivocal relation of polarity which seems the conceptual scheme appropriate for thinking through the system. Each word in itself becomes divided by the strange logic of the "para," membrane which divides inside from outside and yet joins them in a hymeneal bond, or which allows an osmotic mixing, making the stranger friend, the distant near, the *Unheimlich heimlich*, the homely homey, without for all its closeness and similarity, ceasing to be strange, distant, and dissimilar. (454)

The notion of "making . . . the *Unheimlich heimlich*," which translates "making the un-home-like home-like" or "making the frightening familiar," is relevant to a reading of Marlatt's text. Like the guest-host relation, *unheimlich-heimlich* constitutes a double antithesis. The most extended consideration of its operation is Freud's essay on "The 'Uncanny' " – the English translation of the "*Unheimlich.*" Freud's lexicological inquiry shows that "among its different shades of meaning the word '*heimlich*' exhibits one which is identical with its opposite '*unheimlich*' " (345). "*Heimlich*" has two principal meanings: "belonging to the house, not strange, familiar" (342) and "concealed, kept from sight" (344). "*Unheimlich*" designates that which is "eerie, weird, arousing gruesome fear;" it is " '*the name for everything that ought to have remained . . . secret and hidden but has come to light*' " (345). The radical continuity, the contradictory coherence of "*unheimlich*" with the second meaning of "*heimlich*" leads Freud to reject the notion of the *Unheimlich* as simply the *un*familiar. Instead, Freud proposes that the *Unheimlich* or uncanny is "that class of the frightening which leads back to what is known of old and long familiar" (340).

The attention here to the ways in which language differs from itself would be enabling for feminist thought if it were not so tied to the castration complex, Freud's privileged example of the *Unheimlich*. Although Freud does not frame the following examples in terms of the castration complex explicitly, these examples are grounded in the notion that the male subject perceives the female genitals as "other" or "lacking" and that this perception produces fear:

> It often happens that neurotic men declare that they feel there is something uncanny about the female genital organs. This *unheimlich* place, however, is the entrance to the former *Heim* [home] of all human beings, to a place where each one of us lived once upon a time and in the beginning. There is a joking saying that "Love is home-sickness"; and whenever a man dreams of a place or a country and says to himself . . . : "this place is familiar to me, I've been there before," we may interpret the place as being his mother's genitals or her body. In this case, too, then, the *unheimlich* is what was once *heimisch*, familiar; the prefix "un" ["un-"] is the token of repression. (368)

Some of the topoi of this passage – the presentation of the mother as both *heimlich* and *unheimlich*, the attention to beginnings, the notion of "home-sickness," and the return to the mother-body – resonate with Marlatt's text. Although these topoi are inflected very differently in *HHS*, the resonances hint at the possibility of reading the return to the mother in Marlatt's text as a feminist meditation on the uncanny. Before exploring this possibility, however, it is useful to consider the construction of gender within Freud's "The 'Uncanny'."

Freud's text presents the uncanny as a feeling experienced by men at the site-sight of the female genitals. In "The Blind Spot of an Old Dream of Symmetry," Luce Irigaray rehearses this scene:

> Now the little girl, the woman, supposedly has *nothing* you can see. She exposes, exhibits the possibility of *a nothing to see*. Or at any rate she shows nothing that is penis-shaped or could substitute for a penis. This is the odd, the uncanny thing, as far as the eye can see, this nothing around which

lingers in horror, now and forever, an overcathexis of the eye, of appropriation by the gaze, and of the *phallomorphic* sexual metaphors, its reassuring accomplices. (47)

Freud's uncanny, then, elides the female subject and objectifies her body as both frightening and familiar through several strategic displacements: a metonymy that allows a body part to stand in for the woman-mother; a metaphor that substitutes for that part the structures of the home; and a projection that attributes to that same part the otherness of the male onlooker. Freud justifies the status of the female body as *heimlich* on the grounds that it is "a place where each one of us lived once upon a time and in the beginning." This presentation of the female body as a point of origin, the undifferentiated space of all beginnings, allows him to ground the connection between the uncanny and the castration complex. Further, "conveniently" for Freud, the corporeal morphology that guarantees the female body's status as *heimlich* is easily read as the mark of its lack. So, as Irigaray notes, "while '*heimisch*' as a mother, woman would remain 'un' as a woman" (48n). The suggestion in Freud's text is that as "surely" and "naturally" as the female body is familiar to the male subject, it is also frighteningly other.

The terms of the connection between the castration complex and the uncanny foreclose the radical implications of the difference *within* the terms "*unheimlich*" and "*heimlich*." Shoshana Felman's reading of Freud's uncanny is helpful here:

> what is perhaps most uncanny about the uncanny is that it is not the opposite of what is canny, but rather, that which uncannily *subverts the opposition* between "canny" and "uncanny," between "*heimlich*" and "*unheimlich*." In the same way, femininity as real otherness . . . is uncanny in that it is not the opposite of masculinity, but *that which subverts the very opposition of masculinity and femininity*. (41-42)

Felman offers a different reading of that which "ought to have remained secret and hidden but has come to light"; Freud's stake in maintaining unequivocal self-presence for the male subject leaves him blind to the kind of otherness that breaks down sexual difference based on opposition. The "indifference" in Freud's uncanny means that what is viewed as the woman's "otherness" is a function not of her own difference from herself, of the heterogeneity of her own subjectivity, but rather a function of the male subject's self-projection. Further, as Kaja Silverman suggests, the fact that the male subject recognizes the female genitals as uncanny signals that he is structured by lack prior to the moment of registering sexual difference: "what seems to confront [the male subject] from without, in the guise of the 'mutilated' female body, actually threatens him from within, in the form of his own history" (17). In other words, what is uncanny or strangely familiar is *otherness*. This otherness takes the child back to previous splittings or divisions – from the child's feces, from the mother's body. In fact, in the passage cited from Freud's text, it is possible to read the uncanny return as a return to various instances of separation from the mother as well as a return to the castration complex.

Related to the gender indifference in Freud's text is the woman-mother's status as "*Heim.*" What does it mean to *be* the "haunted house" of Freud's uncanny? As Mieke Bal points out, "If the house *is* the mother, in the male fantasy, then there is no place for the mother *inside* it" (194). This "paradoxical state of being confined to and excluded from the house" (Bal 195) hints at a larger problem: the theory of sexuality implied by Freud's uncanny cannot adequately accommodate either the constitution of a female subject or the complexities of a woman's desire to return to the mother-body. To rephrase Bal's question, then, if the mother is the house, how can she formulate the desire to return to it? Like the woman-mother of Plato's cave, she is homesick, in the sense of housebound. This "blind spot" in Freud's uncanny is symptomatic of the fact that the focus of the male gaze is the female body. And within this specular economy a woman is, as Nicole Brossard has it, literally "stuck in matter" (21).

As mentioned above, the castration complex reduces a woman to a part of her body, a part that functions as a blank screen for the projections of the male subject. In locating the uncanny in the female genitals, Freud's theory depends upon that which it cannot see, upon that which is outside the purview of the male subject. For, as Irigaray points out in her readings of Freud and Plato, what the male subject sees is not necessarily isomorphic with the meanings that the female subject attributes to the female body. To return to the paradox identified by Bal, a woman is both confined to and excluded from Freud's theory; in fact, she is confined to being excluded. Nevertheless, as the subject who is both missing and extra, a woman stands in a supplementary relation to Freud's uncanny – that is, she marks its gaps, its logical contradictions. Freud's presentation of the mother as origin has to be re-read, then, in terms of her status as the condition of possibility of the theory. The mother is the term that provides the foundations of the structure but that cannot be accommodated within it.

home-sickness

Marlatt's text offers a radical re-reading of the uncanny. In particular, it marks a significant departure from the economy of desire implied by a metaphor such as "Love is home-sickness." In *HHS*, the idealizing, masculinist frame "Love is" is elided and the trajectory of desire resituated within "homesickness." And although the word itself does not occur in the text, the sense of homesickness is all-pervasive and polysemic. On the level of narrative, Marlatt's text is a turning toward home, home understood as a site – "red dirt of Devon bedrock" (26) and "*the original grotty cotty*" (27). Further, if we let the word "homesickness" drift a bit, the juxtaposition of "sickness" and "home" emphasizes the radical continuity of the foreign with the familiar. "Homesickness" evokes Kit's illness – "allergic to the nearest thing we have to a hereditary home" (24) – as well as his desire "to go home . . . where it's nice & boring" (78). Similarly, the word captures both the trauma of the speaker's return to England and her desire to return to Canada: "it fills me with dread & not for the first time. i think how can we be here for another two weeks. i only want to fly home with him, to keep him safe" (54).

The tension here between Canada as home and England as home suggests that "home" is always already "away." As a site of desire, home is marked by pain and absence. In fact, the word "homesickness" holds this contradiction within it; it is akin to "nostalgia" – from the Greek *nostos* (return home) and *algos* (pain). In *HHS*, the painful longing to return home is never far from the pain of returning home: "star of a shattered system of domestics, memorial orbits of love, spasmodic, reaching far back in the blood – where there is a gap, a black hole somewhere" (34). In this light, Tostevin's assertion that Marlatt's texts "convey a nostalgia for a source, an origin" takes on another meaning. *HHS* takes "nostalgia" out of the realm of the sentimental and reframes it in terms of the uncanny by disrupting the polarity of absence and presence, the familiar and the strange, desire and that which desire rejects – pain, confusion, nightmare.

Freud reads the metaphor "Love is home-sickness" as a euphemism for intercourse. Within the masculinist, heterosexual economy of Freud's text, the metaphor constructs desire in terms of a man's longing to return to the mother. In the context of *HHS*, too, "homesickness" can be read as a longing for the mother: "her i lost, not him in the throng . . . where have you gone? first love that teaches a possible world" (78). But here "love" – uncapitalized – is outside the terms of Freud's "Love is home-sickness." This love inscribes on the level of the enunciation the contradictions of a female subject of desire. For example, the trajectory of desire doubles back on itself: the speaker both longs for and *is* the mother body; she both longs for her origin and is a repetition of her origin. This doubling back, this return, marks the subject of desire as different from herself, and the origin as a repetition. As both a subject of desire and a site of desire, the mother is self-differentiated. And the speaker's return to the mother is uncanny in so far as it is a return, a repetition with difference.

In *HHS*, homesickness – the longing for the mother – is restaged as the female subject's return to the representation of the mother in "The 'Uncanny'." Marlatt's text's stake in exploring the home-mother metaphor, however, differs significantly from that of Freud's text. "The 'Uncanny' " attends to the corporeal referent of the metaphor in so far as the displacement of "womb" by the term "home" reveals something about the male subject's repressed fear of castration, about the *Unheimlich* in the *heimlich*. Marlatt's text, on the other hand, foregrounds the fact that representations such as Freud's use the female body as a prop. By playing with the disjunction between "mother" and "womb," between subject and site, it points to the synecdoche on which the metaphor relies and troubles the tidy metaphorical substitution of "home" for "mother." No longer unequivocally homesick, housebound, the woman-mother can mediate for herself the difference between the dominant meanings attributed to the female body and the meanings she attributes to it. She can explore the haunted house as well as being the haunted house; and as she discovers, the ghostly mother is not at home.

HHS is interested in the particular terms that allow the metaphorical connection between "home" and "womb," terms that have been forgotten or displaced to assure the symmetry and correspondence of "home-mother" or "house-wife." Perhaps the most important and the most prevalent of these is "walls":

> my mother's body soft & angry in its hum, & warm, walls that hold, to go back . . . (18)

> feet on the red dirt of Devon bedrock we go back to the familiar: my mother's trace, these family pathways to negotiate, these still-standing walls of home. (26)

The word "walls" is metonymically related to both "home" and "womb"; it is the necessary third term that facilitates the metaphorical connection. The text's attention to this third term complicates the identity or isomorphism of "home" and "womb" and refigures the metaphor as a chain of metonymic adjacencies. As Irigaray shows in her reading of Plato's parable of the cave, a metaphor is almost always grounded by previous, unacknowledged metonymies:

> It is within the project encircling, limiting the horizon in which the *hystera* is made metaphor, that this dance of difference is played out, whatever points of reference outside the system and the self are afforded for relating them one to another, bringing them together, making them metaphor. For metaphor – that transport, displacement of the fact that passage, neck, transition have been obliterated – is reinscribed in a matrix of resemblance, family likeness. (247)

HHS explores the "points of reference outside the system," the referential similarities – in this case walls – that are the condition of possibility of metaphor. In these terms, "home" can no longer simply replace "womb" and thus elide its corporeal referent.

Like guests and hosts, walls are both foreign and familiar in Marlatt's text. Walls are hospitable – "warm, walls that hold" (18), "clay, straw & pebbles these walls, two foot deep sills where winds from the southeast blow" (27) – and hostile – "Climbing walls (what else are they for?)" (17), "past stonewalled enclosures Dartmoor ponies roam" (33). As Miller suggests, this internal contradiction is "the strange logic of the 'para,' membrane which divides inside from outside and yet joins them in a hymeneal bond" (454). "[T]hese still-standing walls of home," then, are not immune to the passage of ghosts – both ghost-writing and the ghostly mother. The text itself considers the possibility that the walls are not so still-standing:

> out of nowhere we are near the source. a shallow brook ripples by a few crosses at fords, a few stone walls for leaning up against – the Thames, really? not that one. wellspring. dayspring. home – when the walls come down, what kind of source? (69)

Here, the ghostly mother "materializes" in the words of text; "home" is linked to "womb" by the term "walls," and "river" is linked to "womb" by the term "source." The text de-idealizes and demystifies the origin by writing it in terms of the source of a river. Thus, if the mother is a "source" or an "origin," her status as such cannot be read outside the material contingencies foregrounded in this passage – the materiality of the signifier that allows the meanings of "source" and "walls" to proliferate and the referential adjacencies and similarities that subtend the home-womb and source-womb metaphors. The final question "home – when the walls come down, what kind of source?" operates on various levels. If the walls are those of home, how does the mother represent herself when she no longer merely constitutes "home" or "cave"? If the walls are those of the womb, in what ways can discourse acknowledge the contingencies of beginning in the womb without re-centring origins? And if the walls are the limits of a restricted economy of meaning, how does a different economy of language, one which draws attention to the material and to the enunciation, alter representations of sexuality?

In its attention to the corporeal referent of the "home" metaphor, *HHS* seeks a return not to a body outside discourse but rather to a written body in order to explore a different morphology. In a discussion of Irigaray's texts, Anna Munster insists on the status of the body as discursively mediated:

> Anatomy does not *determine* the representation of either femininity or masculinity; these are constructed by the *meaning* the female or male body comes to have in both dominant modes of signification and in their lived meaning(s). Morphology is not concerned with a given biological body, but with the body as meaningful for the subject. Irigaray's texts dislodge the universality of phallic morphology, implying that a different morphology may take shape through different signifying practices, different discourses. (122)

The construction of the female body in *HHS* can be read in these terms. For example, the sequence "the Valley of the Rocks, heathland, uncultivated stone walls & stands of ancient culture *knew* its stone womb" (53, my emphasis) suggests that the the body is a function of representation, of orders of "knowability." And the possibility that "ancient culture" knew its stone womb through "uncultivated stone walls" points toward a different representational order, one in which nature and culture, origin and representation/reproduction are radically continuous because discursively mediated.

Marlatt's text works toward this different representational order by re-reading dominant metaphors for femininity such as "home-mother" and "earth-mother." The following excerpt from "close to the edge," for example, emphasizes the textual status of the traditional collocation of mother and earth:

> in caves. she is in caves. but i don't feel her here. along the causeway, light bouncing brilliants off housefronts, evening strollers, off waves to the

> Dolphin, Fo'c'sle, off the Royal Marine – *we get our storms here*. she is not here, if anywhere, past cliffs to Wild Pear Beach where darkness gathers in cracks, slits, tidal caverns, gathering us up (& fascinated, wanting to go back in all the way, nose up against those walls of rock, musty with sea rank pebbles, sea-wrack fear of old, being trapt by the sea) she said the tide is coming up, if we don't go now we won't get back & i could hear it in her, panic, pan-ic (terror of the wild), shouldn't have brought you here, all three, & the wind rising – risk. to meet it. (55)

Here, *HHS* "plays with a different form of/for sexuality" (Munster 122) by allowing the mother to take shape not so much in the landscape as in the process of reading. The text draws attention to the land-mother or cave-womb connection as metaphorical rather than natural or essential by producing the woman-mother through the unacknowledged metonymies that subtend the metaphors. Further, the text allows for the non-correspondence of "mother" and "womb" by marking the gap between the mother who writes/explores the cave-womb and the mother who is the cave-womb.

Although the signifier "womb" does not occur in the poem, the sequence beginning "where darkness gathers in cracks, slits, tidal caverns, gathering us up . . . " retraces various characteristics or attributes of "womb." Parataxis and ellipsis draw attention to the ways in which terms are linked, that is, the ways in which connections are made. For example, "darkness," "cracks," and "slits" are referentially adjacent to both "cave" and "womb"; they are the metonymies that allow "cave" to stand in for "womb." The term "womb," then, is absent in so far as it is replaced by the term "cave" but present in so far as it can be *traced* through elements contiguous with it: darkness, mouth-like opening, enclosure, wet inside, odour, walls. The contradictory claims "she is in caves" and "she is not here, if anywhere" can be read in terms of this trace structure; the mother's presence is a function of writing and, as such, is also marked by absence. Like "home," the mother is always already "away." Displacing herself throughout the text, she turns up in the strangest places.

known of old and long familiar

In the passage from "close to the edge" cited above, the words "sea-wrack fear of old" hint at *HHS*'s recontextualization of Freud's uncanny – "that class of the frightening which leads back to what is known of old and long familiar" (340). On the level of the enounced, the "sea-wrack fear of old" is the fear of the mother who inadvertently leads her children into danger – that is, it is the speaker's fear of the mother, the speaker's fear as the mother, and the speaker's return to her mother's fear. On the level of the enunciation, contextual marks or shifters such as "I," "she," and "here," verbs without specified subjects, and present participles contribute to this heterogeneity; they situate the reader in the moment of the enunciation and allow for a layering of enunciative contexts. The text directs attention to the reader's role in producing meaning by obscuring the "source" of the fragment "shouldn't have brought you here . . . – risk." Here, the text questions the notion that a speaker is the origin of her/his enunciation. The attempt to recuperate an "original" enunciation is further complicated by the fact that these words make an uncanny return to those of the previous poem – "where does this feeling come from that i have put him at risk" (54).

In Marlatt's text, then, the return to the mother is a return in language, a return that is non-originary in so far as language is a system of *repeatable* terms. As Irigaray shows in *Speculum*, any return or repetition introduces a margin of difference on the level of the enunciation, a space for feminist critique. *HHS* reads the uncanny – "that class of the frightening which leads back to what is known of old and long familiar" – in terms of this margin of difference between seemingly identical terms. In several poems in which the speaker returns to the site of a previous visit, the word "familiar" signals this margin. With its sense of the supernatural as well as the domestic or recognizable, "familiar" has the same "ghostliness" as "guest" and "host." It inscribes the order of the "always already" and traces several instances of enunciation within a "single" enounced.

The poem "by train to Reading" pivots on the familiar, on the position that the speaker shares both with her son and with her mother:

> it is the rackety clacking of the wheels that is familiar, or this sideways motion, this compartment speeding down the line . . . it's my son discovering the window open, staring head out into wind, ecstatic, until the cinder bit in eye:
>
> *didn't i tell you?*
>
> that was it, my vision smeared with soot like some kind of powdered ink, my mother's handkerchief a scalding rubdown. (16)

In this poem, the verb tenses mark a general movement from present action – "it is the rackety" and "it's my son discovering" – to a corresponding line of past action – "the cinder bit in eye" and "that was it." This movement "back to what is known of old and long familiar" is complicated, however, by the words "*didn't i tell you.*" Because these words operate within the present tense of the enunciation, they can occupy simultaneously various instances of production: they are the words of the speaker's mother on the speaker's childhood visits, and the words of the speaker as mother on the 1981 return. Thus, the "i" of the poem and the "i" in italics are both continuous and discontinuous with one another, and the words "*didn't i tell you*" are a repetition within themselves. This doubleness produces the uncanny sense that time has both passed and been suspended, that the subject who visits is both the same as and different from the subject who made the previous visit. Further, the dense layering of moment within the enunciation and the shift in the "i" foreground the reader's production of the text. As the punning title suggests, the reader accompanies the text "by train to Reading," *en train de lire*, in the process of reading.

Note

I am grateful to Danny O'Quinn for his dialogue, and to Barbara Godard and Jim Lyons for their editorial suggestions. Thanks also to Stan Dragland with whom I first read *How Hug a Stone* and to whose words I made an uncanny return. Finally, I would like to acknowledge SSHRC.

Works Cited

Bal, Mieke. "The Architecture of Unhomeliness." *Death & Dissymmetry*. Chicago: U of Chicago P, 1988. 169-96.

Brossard, Nicole. *These Our Mothers*. Trans. Barbara Godard. Toronto: Coach House P, 1983.

Cooley, Dennis. "Recursions Excursions and Incursions: Daphne Marlatt Wrestles with the Angel Language." *Line* 13 (1989): 66-79.

Davey, Frank. "Words and Stones in *How Hug a Stone*." *Line* 13 (1989): 40-6.

de la Mare, Walter. *Come Hither*. Toronto: Longmans Canada, 1962.

de Lauretis, Teresa. "Sexual Indifference and Lesbian Representation." *Theatre Journal* 40.2 (May 1988): 155-77.

Derrida, Jacques. "Différance." *Margins of Philosophy*. Trans. Alan Bass. Chicago: U of Chicago P, 1982. 3-27.

____. "Structure, Sign, and Play in the Discourse of the Human Sciences." *Writing and Difference*. Trans. Alan Bass. Chicago: U of Chicago P, 1978. 278-93.

Felman, Shoshana. "Rereading Femininity." *Yale French Studies* 62 (1981): 19-44.

Freud, Sigmund. "The 'Uncanny'." *Art and Literature*. Vol. 14 of *The Pelican Freud Library*. 15 vols. Trans. James Strachey. London: Penguin, 1985. 339-76.

Gallop, Jane. "*Quand Nos Lèvres S'écrivent*: Irigaray's Body Politic." *Romanic Review* 74.1 (January 1983): 77-83.

Godard, Barbara. " 'Body I': Daphne Marlatt's Feminist Poetics." *American Review of Canadian Studies* 25.4 (1985): 486-96.

Hertz, Neil. "Freud and the Sandman." *The End of the Line: Essays on Psychoanalysis and the Sublime*. New York: Columbia UP, 1985. 97-121.

Irigaray, Luce. *Speculum of the Other Woman*. Trans. Gillian Gill. Ithaca: Cornell UP, 1985.

Johnson, Barbara. "Translator's Introduction." *Dissemination*. Chicago: U of Chicago P, 1981. xii-xxxiii.

Marlatt, Daphne. *How Hug a Stone*. Winnipeg: Turnstone P, 1983.

———. "In the Month of Hungry Ghosts." *The Capilano Review* 16/17 (1979): 45-95.

Miller, J. Hillis. "The Critic as Host." *Critical Theory Since 1965.* Ed. H. Adams and L. Searle. Tallahassee: Florida State UP, 1986. 452-68.

Munster, Anna. "Playing With a Different Sex: Between the Covers of Irigaray and Gallop." *Futur*Fall: Excursions into Post-Modernity.* Ed. E.A. Grosz, et al. Sydney: Power Institute of Fine Arts, 1986. 118-27.

Silverman, Kaja. *The Acoustic Mirror: The Female Voice in Psychoanalysis and Cinema.* Bloomington: Indiana UP, 1988.

Tostevin, Lola Lemire. "Daphne Marlatt: Writing in the Space That Is Her Mother's Face." *Line* 13 (1989): 32-9.

MANINA JONES

Log Entries: Exploring Discursive Space in Lionel Kearns' Convergences

> this is the place
> you reach
> to name
> remember and recite
>
> Eli Mandel, *Out of Place*

In his "Introduction" to *The Writing Life*, Frank Davey comments that one cannot fully understand *Tish* magazine without understanding its sense of community as a "placing" of the individual within the cosmos, physical geography, social fabric, and language (19). When Davey elsewhere assesses Lionel Kearns' writing of the 1960s, it is Kearns' sense of involvement in the particular " 'circumstantial' scene"[1] in his poems that for Davey connects him with the *Tish* group and its interest in the Black Mountain school's "field theory" (*From There to Here* 148).[2] Kearns' recent volume, the long poem *Convergences* (1984), reprises this early interest in place and placing, using the explorer journal as a means of rediscovering a geographical, historical, and linguistic landscape. In *Convergences*, Kearns re-theorizes the Black Mountain/*Tish* emphasis on "stance" and locality as an interactive "communal" process of *reading* that, as Barbara Johnson puts it of another work, transforms "the plane geometry of physical space [and, it should be added here, the Cartesian 'plotting' of historical time] into the complex transactions of discursive exchange" (279).

In Black Mountain poetics the concept of "proprioception" is opposed to the straightforward notion of perception. As Warren Tallman sets forth the distinction, "The perceptive writer sees himself in the midst of the surrounding world as object," while "[t]he proprioceptive writer sees the surrounding world in the midst of himself as subject." Charles Olson, for example, did so when he "subjected himself" to Gloucester, Massachusetts in *The Maximus Poems*, so that "he might incorporate that place into himself and thus become Gloucester" (Tallman 31-2). Frank Davey characterizes this process in Olson's poetics as an assimilation of the scientific ethos of ecology, in which "The poet's self becomes document; his current being – his articulations, breathing, enthusiasms – a barometer of immediate process" ("Countertextuality" 35). The *Tish* writers' concern with the poet's relation to his surroundings, C.H. Gervais suggests (194), is close to the themes Dorothy Livesay sees as characteristic in the Canadian documentary poem: "our narratives reflect our environment profoundly; they are subtly used to cast light on the landscape, the topography, the flora and fauna as well as on the social structure of the country"

(Livesay 269). In them the poet attempts, in Livesay's now-famous formulation, "to create a dialectic between the objective facts and the subjective feelings of the poet" (267). Gervais states that the "relationship of the poet to 'place' [in *Tish* poetics] is of such a nature that it allows the poet to participate and extend himself into that 'place' whether it be geographical or historical" (206).

Convergences, a work Davey calls "the most rigorously 'documentary' of recent Canadian long poems" ("Countertextuality" 38), situates itself within the *problematic* dynamics of this encounter. In it, the status of distinctions between subject and object, self and other, past and present is placed at issue.[3] Kearns' poem points to the changing, contextual nature of place and/as discursive positioning. "Consider that word, *circumstance*," a self-conscious narrating voice in the poem urges us, "the circle in which we stand. But we never stand still" (*34).[4] *Convergences* formulates its tentative approach to the "documentary" through the use of what might here be called "circumstantial evidence": the presentation of provisional, contextualized perspectives, including citations from written records, illustrations, historical narrative, and the contemporary narrator, who confesses to the difficulties of reading and relaying "documentary" information. The various texts that compose *Convergences* are seen as *in*scribing, rather than simply describing, places/positions in the world. "Objective fact" is thus problematized by the various discourses that compose it. Historical and geographical place, in this sense, is always already *dis*-placed; it is situated within a field of often conflicting, literally prescribed systems of meaning.

David Carroll uses the significant metaphor of "grounding" to describe this kind of interrogative approach to history:

> Rather than establishing a *ground*, a critical return to history will inevitably be forced to confront not an abyss, total absence or pure groundlessness . . . but the conflictual interpenetration of various series, contexts and grounds constituting any ground or process of grounding. (66)

The very title of *Convergences* situates it at just such points of interpenetration. Its front cover illustration is a reproduction of one of John Webber's "documentary" engravings of James Cook's 1778 voyage. It sets the poem at a spatial/temporal point of convergence where two cultures intersect: the shoreline meeting of Cook's men with the Mooachaht Indians at Nootka Sound. The perspective of the etching may be identified with European explorers about to arrive on "the scene." In fact, a Mooachaht Indian in the lower right-hand corner of the cover appears to be visually addressing the viewer. As Lianne Moyes observes, while Webber's etchings might be used in a conventional history "to document 'how the West Coast Indians live', *Convergences* uses them to emphasize 'how European history depicts how the native people live' " (27). The presentation of this historical event is not, therefore, simply a detached observation, but one clearly grounded in a particular historical/cultural perspective. The poem's description of the Mooachaht's initial recognition of the European ships on the horizon as a kind of portable landscape, "an island moving on the sea" (*10), reinforces this sense of grounding at the same time as it implies a coincident "figurative" perception arising from another spatial/cultural position, a position that is literally and figuratively represented as marginal to Webber's etching: the "looking" Mooachaht is spatially de-emphasized on the cover, and his viewpoint is not figured by it, or by the explorer's account it illustrates.

Cited illustrations are later used to reveal cultural convergence as a site of *mutual* interpretation. On opposing pages that contain the narrative description of the first European-Mooachaht contact, there are two drawings: one Webber's rendering of a Mooachaht canoe (an extension of the etching that appears on the front cover), the other presumably a Mooachaht rendering of a European ship (*10-11). Cultural difference is inscribed here both as a difference in perspective, and as a disparity in the stylistic conventions of representation. Later in the poem, the contemporary narrator draws attention to the "realism" and "authenticity" of Webber's illustrations as "accurate visual representations," not because they objectively present the truth, but because they "give me a sense of the visual experience of the men on those ships" (*36). Webber's drawings are contrasted to Mooachaht art, which "was more sophisticated in approach, more serious in intent, though the Europeans, their appreciation numbed by their judgement, found it primitive, barbarous, and crude" (*36). This observation may well turn readers back to their own earlier reaction to the Mooachaht drawing in order to see that assessment as embedded in a European tradition of judgement.

The contemporary speaker in *Convergences*, similarly, expresses an awareness of his own historicized responses to the situation he attempts to articulate. Just as the explorers' view of the coastline is determined by their European perspective, the narrator comments on his own historiographic encounter: "And I too find myself here at the edge of the continent, an expression of genes that have drifted westward through generations. I am the newcomer encountering those others who have been here all the time or have come in the other direction" (*13). Subjectivity itself is both textualized and historically embedded. It is, in fact, literally "relativized," since the individual's subjection to historical and cultural pretexts is imaged in terms of the genealogical inheritance of genetic codes. As described on the first page of the poem, the "new" arrivals at Nootka Sound are involved in a process of coding which is determined by the past, and which in turn generates the subjectivity of those who follow: "Their genes move into positions on old chromosomal chains, composing and encoding characteristic details of following generations" (*1).

The genetic process is also formally associated with the inheritance of a European "empirical" tradition that propagates a geographical empire, founded (empirically) on its own "knowable" experience. On one page, the left-hand column begins, "Science and empire inspire this expedition. They chart the unknown seas and coastlines, claim in the name of the British Crown whatever they find, and gather information" (*19). Language, in this use of it, is significantly empirical; in representing the environment, the explorers assert ownership. The right-hand column draws attention to the contemporary narrator's parallel attempt to interpret history, an attempt situated both geographically, and within a genealogical process of inheritance and reinscription of historical codes, which finally gestures toward future "generations" of readers:

> The patterns persist. Moving, shifting, the repeated genotypes converge and combine in endless variety to express the unique and individual forms of the actual: persons, situations, events, institutions, cultures, states of mind. I sit on the porch listening to the sound of the creek in the evening stillness, dogs barking in the distance, and beyond that the monotonous murmur of city. As these words fall into the formal patterns of my given language . . . . I wonder what is happening around you as you read these words. (*19)

Convergences's use of quoted documents stresses the importance both of "given" codes and their "embedded" or contextualized reception. As Martha Rosler perceives, the formal gesture of citation may point to our inheritance of "a received system of meaning, a defining practice" (80). *Convergences* both acknowledges its indebted stance in relation to inherited accounts, and undermines readings that would allow them to function simply as authoritative empirical evidence of historical events. By fragmenting and recontextualizing documents, in effect, the poem alters its own heredity, creating recombinant genetic codes. It also displaces the "given environment" by undermining the document's cognitive "ownership" of the landscape. Further, it violates the boundaries of textual property in its appropriation of the historical text in much the same way crewman John Ledyard "cribbed whole sections" from a fellow-traveller's journal, "and elaborated on these with his own personal testimony" (*66). The volume's cover, for example, as we have seen, is not simply a representation, but the poetic "re-citation" of a representation, whose meaning is dependent both on the interplay of its internal perspectives, and on the context of its reception: it functions quite differently in its role as an element of Kearns' poem than it does as one of the illustrations to Cook's "authorized version of the voyage" (*37).

The self-conscious act of quotation, Rosler asserts, "can be understood as confessional, betraying an anxiety about meaning in the face of the living world, a faltered confidence in straightforward expression" (81). The contemporary narrator in *Convergences*, located spatially at a desk covered in papers and temporally at a point in an as-yet-undetermined history – both places circumscribed by historical texts – explicitly confesses his discomfort with these texts: "My desk is covered with papers that I do not want to see. What will I do with them? What will I do with all this information?" (*1). When the Mooachahts are confronted with the foreign European presence, "[n]o one knows which voices to listen to. No one knows which rules apply in a case like this" (*11). The contemporary narrator – and the reader of *Convergences* – is similarly confronted with the various voices and sign-systems represented in the poem. He may therefore engage in a kind of conversation with the past, a conversation that stands in marked contrast to conventional history's "monological idea of a unified authorial voice providing an ideally exhaustive and definitive (total) account of a fully mastered object of knowledge" (LaCapra 36).

Citation, as Rosler remarks, "can reveal the thoroughly social nature of our lives" (80). *Convergences*, then, does not just depict a place of social interaction – the shore at Nootka Sound – it *is* a place of social interaction. Poem and land are seen as parallel loci whose very identities are dependent on verbal relations. The name

"Nootka Sound" might itself be seen as an emblem of this parallel. "Nootka," we learn, is a name marked by the process of transmission and reception. In an inaccurate translation, a displacement of language between cultures, "[t]he English hear the Mooachahts repeating *nu-tka-sshi'a, nu-tka-sshi'a,* meaning, *Come around the point into the cove.* They hear the sequence of syllables and think it is the name of this place" (*16). When the explorers record the name on their charts, they perpetuate their misapprehension.

"Sound" is a geographical term meaning a passage of water connecting two seas. It is also an utterance, or the production of an utterance. The first page of the poem describes the arrival of "newcomers" by asserting that "Their talking and groaning and shouting augment the *volume of sound* echoing and fading here in this place" (*1, emphasis added). While presence and place are clearly important to the "passage" (both as quoted text and as geographical space), precisely who is arriving and where remains remarkably indeterminate. As Lianne Moyes points out, in *Convergences,* "temporal and spatial indicators such as 'here', 'in this place', and 'now' are vague and shifting; their point of reference lies in the ever-changing context of enunciation" (22). Emile Benveniste calls such indicators " 'pronomial' forms," pointing out that they "do not refer to 'reality' or to 'objective' positions in space or time but to the utterance, unique each time, that contains them" (219). The passage from *Convergences* could conceivably be read as describing the European arrival at Nootka sound, the European sighting of the Mooachahts, each reader's arrival in the contextual space of the poem or history, and perhaps most appropriately for this argument, all three (or more) together, in which case context itself is placed at issue.

If "here," "in this place" is potentially the present reading of *Convergences,* where the word is defined by the context of its enunciation, then the poem may well be labelled "a volume of sound" – both because it is a book that "contains" a geographical place (Nootka Sound), and because it is a polyphonous point of convergence of historical utterances which the reader may augment, and in which, as Moyes puts it, "[t]he permanence and authority of the written word are threatened by the fact that meaning cannot be pinned down" (23).[5]

The performative processes of transmission and interpretation of even written texts in *Convergences* are thematized in the recurring image of "sound waves," a motif that incorporates both geographical and acoustic resonances. For example, a passage by the contemporary narrator is placed in apposition with a citation from the crewman Ledyard's journal that likens the Mooachahts' physical appearance to the more familiar eastern Amerindians, and their dress to that of the Chinese. Ledyard literally "orients" his understanding of an alien presence with known points of reference. The narrator describes his own similar "translation" of the cited passage itself into the familiar "scientific" terminology of the academic:

> Extending outward in space and time, these *wave patterns* induce in my mind abbreviated images of their own condition, which I dissect and analyse, smudge and slur into general concepts, and so speak of geography,

> history, culture, heredity—the counters of convenient conversation and classroom drudgery, ... (*21, emphasis added)

Reading is seen here as a "civilizing" process that filters perception through familiar texts. Civilization, we are later told, involves "people behaving in pleasingly *predictable* ways" (*38, emphasis added). That is, it is a conformity to already-articulated linguistic conventions.

Later, the speaker comments that the physical convergence at Nootka Sound will be followed by

> a scattering, and other mergings and scatterings of material and personality, the segments of a rhythm, a pulse, *generating and broadcasting waves* in every direction, to *interfere* and merge in patterns beyond our present focus, just as these lines will interfere with the words and images already in your mind, to emerge as shapes and shadows and sounds that I will never perceive or imagine. (*63, emphasis added)

Interpretation becomes a social process that transpires through time, and involves the "interference" of various signals. Meaning might, in fact, be defined both historically and socially as a moment of intertextual/intersubjective convergence: "If these words of mine become words in your head and so connect our lives for a moment, this will be meaning" (*30). "This" meaning, of course, is another pronomial form whose significance is generated at the site of "interference" of its production and reception, a point of convergence.

Such convergence is represented in explicitly spatial terms on the first page of the poem: "At this moment, I know only that I am here and that others have been here before and have left something for me, as I leave something for you. Time is a ritual exchange, though the gifts move in a single direction" (*1). Location itself (the contextually ambiguous "here") is marked by the traces of previous presences. This passage also uses the image of the "present" text as gift, perhaps even suggesting the potlatch (a celebration notably foreign to imperialist/capitalist ideas of property ownership), in which the giver distributes his material goods "in a single direction."

Dominick LaCapra encourages a "rhetorical" reading of past writings that includes the notion of gift-giving. Such a reading would attend to the ways documents rhetorically re-work rather than simply represent "reality." LaCapra likens rhetoric to a "performative" verbal display, which

> may be seen as the discursive analogue of the process of gift-giving as analyzed by anthropologists such as Marcel Mauss. Like the gift, rhetorical usage has the quality of being both deeply gratifying and threatening or anxiety-producing, notably with reference to scientific criteria of meaning (such as univocal definition of terms). It also provides a larger setting for the role of tropes as turns of language that manifest a playful and sometimes uncanny potential. (39)

The members of the scientific expedition led by Cook are unable to identify the function of a "curious" object that appears in a Mooachaht long house in one of Webber's etchings. Given its signifying role as a spectacular object of exchange – it is a *trophy/trope* – their anxiety about its meaning is understandable (*55).

As we have seen, "Nootka Sound" is both a geographical setting, and a kind of poetic gift, that provides a setting for linguistic play. Barbara Hernstein-Smith observes that when we re-read a verbal structure as something other than what it was given as, we have, in effect, "regiven it to ourselves" (50). By re-citing quotations from the journals of Cook and his men in the format and context of poetry, *Convergences* "gifts" them to its readers, encouraging a self-conscious rhetorical reading of a text that might not ordinarily be seen as rhetorically impressive. "Poetry," the contemporary narrator notes,

> is language focussed on its own form, yet our focus here is upon the facts as I try to include them all before it is too late. The challenge is to disguise this unpoetic material in such a way that you will approach it as poetry, a task which is almost impossible because the content of this language is more compelling than any formal flourish I can generate. (*51)

Cited texts are, then, "ambivalent words," caught between empirical and poetic sign-systems (see Kristeva 73). They demand a dual focus, both a "factual" reading, and a rhetorical re-reading. For example, in a cited journal entry, Ledyard describes the Mooachaht tools for fishing:

> *They have near a dozen different kinds of fish-hooks*
> *all made of wood,*
> *but was a European to see any one of them*
> *without previous information*
> *of their design,*
> *he would as soon conclude they were*
> *intended to catch men as fish.* (*50)

The narrator's commentary – as well as the journal excerpt's formal presentation and placement in the volume of poetry – draws out the metaphorical potential of Ledyard's simple description, at the same time as Ledyard's description reflects on the contemporary notation, turning the idea of fishing for men on the coast/line into a kind of double hook that links the two passages, and thus suspends linear chronology. The commentary, arranged as prose, reads:

> On this coastline two waves are beginning to converge. Two worlds are about to move together to produce the eventual ambiguous contingencies of my life. I walk the beach at evening, attentive to the sound of the sea breaking on the rocks out past the point, watching the sand-laden rivulets

of seawater trickling back down the slope of the shore between each slap and rush of water. At this moment I do not know which way the sea is running. Fishing is good at the turning of the tide. (*50)

A reading of the cited explorer's log that exceeds its denotative "content" might well be said to be "attentive to the sound . . . out past the point." The rhetorical reading of either passage does not eliminate the denotative qualities of its language, but it does relativize them by introducing other possible contexts beyond the "objectively" grounded setting: for instance, the context of cultural convergence as reading, in which Ledyard struggles to interpret and record the life-signs of an alien people; the contemporary narrator's parallel interpretive encounter with Ledyard's journal in which he is "fishing" for an understanding of past men using a poetic line (of enquiry); and the ambivalent convergence of "figurative" and "denotative" language in the physical/discursive space of the page that produces *contingent* settings – neither objectively grounded "on shore," nor subjectively "at sea" – for both the contemporary and historical speaker.

In *Convergences*, the "log" is both a descriptive device used by the explorers, and a poetic play on "word(s)" (*Logos*) in which an authoritative naming of place and time is undermined in favour of attention to the "ambiguous contingencies" of rhetorical exchange. The contemporary narrator's comments may be seen as "log entries" in that they are an account of a reading of historical documents. They are simultaneously the record of a "poetic" exploration of the historical text and/as linguistic landscape, and an "entering in" and undermining of authoritative positions.

Frank Davey has drawn attention to the fact that exploration frequently functions in Western Canadian aesthetics as a metaphor for the writer, "often both in terms of exploring experience and exploring language" ("The Explorer" 147). As *Convergences* demonstrates, exploring experience *is* exploring language. The poem allows us to see both historical explorers and explorers of history as engaged, not just in discovering a landscape, but in the rhetorical project of discursively (re)constructing that landscape, and situating themselves within it. As Leslie Monkman comments, exploration narratives are frequently seen by contemporary writers like Kearns as expressions of a European vision: "the language of the narratives becomes the focus for examination of a whole range of tensions stemming from the meeting of a European discourse of conquest – whether eighteenth-century or twentieth-century – with the North American continent and its peoples" (80-81).

The European explorers claim a position of authority associated with open representational space, literally, a "*carte blanche*" in Second Lieutenant John Rickman's words, the ships "*have reached that void space in our maps / which is marked as / country unknown* (*14). In a parallel column, the contemporary narrator reminds the reader of a connection between geographical and cognitive space[6] when he taunts him for attempting to silence the "nattering voices" in his brain:

> The right hemisphere always gave you problems, didn't it? God, those dreams! So much interference up there in the corpus callosum. But we are considering Cook and his crew as they approach the North West Coast of America. They had other hemispheres to worry about, though they were otherwise much like you. (*15)

Cook and his crew are like the reader addressed here, "*other/wise*," that is, in their attempt to establish a position of "knowledge" in relation to "others." Just as this reader uses alcohol to silence the dissension within himself (the voices of his creative right hemisphere) in order to make sense of his life, the explorers must suppress "other" alter-*native* voices that constitute the Western hemisphere (America), because they "interfere" with a monological model of knowledge. This parallel reinforces LaCapra's assertion that "[a]lterity . . . is not simply 'out there' in the past but in 'us' as well" (140). *Convergences* suggests a negotiation between "others" both outside and inside ourselves in its self-conscious questioning of the authority of historical writings and/as historical readings.

In conventional readings of history, map and mapmaker are authority figures; in *Convergences* they are also revealed as *figures* of authority – emblems of privilege in the *rhetorical* production of historical knowledge. Webber's representation of Cook, significantly, has him holding a map; the passage placed next to it describes the captain as a powerful and enduring signifier of the voyage itself: "Cook is commander, father, old man, whose life and role and name all identify and characterize this expedition, then as now" (*6).

The "character" of the expedition is produced within texts and their consumption: "Cook *belongs* to his public image, to the portraits and newspapers and history books" (*6, emphasis added). It is almost as if Cook is the (historical) word made flesh. His demise, then, enacts a kind of "poetic justice," since it is seen as an ironic communion, a violent "festivity," in which "his flesh [is] eaten by those he most impressed" (*6). *Convergences* enacts its own textual "poetic justice" that counteracts the empirical authority of Cook's historical words. By poetically re-citing historical accounts, it effects what Mikhail Bakhtin would call an anti-authoritarian, "carnivalistic" strategy of textual dismemberment that counteracts monologic history (24). The poem does not present the "Cooked" comprehensive narrative of the voyage. Rather, it self-consciously *re*presents the dis-ordered "raw" materials of "historical fiction."

Convergences (re-)places Cook in context. The explorer's recording of his passages through space and time may be seen as "accurate," but only within a culturally Eurocentric, ideologically empirical frame of reference: "With his new Harrison chronometer set on Royal Greenwich Observatory time Cook calculates his geographic positions and navigates with an accuracy never before attained" (*4). This is a mapping of history that installs powerful new fictions. The European mapmakers "compose an intricate shoreline on paper" (*47) in much the same way the log "plots" its empirical observations on a narrative line. "They" – explorers and/as historians – "bring pen and paper, instruments to confer permanence to the momentary act of reflection. They come with the power to make history and they begin to make it" (*46).

For those who engage in such a project, the contemporary narrator comments, writing determines the structure of historical chronology: "time becomes a line" (*17). Just as the unity of the coast/line is disrupted by the poem's contextual representation of space, so too is the simple linearity of historical narrative disrupted by the multiplication, fragmentation, and disordering of documentary accounts, and the "present" reader's dialogic encounter with them in *Convergences*. The poem allows its readers to see any "given" narrative in the context of other possible readings. "Do not fasten on that line," the narrator warns us, "[t]he fascination lies in the living" (*17). One interpretation of this appropriately multivalent passage might be that a spellbound attachment (fasten-ation) to a prescribed time-line, *lies* – is both a fiction and a tie (*lier*, Fr. "to fasten") that binds us to experience.

While writing makes time a line, we are warned not to let it string us along. *Convergences* suggests the dangers of an unreflective acceptance of the "official story." An excerpt from the journal of Charles Clerke, whose name stresses his role as recorder, tells us of – and reinforces – irreconcilable differences in taste between the explorers and the Mooachahts. The explorers turn down the "hospitable offers" of the natives, because their

> *. . . idea of what is good and palatable*
> *would not permit us to avail ourselves*
> *of this part of their kindness.*
> *However, we were very social.* (*30)

The historical narrative adds ironically that Clerke was indeed "social," "having left behind him in the house of his hosts a deposit of tuberculosis bacilli, an invisible but telling memento of this first wave of European culture on this coast" (*30). Clerke's "distasteful," detached cultural perspective as a member of the scientific expedition contrasts with his literal contamination of the Mooachahts.

His objective rhetorical stance is similarly contradicted. The infection of the Mooachahts by tuberculosis is potentially parallelled with another "*invisible* but *telling* memento" left by the Europeans: historical writing itself. "History," we are reminded in the poem, "covers its tracks" (*53). It is discourse that suppresses the marks of its discursivity. Asserting authority by concealing its own contingencies, and the textual/cultural impressions it *makes*, it appears only to record impressions objectively. Such "invisible" writing and its strategies are made tangible by the citational method of *Convergences* that reinserts historical writings into a discursive setting.

The poem draws attention to the continuing textual/geographical displacement of the Mooachahts to the margins of contemporary "Canadian" society:

> The Mooachahts still live on this coast.... But the land, more polluted, less productive, though in many ways the same, is no longer their land. They live

> only on the fringes, licking Canadian stamps for their occasional letters . .
> . . There have been no wars of conquest, no treaties; only waves of people
> coming and staying and occupying this space and taking control. (*56)

The European colonizing of geographical space (now represented as non-native Canadian) is a corollary of its occupation of "this" discursive space.

The stamps the Mooachahts lick might be seen as stamps of (the) authority that relegate(s) them to a position on the fringe of contemporary society by regulating the circulation of signs. The stamp that *Convergences* reproduces (courtesy of the *Post-Master General of Canada* [iv]), reinscribes Webber's etching of a Mooachaht longhouse into the contemporary world without any attempt historicize it. *Convergences*, on the other hand, might be seen as a kind of "occasional letter" (complete with, but subversive of, its stamp) since it clearly calls for an aesthetics of reader-response of "correspondence," and since it draws attention to the "occasional" context of linguistic production and reception. Its recirculation of authoritative signifiers like the stamp places their authority in context, allowing ironies to emerge. For example, although the narrator notes that the Muchalahts and the Ehatisahts and the Nuchatlahts and the Kyuquahts and the Ahts also live there, the stamp claims to be a depiction of generalized "Indians of the Pacific Coast" (*56). This title effaces cultural differences *between* native groups, making all West Coast Indians a generalized "other." The stamp also sets them in diminished relation to the national and financial considerations signified by the large-print "Canada 8" on the stamp.

Convergences encourages its readers to accept their continuing implication in historical discourse, and to re-explore that position with a self-consciously "uncivilized," challenging attitude. The narrator comments: "Civilization is fully knowing a situation. It is always the others who are savages. Come here my little savage" (*38). The reader of *Convergences* may be an "other" who stands both within and outside the social process of making sense. This is an unstable position indeed, but it is also an ideal place from which to question that process. If, as Martha Rosler asserts, quotation is "alienated sensibility" (81), the literally "documentary" quotations in *Convergences* are a key element in the poem's general strategy of "[d]eliberate alienation" (Mandel, "Imagining Natives" 36). In re-citing the explorers' accounts, *Convergences* also "re-sites" the landscape they describe, displacing the very discursive/geographical ground on which the explorers – and the contemporary speaker and reader as their heirs – stand. In a continuing process of establishing its "setting," the poem refuses access to history or geography as an extra-discursive product, thus unsettling the reader's conventional position of comfort in a "home and native land."

Notes

[1] The title of Kearns' first book of poems is *Songs of Circumstance* (1962).

[2] Warren Tallman writes that when George Bowering, Frank Davey, David Dawson, James Reid, and Fred Wah decided to start *Tish* magazine, Kearns declined to be an editor, but acted as one for all practical purposes (53).

[3] Lianne Moyes describes the formal arrangement of the poem:

> the columns of large typeface present a discontinuous "historical narrative" written in prose with a ragged right-hand margin; the columns of italics are "historical documents," direct quotations from explorers' journals written in prose but transformed into verse with ragged left and right margins; and the columns of small typeface present a self-conscious discourse written in prose with justified margins. (16)

[4] *Convergences* is strategically unpaginated: the narrator comments, "You are free to shuffle these pages and browse, but I cannot answer your questions because I am too busy answering my own questions and posing new unanswerable questions." Since I quote extensively from the poem, for the sake of my own convenience, I have commited the self-conscious injustice of numbering its pages. I acknowledge that injustice by marking each page reference with an asterisk.

[5] George Bowering points out that as early as *Songs of Circumstance*, Kearns "employed a Saussurian idea of the transcription as transmission between ear and ear" (117). *Convergences* does not seem to valorize the "originality" of the oral, as Saussure does. Rather, as I will argue, orality becomes a "provocative" image, stressing the performative quality of language in general.

[6] Fredric Jameson uses the term "cognitive mapping" to indicate the ideological implications of spatial perception.

Works Cited

Bakhtin, Mikhail. *The Dialogic Imagination*. Ed. Michael Holquist. Trans. Caryl Emerson and Michael Holquist. Austin: U of Texas P, 1981.

Benveniste, Emile. *Problems in General Linguistics*. Trans. Mary Elizabeth Meek. Coral Gables, Florida: U of Miami P, 1971.

Bowering, George. "Metaphysic in Time: The Poetry of Lionel Kearns." *The Human Element*. 2nd ser. Ed. David Helwig. Ottawa: Oberon, 1981. 113-31.

Carroll, David. "The Alterity of Discourse: Form, History, and the Question of the Political in M.M. Bakhtin." *Diacritics* 13.2 (1983): 65-83.

Davey, Frank. "Countertextuality in the Long Poem." *Open Letter* 6th ser. 2/3 (Summer-Fall 1985): 33-44.

———. "The Explorer in Western Canadian Literature." *Surviving the Paraphrase: Eleven Essays on Canadian Literature*. Winnipeg: Turnstone P, 1983. 137-49.

———. "Lionel Kearns." *From There to Here: A Guide to English-Canadian Literature since 1960*. Erin, Ontario: Press Porcépic, 1974. 148-50.

———. Introduction. *The Writing Life: Historical and Critical Views of the Tish Movement*. Ed. C.H. Gervais. Coatsworth, Ontario: Black Moss P, 1976. 15-24.

Gervais, C.H. "*Tish*: A Movement." *The Writing Life: Historical and Critical Views of the Tish Movement*. Ed. C.H. Gervais. Coatsworth, Ontario: Black Moss P, 1976. 193-207.

Hernstein-Smith, Barbara. *On the Margins of Discourse: The Relation of Literature to Language*. Chicago: U of Chicago P, 1978.

Jameson, Fredric. "Cognitive Mapping." *Marxism and the Interpretation of Culture*. Urbana and Chicago: U of Illinois P, 1988. 347-57.

Johnson, Barbara. "Thresholds of Difference: Structures of Address in Zora Neale Hurston." *Critical Inquiry* 12.1 (Autumn 1985): 278-89.

Kearns, Lionel. *Convergences*. Toronto: Coach House P, 1984.

Kristeva, Julia. "Word, Dialogue, and Novel." *Desire in Language: A Semiotic Approach to Literature and the Arts*. New York: Columbia UP, 1980. 64-91.

LaCapra, Dominick. *History & Criticism*. Ithaca: Cornell UP, 1985.

Livesay, Dorothy. "The Documentary Poem: A Canadian Genre." *Contexts of Canadian Criticism*. Ed. Eli Mandel. Chicago: U of Chicago P, 1971. 267-81.

Mandel, Eli. "Imagining Natives: White Perspectives on Native Peoples." *The Native in Literature: Canadian and Comparative Perspectives*. Eds. Thomas King, Cheryl Calver, and Helen Hoy. Oakville, Ontario: ECW P, 1987. 34-49.

———. *Out of Place*. Erin, Ontario: Press Porcépic, 1977.

Monkman, Leslie. "Visions and Revisions: Contemporary Writers and Exploration Accounts of Indigenous Peoples." *The Native in Literature: Canadian and Comparative Perspectives*. Eds. Thomas King, Cheryl Calver, and Helen Hoy. Oakville, Ont.: ECW P, 1987. 80-98.

Moyes, Lianne. "Dialogizing the Monologue of History and Lyric: Lionel Kearns' *Convergences*." *Open Letter* 7th ser. 5 (Summer 1989): 15-27.

Rosler, Martha. "in, around, and afterthoughts (on documentary photography)." *Martha Rosler, 3 works*. Halifax: The Press of the Nova Scotia School of Art and Design, 1981. 59-86.

Tallman, Warren. "Wonder Merchants: Modernist Poetry in Vancouver During the 1960's." *The Writing Life: Historical and Critical Views of the Tish Movement*. Ed. C.H. Gervais. Coatsworth, Ontario: Black Moss P, 1976. 27-69.

DOUGLAS BARBOUR

Tish/*Afterword* &
Notes on Contributors:

In the thirty years since *Tish*, "A Magazine of Vancouver Poetry," first landed in some chosen mailboxes (it only became "A Poetry Newsletter" with number 4), the youthful, rambunctious, yet highly committed bunch of student writers who put it out have had an impact on Canadian writing far greater than their numbers would have led anyone, even them, to suspect at the time. For all the controversy about American imperialism, unCanadian literary activities, or just plain obscurantism, which have been leveled against them, writers like George Bowering, Frank Davey, Gladys Hindmarch, Lionel Kearns, Daphne Marlatt, and Fred Wah have taught and inspired other writers for three decades, and have always remained faithful to the originating impulses of *Tish*: a commitment to language and locale which each has supplemented in his or her own way. As an interested observer during those three decades, I have often found inspiration in their work. In their continual striving to improve their craft, to transcend what they have already achieved, to expand the range of options open to the writer, these writers have always understood the work of art.

When Harvey De Roo, the then editor of *West Coast Review*, first approached me about the possibility of putting together a special issue on what the members of the original *Tish* group had been up to lately, it struck me as a great idea. As in all such endeavours, the results are far different, and I believe more interesting, than we originally planned. In the years since, as *West Coast Review* and *Line* joined together to become *West Coast Line* under the editorship of Roy Miki, I have had a great deal of help from the magazine's editors, as well as from the original *Tish* editors. The latter kept finding people and writing that I would not have been able to track down on my own; some of the responsibility for the new writing herein is theirs, then, and surely that is how it should be. It's especially gratifying to have new work from some of the early editors and contributors who have not been publishing recently. The range of the new writing reveals just how far these writers have travelled during those decades, and how different their writings are, despite the continuing critical attempt, in some quarters, to brand them as alike (and somehow bearing obvious traces of US colonization). The interviews and critical essays, the latter especially interesting because they include contributions from at least three generations of critics, range widely in approach, and provide a number of differing views of the work these writers have accomplished in the last decade or so.

Frank Davey recently became Carl F. Klinck Professor at the University of Western Ontario in London; Turnstone Press published *Reading Canadian Reading* in 1988 ... George Bowering's *Harry's Fragments* was published by

Coach House last year; like many of the *Tish* group he still lives in the Vancouver area ... David Bromige lives and teaches in California; *Desire: Selected Poems 1963-1987* (Black Sparrow 1988) won the Western States Book Award ... David Cull recently returned to BC from New Zealand ... David Dawson lives and teaches in Seattle ... Gladys Hindmarch teaches writing at Capilano College; *The Watery Part of the World* was published by Douglas & McIntyre in 1988 ... Robert Hogg lives on a farm outside Ottawa and teaches at Carleton; *Heat Lightning* appeared from Black Moss Press in 1986 ... Lionel Kearns makes his living as a consultant in Interactive Multimedia; his principal interest at the moment is the literary and creative potential of VR (Virtual Reality) ... Daphne Marlatt now lives on Salt Spring Island; *Salvage* will be published by Red Deer College Press in the fall of 1991 ... Jamie Reid lives in BC; he has performed "Homage to Lester Young" with jazz accompaniment ... Fred Wah teaches Creative Writing at the University of Calgary; *Limestone Lakes Utaniki* appeared last year from Red Deer College Press.

Pamela Banting has joined the English Department at the University of Western Ontario ... E.D. Blodgett teaches Comparative Literature at the University of Alberta; *Da Capo: The Selected Poems of E.D. Blodgett* was published by NeWest Press in 1990 ... Brenda Carr and Manina Jones live and teach in London, Ontario ... Jeff Derksen lives in Vancouver where he edits *Writing* magazine ... Ed Dyck lives in Manitoba; Oolichan Books published *Apostrophes to Myself* in 1987 ... Lynette Hunter teaches Canadian Literature at the University of Leeds in England ... Tim Hunter edited the Olson/Layton correspondence published in *Line* #13 ... Turnstone Press is publishing Roy Miki's *Saving Face* ... Lianne Moyes is completing her PhD at York University in Toronto ... Irene Niechoda's *A Sourcery for Books 1 & 2 of bp Nichol's The Martyrology* is forthcoming from ECW Press ... Ken Norris teaches Canadian Literature at the University of Orono, Maine; Quarry Press is publishing the latest installment of his ongoing *Report on the Second Half of the Twentieth Century* ... Sharon Thesen teaches at Capilano College in North Vancouver; McClellend & Stewart published *The Pangs of Sunday* in 1990 ... Warren Tallman has retired from the English Department at the University of British Columbia, but he still makes sure that things continue to happen on the poetry scene in Vancouver ... Janice Williamson teaches in the English Department at the University of Alberta; a book of feminist fictions, *Tell-Tale Signs*, will be published by Turnstone Press ... Geoffrey Zamora grew up in New Westminister and studied Canadian Literature at Simon Fraser University; he now lives in California.